# THE KID FROM GOLDEN

From the Cotton Fields of Mississippi to
NASA Mission Control and Beyond

JERRY BOSTICK

# THE KID FROM GOLDEN
## FROM THE COTTON FIELDS OF MISSISSIPPI TO NASA MISSION CONTROL AND BEYOND

Portions of Chapters 1, 2, 3, 4, and 5 were adapted from Jerry Creel Bostick, "Trench Memories," appearing in "From The Trench of Mission Control to the Craters of The Moon"

iUniverse books may be ordered through booksellers or by contacting:

iUniverse
1663 Liberty Drive
Bloomington, IN 47403
www.iuniverse.com
1-800-Authors (1-800-288-4677)

ISBN: 978-1-4917-8541-6 (sc)
ISBN: 978-1-4917-8540-9 (e)

Library of Congress Control Number: 2015920676

Print information available on the last page.

iUniverse rev. date: 03/11/2016

# Contents

# PREFACE

This book is written for my grandchildren, who now number ten. In the order of their birth, they are Lauren Joy Ray, Dylan Travis Bostick, Jordan Taylor Bostick, Preston Thomas Ray, Ryan Tanner Bostick, Cole Alexander Castañeda, Patricia Grace Ray, Case David Castañeda, Rose Faith Ray and Clay Robert Castañeda. Patricia and Rose were officially adopted on May 21, 2010, from Uganda.

It is presumptuous enough to think that my grandchildren might find my life story interesting, let alone anyone else. I am writing this primarily because three of my grandparents died when I was very young, therefore I do not know or remember much about them. I have often wished that there were more of a record of who they were, what they did, and what their thoughts and beliefs were.

So, Lauren, Dylan, Jordan, Preston, Ryan, Cole, Patricia, Case, Rose and Clay, herewith is more than you probably want to know about your Grandpa Jerry...the kid from Golden.

# Chapter 1

# THE EARLY YEARS

I was born June 9, 1939, in the front bedroom of my parents' home in Golden, Tishomingo County, Mississippi, an unincorporated community of about 300 people. In attendance were, of course my mother, Annie Lois Creel Bostick (she unofficially used Lois Ann Bostick), my father, Orville Erastus Bostick, and my great uncle Dr. Erastus (Uncle Ras) Bostick. My parents have told me that they let Dr. Bostick name me, which apparently was the tradition then. He had delivered my sister Mary Nell about four years earlier and named her for his wife Mary. I am thankful that my father had already been given the doctor's name, so I escaped being named Erastus. For reasons known only to the good Dr. Bostick, he named me Jerry Creel, the second name being my mother's maiden name. In my youth, I was not exactly fond of my middle name, but now I am proud of it.

As I reflect on my life, it becomes more obvious that what I am today, what my beliefs are, and what my values are, were all influenced greatly by my environment and experiences as a youth. Growing up in rural northeastern Mississippi was comfortable for me. The comfort came primarily from the love shown me by parents, relatives, and friends, rather than physical amenities. We had plenty to eat, as long as it was grown on our farm. This meant a lot of chicken, eggs, some pork, fresh milk, and plenty of fresh vegetables. Beef was a rarity, because we had dairy cows, not beef cattle. We did not have indoor plumbing, which meant drawing all water for drinking, cooking, washing clothes, and bathing from a well and using an outdoor toilet. As crude as this may sound to you now, it was normal then, so I had no complaints. I would later learn that the lack of physical amenities was not due to my parents' lack of money. During the great depression of the 1930's, my parents were fortunate and smart enough to have jobs as schoolteachers, so they did have a little money. They were just determined to save it, invest it wisely, and not spend it on themselves. They used all the money they could save to buy land, some for as little as $5 an acre, because there were many people around then who needed the money more than the land. Most people saw the land as useless if they didn't have the money to buy the necessary seed, fertilizer, and farming equipment. My parents saw it as a good investment in the future.

I mentioned in the preface that three of my grandparents died when I was young. Papa Creel (John Franklin), Mother's father, died first, in 1944. I remember him as being kind and gentle and always with time to give me attention. He had pear trees in his side yard and would hold me high enough to pick a couple of pears for us to eat. When I started to school, my parents would occasionally let me ride the school bus to Papa and Mama Creel's house to spend the night, then ride the bus to school the next morning. I loved those visits!

Pa-Pa Bostick (Dolphus), Daddy's father, died in 1947. Our house was between his and the town of Golden so he would frequently stop by. Just before he died, his dog had five puppies, which he named after Santa's reindeer. He let me choose one named Dancer to replace my dog Tuffy, who had recently been killed. After that, it seemed as if he stopped by more often to check on his two boys, Jerry and Dancer. When I was about six years old, Pa-Pa Bostick held a 22-gauge rifle and let me pull the trigger to kill a hog in our back yard. Hog killing was a big day. A 55-gallon barrel was filled about half full with water and tilted at a 45-degree angle over a really hot fire. When the water started boiling, the dead hog was lowered into it for just a few minutes then pulled out so that all the hair could be scraped off with knives. The men did all this work including cutting the hog into manageable pieces after the hair was removed. The women were all in the house getting ready to do the final butchering and making sausage and cracklings (in Texas they're called *chicharrones*, which is fried pork fat). Once the sausage making started, the air was filled with a wonderful aroma, which I can still smell today. Since I was so young, these are about my only memories of my grandfathers other than the day they each died and their subsequent funerals.

When I was about five or six years old, Pa-Pa Bostick and his brother Aderine drove in his Model A Ford to the Lubbock, Texas area in search of good but cheap cotton-growing land. Word was out that there was some of the best land for growing cotton available at reasonable prices. They were gone for about a month. When they got back home, friends, neighbors and relatives would gather at his house two or three nights a week to hear them tell of their journey. The roads were pretty bad then, so they were happy to travel an average of 100 miles per day. They usually slept in the car but occasionally were invited inside by locals along the way. They had a dozen or so flat tires during the trip, which presented a big problem. I sat and listened to the tales of their adventure and hoped that someday I could do something like that. They didn't buy any land.

**Pa-Pa (Dolphus)**   &   **Ma-Ma (Ida) Bostick**

Ma-Ma Bostick (nee Ida Bell Rea) passed away in 1954, so I also remember little of her. One of my fond memories is watching her cook on a wood-fueled stove and getting to sample whatever she was cooking. I loved spending the night at her house and getting to sleep on her screened-in porch. When I was young, we traveled to Vina, Alabama, to see her parents, my great-grandfather Nathan and great-grandmother Dora Rea (pronounced Ray). Even though Vina was only about 12-13 miles from Golden, it was a thirty-minute trip over narrow unpaved roads. I was at their house for Easter 1940 and hunted eggs in their front yard.

**Hunting Easter Eggs at Great-grandmother Rea's**

Mama Creel (nee Florence Alice Underwood) lived until 1964. Soon after Papa Creel died, she moved next door to our original house in Golden, so I saw a lot of her. She was very active in the church, teaching Sunday School and singing in the choir. She wrote poetry and songs and read a lot. She had an old wind up clock, which she left to me in her will because I had fixed it for her a couple of times. It is now a proud possession.

I have distinct and very fond memories of my aunts and uncles. Bernice (Aunt Beece) and Uncle Charlie Mink lived just up the road from us. If I needed a different adult opinion about anything or if I just needed to get away from home for a little while, I could be at their house within a couple of minutes. They were always there for me and I will never forget the love they showed me. Uncle Charlie was the rural mail carrier in Golden. I rode with him on many occasions and thoroughly enjoyed it. There was a gas station about halfway through his route and we would always stop there for a Coke and peanuts. He taught me to pour the peanuts in the Coke, which I thought was a wonderful idea. My Aunt Carmel and Uncle Paul Barbour lived in Birmingham, Alabama, about 100 miles away. I loved to visit them in the "big city." Their son Jimmy and I were about the same age (he was one month and two days older), so we always enjoyed each other's company. Aunt Carmel introduced me to coffee and grits. We had neither at home in Golden, so these were real treats for me. I can still taste the grits in my mind, and all these years later, I have not found any as good. Aunt Beece and Aunt Carmel were my mother's sisters, along with Aunt Maxine who lived in Iuka. She and her husband, Uncle Everett Cutshall, owned a funeral home there. When visiting them, cousin Jimmy and I used to get into the caskets and see how long we could stay before panicking. It is very dark in a closed casket and there is no way to open the lid from the inside! Maxine was the youngest of the Creel daughters but we were never as close as I was to Beece and Carmel. My daddy's brother and sisters all lived further away and I only saw them once or twice a year. I loved them all, but Beecc and Carmel were my definite favorites.

**CREEL FAMILY**
**Front: Papa (John Franklin), Maxine, Mama (Florence)**
**Rear: Carmel, Lois, Bernice**

When I was about eight years old, we had indoor plumbing installed. I felt as if we were living in the lap of luxury. My mother was obsessed with always completely closing the lid on the commode, because "That's a nasty thing to have in the house." Closing the lid is a habit which I still have today. We didn't have a lot by today's standards but, again, I had no complaints. In all of my early years, the only things I can recall really wanting badly were a bicycle and a Boy Scout uniform, both of which I finally got. We didn't have a TV, but few of my friends did either, so it really wasn't a big deal.

Even though eight generations of my ancestors, on both my father and mother's sides, had been farmers since arriving in the United States, I definitely did not want to continue the tradition. I very vividly remember working in the cotton fields watching cars pass by on the nearby road. I wondered what kind of occupation the people in the car had that allowed them not to be in my position. *Where were they going? What were their jobs? How much does a car like that cost? Will I ever be able to afford a car of my own?*

What I did not appreciate until much later was that I was learning a work ethic, which would serve me well for the rest of my life. My parents, of English, Scottish and Irish descent, were teaching me valuable lessons, like "Nobody owes you anything. You have to earn everything for yourself. Any job worth doing is worth doing right. You can accomplish anything you want, but it's up to you to work hard for it. If you want to earn the respect of others, always tell the truth, even if it hurts." My mother often said "Whatever you do, always aim for the moon." Of course back then, that was like saying aim for the impossible. They also taught me a general distrust of government. One of Daddy's favorite sayings was "The further government gets from my front door, the sorrier it gets. There is no way people hundreds of miles away can understand our problems, much less solve them."

My heroes were local men who I greatly respected. Hollis Long, a house painter by trade, was my scoutmaster and someone to whom I looked up. As a painter, he taught me how to make brush strokes (all in the same direction, as few as possible) and how to clean a brush ("If you can look at the brush and tell what color of paint you used, it's not clean.") He was also a musician, who along with his brothers, often performed at school and church events. Hollis played a variety of instruments, including the dulcimer. In later years, he made one for me as a gift to Vickie. As my scoutmaster, he reinforced the moral and ethical teachings I received at home. Another hero was Etha Mann, the local Texaco gas distributor. Even though he had a "dirty" job, pumping gas from his delivery truck into customer gas tanks, he was always dressed neatly. Every chance I got, I would talk to him while he was working. In later years, he bought the theater in Belmont, a town near Golden, and hired me to sell popcorn, then later promoted me to the job of projectionist. The fact that one of my heroes had confidence in me was very comforting. My third hero was Noonan Deaton, owner of the funeral home in Belmont. He, like Etha Mann, appeared to be very successful in something other than farming. He also had a quartet which sang at several church events. I greatly admired someone with that kind of talent. Once in High School at Belmont, his son Dean and I became good friends. Later, we were fraternity brothers at Mississippi State.

– – –

Later in life, while working at NASA, I was honored to be invited to speak at a "Mississippi Models" symposium on the subject *"Conditions in Mississippi which inspire achievement in the field of science and technology."* The series of three symposiums was funded by The Mississippi Committee for the Humanities and sponsored by Phi Theta Kappa, the international honor society of two-year colleges and academic programs. My symposium on science and technology was the first one, with two others on the subjects of literature, delivered by famed author and editor-in-chief of Harper's magazine, Willie Morris, and politics, delivered by Hodding Carter, III, journalist/ commentator and assistant secretary of state under President Carter. Preparing for the symposium made me reflect a lot on the subject, and I have thought more about it since. My parents, my relatives, my teachers, my ministers, and my friends, knowingly or unknowingly, taught me to have respect for all others. They taught me that anything is possible if you are willing to work hard enough for it and that there should be no limits to my dreams. They also taught me that there is a God, and everything you do should be guided by Him. It was a great thrill to see my former Scout Master and one of my heroes, Hollis Long, in the audience the night I gave the speech at Northeast Mississippi Junior College in Booneville. At the conclusion of my rather long diatribe, the program called for three "reactors", all college professors, to each spend 10 minutes reacting on what I had said.

The first two, from Mississippi State, just stood up and said "Amen." The third, an Associate Professor of Philosophy from Ole Miss, used his entire 10 minutes to talk about how deeper the problems in Mississippi were than my "naïve" assessment.

- - -

I jokingly have called my mother "Pollyanna." She invariably looked for the bright side of everybody and everything. A person could be a serial killer and she would say, "Well, he's not all bad, I saw him feed a stray dog one day." She lived that philosophy every day and a little bit of it rubbed off on me, albeit I wish more had. As I mentioned earlier she and my father both taught me, more by action than words, that no matter what you do, do it as well as you can. Don't take shortcuts and don't say, "Well, that's good enough". Their philosophy was, "If it's worth doing, it's worth doing right." People have accused me of being a perfectionist, which I unfortunately am not, but a little of their philosophy did carry over into my style of doing things. Some have interpreted this to be competitiveness, but I definitely do not consider myself competitive in the sense that a competitor gains satisfaction from winning over others. My only competitor is myself. I find satisfaction from doing any task as well as I can and worry little about whether someone else does it better.

I have been amazed and dismayed by some of the government social programs over the past several decades that have been advertised to "help" people. My upbringing taught me that nobody owes you anything: especially the government. I was taught to believe that help comes to those who help themselves. In those days, if our neighbors or we really did need help, everyone pitched in and helped. No one ever even thought that the government should step in and "help."

Most of the memories of my pre-teen years are of either good things or bad things. I suppose it is natural for the ordinary things to fade as time goes by. All of my elementary school teachers were good. Two of them, Bonnie Mae Warren and Lalla Byram, stand out as the very best. They taught me not only the basics but also a great deal about how to get along with other people. A consistent thread was encouragement. They stressed that there is no limit to what an individual can achieve... "If you can dream it, you can do it."

I did very well in school because if my teachers believed in me that much, I surely did not want to let them down. Also, I did not want to embarrass my mother, because she was a teacher in the same school. The only bad thing about school was that if I did anything that warranted punishment, not only did my teacher at school punish me, but also my mother at home once she found out about it.

I remember my friends and playmates, Harold Ginn, Bobby Woods, Dolan Taylor, Jerry Stephens, and John Denson, plus my first "sweetheart", Mable Hall. We guys were inseparable during recess, usually playing marbles, basketball, or softball. I was not very good at hitting a softball, but I figured out that most opposing pitchers could not throw three strikes, so I usually walked. I thought that was as good as a hit. I was a good pitcher and enjoyed some success until one day Dolan Taylor hit a line drive straight into my stomach. I lay on the ground not able to breath. That was the end of my pitching career. John was an electronics wizard. He built a radio from an oatmeal box and some wires! He started repairing TVs while still in high school. One day Bobby found a small round shiny object on the playground that none of us could identify. We all held it, rubbed it, picked at it, and tossed it around between us. Finally, Bobby started beating on it with a piece of coal. Coal was used to fire the boilers to heat the water that circulated though the radiators to heat the school, so there was plenty of it around. As Bobby was beating on this newly found object with a large piece of coal, the bell rang signaling us to go back inside for the resumption of classes. When the second bell rang, meaning we should already be back at our desks, I told Bobby I was going inside and he should come. As I ran toward the door, I heard a loud bang behind me. When I turned around there was Bobby, covered with blood and coal dust and screaming at the top of his lungs. The "object" turned out to be a blasting cap and had exploded when he hit it hard enough with the chunk of coal. The school Principal rushed him to the local doctor, (the nearest hospital was about fifty miles away in Tupelo) while all of his friends worried that he would die and we would all go to prison because we had done something bad. He didn't die, but he did miss several days of school and for a long time thereafter had black marks on his hands and face from the embedded coal fragments.

Most of my good memories from the early years are associated with either church or school. I guess that is an indication of how society in the rural south was so closely tied to those institutions in the 1940s. A distinct memory is from May 8, 1945, VE (Victory in Europe) Day, when Germany surrendered during World War II. Mother and I went to our church to ring the big bell. I was just short of my 6th birthday, so she had to lift me up so that I could grab the bell rope and swing back and forth, ringing the bell. We did the same thing again in August 1945, on VJ (Victory over Japan) Day.

Daddy owned the land across the road from our house and spent a lot of time clearing a few large trees that were growing there. I usually helped him dig up the roots. The last one was so large that we spent several hours trying to dig out the stump and roots. Finally, Daddy gave up and went to the hardware store to buy some dynamite. They told him that half a stick should do the job. He bought two sticks and placed them underneath the stump. He lit the fuse and then came running back across the road where I was watching from our front yard. The dynamite went off, the stump flew about 30 feet into the air, came over the road, over our house and landed behind our barn. Daddy just said, "Well, I guess half a stick would have been enough." We were lucky that no one or no property was hurt.

A memory that I still sometimes have dreams about is getting stuck in a culvert that ran under the road in front of our house. In the 1940s, the Works Progress Administration had built a rock-lined ditch from behind our barn, down to the road, and then from the other side of the road down to a creek (Epps Branch). My friends and I had crawled through the culvert many times with little or no problem. One day Joe Ginn and I decided to crawl through, with me in front. It had been raining a lot and there was a lot more mud in the culvert than usual. About half way through, I got stuck and couldn't go forward or backward. Joe backed out and ran to get Daddy, who crawled in and pulled me out, covered with mud. To this day, I am not actually claustrophobic, but have a fear of being stuck somewhere and can't move.

At around age 10, my parents let me go on a church bus to Nashville, Tennessee, to see the Grand Ole Opry. One of my very fond memories is seeing Hank Williams perform the song "Cold, Cold Heart." He got down on his knees during the song and appeared to be crying. It was also on this trip that I saw my first escalator in Harvey's department store. It was the first one in the south. Another highlight of the trip was a visit to the Parthenon, a full-scale replica of the original in Greece.

There were many non-school events held at the schoolhouse. Since my mother was a teacher, the school was right next door to our house, and there was little else to do, we attended most of them. There were political candidate debates, gospel singers, cakewalks, and "box lunch suppers" (I realize that is a contradiction of terms, but that is what they called them!), all involving lots of food. There was never any dancing because that was considered evil. While the parents listened to or participated in whatever was going on, we kids would play and see what kind of mischief we could get into.

The gospel singers were mostly local groups, but frequently featured more established quartets such as the Blackwood Brothers and the Jordanaires, both based in Memphis, Tennessee, and who later both made records with Elvis Presley. Over a nine-month period in 1953 and '54, both of these quartets spent the night at our new house after their concerts. A couple of them had to sleep on the couches, one in the den and one in the living room, but they didn't seem to mind because it was free and Mother fed them a great breakfast. Their only mild complaint was about the "train that ran under my bed", referring to the Illinois Central Seminole which ran about 100 yards behind our house. Years later, Mike and Kristi would enjoy running to the edge of the back yard to wave at the train engineer who would usually blow the whistle if he saw them.

As I grew older, the cakewalks and box lunch suppers were especially entertaining. I doubt if they have events like that anymore. The cakewalk was a simple way to raise money for the school. Women of the community would bake cakes and donate them to the affair. On the stage of the school auditorium, someone would draw a circle of square blocks, one with the word "cake" written in it. For a fee of a dime each, about ten people at a time would get in the circle and begin to walk slowly from square to square while someone played the piano. When the music stopped the lucky person in the cake square won the cake.

By age 11 or 12, the box lunch suppers were even more interesting to me. Young ladies of the community would prepare a complete meal, put it in a box about the size of a hatbox, and then decorate the box elaborately. The box would be auctioned and whoever bought it got to eat the meal with the preparer. Of course, the preparer of each box was supposed to be anonymous until after it was sold, but half the fun for boys my age was to find out who had prepared which box, and then try to buy the box belonging to the girl with whom you wanted to have dinner. As I remember, the most I ever paid for a box was about five dollars, which was a lot of money then, but it was worth every cent.

As for the church, I mostly remember the revivals. These usually went on for a week and were always a big community event. We were Methodists, and our revivals were a lot calmer than the Baptist revivals, but they were still a big event. The visiting preacher usually stayed at our house for some reason, and I liked that because it meant we had special meals and I got to sleep on a pallet because the visitor got my bed. It was at one of these revivals that I made my commitment to Jesus Christ.

A very bad memory is also associated with the schoolhouse. One summer when I was about 11 or 12 years old, my cousin Jimmy Barbour who was the same age and from Birmingham, Alabama, came to spend a week with us on the farm. I think he actually enjoyed those visits, but he always complained about what hicks we were and that there was nothing to do. One day Jimmy, Jerry Owens, and I were playing together and trying to come up with new and exciting things to do. We ended up playing basketball on the dirt courts behind the school. After a while, we rested in the shadow of the backside of the building. Somehow the conversation got into "I can do anything better than you." One of us, I swear I do not remember which, had been idly pitching small rocks against the side of the brick building and catching them. This led to who could catch the most rocks without missing, who could catch the biggest rock without missing, who could stand the farthest from the wall and catch the most rocks, who could bounce small rocks off a window and catch them, to who could hit a window the hardest without breaking it. Of course, the final proof of this last game resulted in a broken window, which then led to "Since I broke a window, you have to also." The result was that every single window on the backside of the school was broken.

For several days, the talk of the town was the terrible vandalism that had taken place at the school. Who could do such a horrible thing? Why would anyone do such a thing? My mother was the Principal of the school at the time, so there were many visitors to our house and a lot of conversation about how the windows got broken and how to get them fixed. I had such a feeling of guilt I could hardly stand it. I imagined all sorts of torture if we, I, were ever found out... jail, prison, banishment for life. Just before acting on the only solution that seemed viable at the time...running away from home...a man who lived on the other side of the school reported to my mother that he had seen me, Jimmy, and Jerry playing behind the school the very afternoon the windows were broken and maybe we might have seen who did it. When mother asked me about it, I immediately confessed. What a relief. Even the worst whipping I ever received from my daddy was a relief. The great guilt was over and now I could sleep. Of course, our parents paid to fix the windows and each of us had to repay them. I don't remember the dollar amount, but I remember thinking it would take the rest of my life to earn that much money. In fact, I think it only took about two years.

Another bad memory was the burning of our garage. We had a single car garage with a storage room on the back, separate from our house. In 1948, my father finally was able and willing to buy a new car, a 1948 Chevrolet Fleetline. A beautiful white four door with fender skirts and a windshield visor. We all thought it was the most beautiful car we had ever seen! One day not too long after we had bought the new car, I was in town (If it's proper to call Golden a town) and heard the fire truck coming from Belmont, about two miles away. The fire truck was always a source of excitement, so I stepped out to the side of the road to watch it pass. Just as it went by, I heard someone say, "It's Orville Bostick's garage." I started running toward home as fast as I could and almost beat the fire truck there. The garage doors were open, with flames and smoke streaming out. My mother was shouting "Orville, Orville" as loud as she could, looking into the garage. Then I saw the car come rolling out. Daddy had gone inside the burning garage, put the gear into neutral, and pushed the car out. Nothing was going to take away his new car!

There was talk around town that I had accidentally started the fire by smoking cigarettes in the storage room on the back. My folks asked me if that were true, and believed me when I told them no. I had only smoked one cigarette at that point in my life, and that was several months before, behind a tree in the front yard. My Aunt Carmel had left a pack of Camels lying around so I snitched one and tried it. I was so sick I swore I would never do it again, and didn't for several years.

Anyway, an insurance investigator said the fire had started by spontaneous combustion of some rags soaked with paint thinner, so I felt relieved, but there are still people in Golden who will tell you "Jerry Creel burned down that garage by smoking cigarettes in there!"

Not too long after the garage fire, my parents started talking about building a new house across the street in a pecan grove that they owned. There was an old run down house at the front of the lot that we used to store fertilizer and to temporarily store picked cotton before taking it to the gin. My parents ordered the plans for a three bedroom, two bath, brick house with an attached two-car garage from Progressive Farmer magazine. No one around there built houses from such plans. They usually just sketched out a plan and started building, but my parents insisted that it be built exactly according to the specifications. Daddy and I laid out the plan for the foundation and started digging. It was a lot of work for just two people, especially when one of them is a 12 year old. After we finished the trenches for the foundation, we started digging a basement (usually called a storm cellar in those days) which was not a part of the plans, but which my parents wanted anyway. After several long days of digging on the basement, Daddy realized that we would never finish it on time if they wanted the house to be completed that year, so we filled it back in and gave up on the idea of having a basement.

Daddy hired a master carpenter, Delmon Ozbirn, one of the best in the area, but he and I ended up doing much of the work ourselves. He paid cash for all the materials and to the carpenters, plumbers, bricklayers, etc., so he had to keep several thousand dollars on hand most of the time. Afraid of robbers, he slept each night with the cash hidden inside his pillow. On several occasions, Delmon would want to do something slightly different from the plans, but Daddy always insisted that it be built exactly as specified, which resulted in probably the best-built house in Tishomingo County. Any changes in specifications or material were only for improvement, never to "cut corners." For example, the plans called for sheet rock interior walls, but Daddy wasn't convinced that they would be strong enough, so all the interior walls were covered first with 1 x 4 center-match wood, then with sheet rock. He wanted to be sure that no one would bump into a wall and knock a hole in it. Before any of this went up, the interior walls were filled with insulation, because they wanted to be able to heat only one or two rooms if they wanted to. One result of all this stuff inside and on the walls was that each room was almost soundproof. Also, the plans called for a solid 4 x 8 inch roof beam spanning the entire width of the house, about 50 feet. Delmon tried to convince him that he could splice several 2 x 8s together and it would save a lot of money and even be stronger. It made sense to me, but Daddy insisted on exactly following the plans, so he found, with the help of Roy Allen the owner of the Belmont hardware store/lumber yard, a lumberyard in Wiggins, Mississippi (over 300 miles away) that would cut a single beam to the specifications. I hate to think how much it cost to buy it and have it shipped to Golden! Occasionally Daddy got a little carried away with the material selection. The plans called for knotty pine walls in the den, which were all the rage in the 1950s, but Daddy hand selected each piece of lumber, so we ended up with probably the only knotty pine paneling in the world that had no knots in it! In August of 1953 we moved into what I thought was the most wonderful house in the world.

**Me, Age 14, in front of new house**

"We", at this time consisted of just Mother, Daddy, and me. A couple of years earlier, my sister Mary had eloped and moved to Zion, Illinois, which is where many local people were moving in order to find decent paying jobs. It was on a visit to see her there in 1951 that I saw Gen. Douglas MacArthur in a local parade. While there, I also entered a contest to name the streets in a newly planned subdivision. I submitted names of Mississippi counties; American Indian names and won the contest! The prize was $50 and I thought I was rich. I have since wondered if those street names are still there; Tishomingo, Itawamba, Chickasaw, Choctaw, Pontotoc, etc. Sometime in 1951 Mary and her husband separated and she moved back home. Soon afterward, she gave birth to Robert. I waited in the parking lot of the Tupelo Hospital while he was being born. Mary started to college and Robert stayed with us, so he always seemed more like a brother to me than a nephew.

Of course, while the new house was under construction, farming had to continue. We had several dozen head of cattle including four or five milk cows that had to be milked every morning, fifteen to twenty acres of cotton, and ten to fifteen acres of corn. The rest of the acreage Daddy leased to other farmers. At the time, I thought I was being worked to death, but upon reflection, I had it pretty easy. Daddy frequently took care of the milking himself while I was still asleep. Usually I would help him round up our two horses, put their gear on and then hitch them to the wagon, plow, mower or whatever equipment we needed to use that day. I always thought, "Why can't we have a tractor like everybody else!"

Rounding up the horses or cows was always a real treat for me. I had a collie dog named Tuffy, who had to be even smarter than Lassie. When Daddy wanted to load a cow on the truck to take to market, he would go out into the herd, pat the cow that he wanted, and Tuffy would drive it to the truck. He would do the same with the horses when we needed them. Late one afternoon, someone shot Tuffy from a passing car. That was one of the saddest days of my life.

In August each year the schools had a "Harvest Holiday" when we had a couple of weeks to gather the crops. This usually involved long days of picking cotton, dragging a sack behind you. I thought I was big when I started picking two rows at once. This was the way the grown-ups did it and I managed to pick an even 200 pounds one day. At 10 cents per pound, this amounted to $20 for about a ten-hour day. Doesn't seem like much now, but that was a lot of money at the time. We hired almost anyone who was willing to work for 10 cents a pound, including several of my classmates including Linda Tiffin, Margaret Yarber and Clytee Smith. They usually only lasted a day or two.

One of my favorite things was going with Daddy to take the cotton to the gin in Belmont for processing. I loved all the machinery involved: a big vacuum tube to suck the cotton out of the wagon; the machine that extracted the seeds; the huge compressor that pressed the processed cotton into bales; and then applying the bagging and ties. Once this was all completed, a sample was taken from each bale and encased in a round cylinder approximately a foot long and 5 inches in diameter. Each sample was then taken to buyers who would evaluate them for cleanliness and staple (fiber) length. The cleaner it was and the longer the staple, the higher the price. This is the derivation of the term used when someone asks how you are. A standard answer in the South was "Fair to Middling" which was an average grade of cotton meaning it was fairly clean and middling in staple length. So, "Fair to Middling" means you are average.

I have both good and bad memories of pulling corn. The good memories are of riding to the field in our wagon with Daddy and me sitting up front on the scoop board. Before putting the corn in the wagon, the scoop board would be installed at a 45-degree angle and serve as a starting point for shoveling the corn out of the wagon with what we called a scoop, about the size of a snow shovel. When the wagon was empty, the scoop board would be placed across the top of the side frames making a seat for the driver and passenger. Daddy and I would sit up there as we rode to the field and discuss all sorts of things, like religion, school, the "birds and the bees," politics, etc. I'm not sure how we got into these discussions, but I never thought of them as lectures. It was just me and my Daddy having a discussion, and I enjoyed it.

One thing I didn't enjoy was how long it took to fill up the wagon. Daddy would get on one side of the wagon and me on the other, pulling ears of corn and throwing them into the wagon. Amazingly, the horses would just stand there and wait until Daddy told them to move up a few yards. Just when I would think the wagon was getting full, Daddy would raise the sideboards by putting an ear of corn at each corner between each board, making the wagon sideboards a foot taller.

We would take some of the corn to a gristmill on Moore's Mill Road to have it ground into corn meal. It was powered by a huge water wheel that turned the grinding stones. I always loved going there. Some of our corn was shelled in a hand-operated sheller where you inserted the ear of corn, minus the shucks, into the top and turned a crank. The shelled corn came out into a wooden box underneath and the bare cob was expelled on the ground outside the box. I spent many hours doing this. The sheller is now a prized possession of mine, proudly displayed in our den.

OUTSTANDING — Jerry C. Bostick, son of Mr. and Mrs. O. E. Bostick of Golden, Miss., has been awarded a watch for being the outstanding 4-H Club boy in Tishomingo County for 1954.

**Outstanding 4-H Club boy in Tishomingo County, 1954 Courtesy The Belmont & Tishomingo Journal**

I was a member of both the Future Farmers of America and the 4-H Club, involving several different farm related projects. I usually did very well with these projects and in 1954 won a Tishomingo County 4-H Club award for growing 200 bushels of corn per acre.

As I was growing up, I thought of my Daddy as being very stern. Now as I look back, he was stern, but also the source of many good memories. In addition to farming, he frequently worked at the Farmer's Co-Op in Belmont and in Iuka, a town about 25 miles away. I always enjoyed going to work with him, especially to Iuka. There, we usually ate lunch at Claude's (Edmondson) Hamburgers, where hamburgers were only five cents each. They were small, but at that price, you could eat two or three and it was still a great bargain. I remember them as the best

I have ever eaten. When Daddy worked in Belmont on Saturdays, I would always go with him because the theatre was just across the street and it only cost ten cents for admission and five cents for popcorn. What great memories I still have of Roy Rogers, Gene Autry, and Lash LaRue!

The stern side of Daddy really showed when Mr. John Epps, the owner of a local grocery store, told him that I had been charging candy to his account. I would go there frequently with my friend Jerry Owens, who would get candy, just say, "Charge it," and walk out. I witnessed this several times and thought this was a great thing, having no idea what it meant. So, I tried it. It worked. What a deal. Free candy! It would be an understatement to say that Daddy was not too happy when he explained it to me. No more free candy and another lesson...there are no free lunches.

Chapter 2

# HIGH SCHOOL DAYS

Beginning with the 9th grade, I went to Belmont High School, a whopping two miles away. It did seem like a long way, because I had to ride a bus rather than walk the 100 yards or so that I had done for the first 8 years of my schooling. All of the kids from surrounding elementary schools such as Golden who showed up for high school in Belmont were at first outsiders, but were accepted fairly quickly and blended right in with the "city" folks.

Moving to a new school with new classmates meant that I had to study harder and not be thought of as an inferior kid from the farm. I saw right away that the ones who were making the best grades were Margaret Yarber and Linda Tiffin from Belmont, and Dolan Taylor, my friend and classmate from Golden, so I tried to at least stay up with them. There was a competition my freshman year for whoever had the best grade average to get to serve a month as a Page in the state legislature. I thought this would be really neat, so I hit the books a little harder and won. More about my experiences as a Page later.

Margaret was my first high school sweetheart. Her dad owned the drug store in Belmont. She worked there after school and on weekends, so I tried to spend as much time as I could hanging around the drug store. I started going to the movies each Saturday night and usually got to sit by Margaret. Later, I got a job selling popcorn at the theater, so I got to see her more frequently. One night during my sophomore year, I was in front of Yarber's Drug Store and Linda, who was Margaret's best friend, came out to talk. She told me that she had broken up with her boyfriend. I took this to mean that she was then available for dating, so later I asked her for a date and she accepted. We continued to date off and on during high school and got married just before our junior year in college.

The transition into high school at Belmont was made easier because there were many outstanding teachers. The very best of the best was Ruth Mann, my English teacher and wife of my hero, Etha Mann. She made learning fun and she really cared about her students. I will always remember her teaching us; "Never use a preposition to end a sentence with." Other than my parents, Ruth Mann had more influence on my life than any other person.

At age 13, I began to seek outside employment. My folks said that would be okay as long as it did not interfere with my home chores, which mostly involved helping Daddy with farming. At first, I got a job delivering newspapers. This involved getting up early to pick up the papers by 6:00 a.m., then riding my bicycle to deliver them, which took about an hour. I also got a job selling magazine subscriptions. This also involved a lot of bike riding. My parents restricted my sales route to a two mile radius of home, so in a rural community, that limited my prospects.

My first real paying job was pumping gas at the grand opening of a new service station. During my freshman year in high school, I was at home mowing the yard one day when a car came by with a loud speaker advertising the grand opening of a new Texaco station in Belmont. I was looking for a way to make more money, so I called Buster Davis, the owner, and told him I would work for no pay on the day of his grand opening and if he liked my work, I would like to get a job working weekends. He said come on down and I guess he liked my work that day because he hired me after that. I pumped gas, washed cars, and did oil changes. As I recall, I made $5 a day and I thought I was rich.

One of the first things I purchased was a transistor radio. Little did I know that one day I would meet and spend time with the co-inventor of the transistor, Dr. William Shockley. I would take it to bed with me at night and play it at a very low volume under the covers, so that Mother and Daddy couldn't hear it. I was really into Rhythm and Blues, but they thought it was "race music." I listened to WLAC, Gatlinburg, Tennessee, XERF, Del Rio, Texas, and WHBQ, Memphis, Tennessee. At night, they played a lot of R&B...LaVern Baker, Fats Domino, Ruth Brown, and Little Richard. I didn't care what they called it or who sung it, I just loved the music! WHBQ had a nighttime show, "Red Hot and Blue" hosted by Dewey Phillips. One night in 1954, he played a recording of *That's Alright Mama* by a young truck driver by the name of Elvis Presley, origanally from Tupelo, Mississippi. I couldn't believe how good it was! Phillips must have liked it also, because he played it about ten times in a row. Elvis was revolutionary for my friends and me. He wasn't country and he wasn't R&B. Radio stations didn't really know how to classify him. So called "Popular" music at that time was songs like *How Much Is That Doggie in the Window* by Patti Page and R&B was only played late at night.

Another thing I purchased was a .22 gauge rifle. I bought it from Hobson Tiffin, Linda's dad, who owned a grocery store in Belmont and also sold guns. My dad had a shotgun that he used mainly to shoot blackbirds who loved the pecans on our trees. I had never fired a rifle before but became pretty good at it. I could hid birds and squirrels with it and also could throw a Coke can in the air and hit it before it hit the ground. My dad told Vickie in later years that I could hit the can twice before it hit the ground, but I don't remember if I was able to do that. One day I was shooting at birds in our back yard. A few minutes later, the phone rang. Mr. Long, who lived about a half-mile behind us called to say that he was walking toward his barn carrying a big piece of tin roofing and one of my shots hit the tin. I was forbidden to shoot the rifle at home any more.

For Christmas, 1953 my sister Mary gave me one of the best presents ever; a $5.00 gift certificate to Deaton's Café in Golden. Each day after school I would get off the bus in Golden, which stopped at the café, and have a Purple Cow...a small Dixie cup of vanilla ice cream with NuGrape soda poured on it (five cents each). I enjoyed this concoction every day for the rest of the school year.

- - -

During the summer of 1954, I was fortunate to get to go to Philmont Scout Ranch near Cimarron, New Mexico. Friends Dean Deaton, C. M. Harris and about 20 other boys from northeast Mississippi made the long four-day trip in a school bus. We called it the "Yellow Dog." It was a long, hot ride. We went by way of Texarkana (where we all got out and stood with one foot in Texas and the other in Arkansas), Abilene (where we spent the night sleeping on a high school gymnasium floor), and El Paso (where we made a side trip to Juarez, Mexico). This was my first time to go outside the United States. One of the other boys was Robert Moorehead from Hickory Flat, Mississippi. Later we would both be Civil Engineering students at Mississippi State and both of us joined NASA upon graduation. At Philmont, we were on the "Lucian Maxwell Trek." I soon found out what a "trek" was...lots and lots of hiking with a very heavy backpack! Each night we had to pitch our tents and cook our own food. One night a bear broke into our food tent and did a lot of damage, but fortunately didn't get away with very much food. We pitched camp one night beside a beautiful lake near the top of one of the highest mountains in New Mexico. We also hiked up to the wreckage of a World War II B-24 Liberator airplane, which had crashed there while on a training mission. Unfortunately, all seven men on board were killed. After about two weeks at Philmont, we returned by a more direct route through Oklahoma, which only took three days. The entire trip was a great experience. Some of the most beautiful scenery I had ever seen.

**Philmont Scout Ranch, New Mexico, 1954**

— — —

As I mentioned earlier, my sophomore year I got a job selling popcorn, then running the projector in the theater in Belmont. Projectionist was a great job because I got to see all the movies, it paid more than the gas station, and it wasn't nearly as dirty. I played records before the movies started, but the records on hand were pretty old and boring. With my own money, I bought a Bill Haley and the Comets record and started playing *Rock Around the Clock*. After several days Mr. Mann, asked where I got "that loud music" and told me to turn the volume down if I had to play it. Pretty soon, he realized that the kids liked that kind of music, so he gave me money and sent me to buy some newer records. I was in heaven.

On Friday nights at the theater we had local talent night. This usually was such stuff as "Shorty Ginn and His One Man Band", a local guy who played the guitar, blew a harmonica, played drums with foot pedals, and banged symbols between his knees all at the same time. Occasionally we would have a gospel group from Memphis or Lash LaRue, a cowboy actor who sang and twirled a rope. One day Mr. Mann asked me who he should book for an upcoming date, Elvis Presley or Johnny Cash, since he had never heard of either. My answer was, "Get Johnny Cash, he's much more popular than Elvis." So much for my ability to pick talent! When Johnny Cash showed up for his performance, he was passed out in his car and unable to even walk. We turned out the lights in the theater so that the people could not see that Etha Mann, The Tennessee Two (Marshall Grant and Luther Perkins), and I were lifting Johnny to the stage. We stood him up behind the microphone, ran off the stage, and then turned on the lights. I just know that I was going to be fired for suggesting a drunkard for the talent that night. When the lights came on however, he performed a 45-minute set without any sign of anything being wrong. I found out in later years, from Johnny's book, that he wasn't drinking then but was heavy into amphetamines.

Another job I had in high school was reporting on basketball games for the Tupelo Daily Journal. This meant I had to go to all the games, both home and away, and call the scores and stats into the paper afterwards. I wasn't good enough to play, so this was the next best thing. I had played basketball in elementary school at Golden, but couldn't make the team in high school. We didn't play football in the Tishomingo County schools then because a player broke his neck in a game years earlier, so football was outlawed. My Daddy was playing in the game when it happened.

For the away games, I had to get a ride with someone. One night the Belmont girls' team was playing Marietta, about 25 miles away. I hitched a ride with Ellis Carr, who had already graduated from high school and was dating Shirley Yarber, the star of Belmont's girls' team. After the game, we waited until the team bus was loaded and then started following it back home. The roads were pretty crooked and the bus was going very slow, so Ellis decided to pass it. What he did not foresee was a sharp turn in the road ahead. Just about the time we were beside the bus, with all the girls waving at us, we were going too fast to make the turn and went down a rather steep embankment. The car turned over several times and ended up on the driver's side. This was before the days of seat belts, so I was down against Ellis. We laid there for a few seconds, and then Ellis turned to me and said, "Jerry, I think we turned over." I replied, "Yea, I think we did. Do you think you should turn the engine off?" Neither of us seemed to be hurt, but because we were lying on our sides, we had a difficult time determining what was "up" or "down." At about that time we heard Shirley coming down the embankment screaming, "Ellis! Ellis! I love you!" He then turned to me again and said, "Tell her I'm dead." We found a farmer who, with his tractor, turned the car back on its wheels and pulled us back up on the road. Amazingly, the car started fine, so we got back in and headed home. One big problem was that there was no windshield! Even driving very slowly, the wind was pouring in on us, but we made it home safely. That was my first automobile wreck.

In the summer of 1955, between my sophomore and junior years, I bought my first car. I paid $300 for a black two-door 1950 Ford and thought I had the finest car in the world. If I wasn't driving it, I was washing and waxing it.

**1950 Ford 2 door, like my first car.**
**Courtesy Ford Motor Co.**

In Mississippi you could get your driver's license at age 15, so for a year prior to that, I had been driving my parents pickup truck. Several of my friends (Harold Ginn, Bobby Woods, and Dean Deaton) also had access to their parents' trucks so truck racing was one of our favorite pastimes. We raced against the clock rather than against each other. We would select a little traveled, unpaved back road and time how quickly we could go from one point to another. A pretty dangerous pastime in retrospect, but there was not much else to do in rural Mississippi and thankfully, none of us were ever hurt. When I got my own car, I stopped doing this. It was too precious to possibly damage.

After about six months of owning the Ford, I stopped one night to get gas and the attendant, Blake Moore, offered me $400 cash for my car so I sold it on the spot. Within a few days, I paid $300 for a black four-door stick shift 1950 Chevrolet Fleetline. It was not quite as sporty as the Ford, but I had made a profit of $100 so I felt like a successful businessman. One of the first things I did was have exhaust headers and twin pipes installed by my Uncle Tom Segars. If you got it up to about 60 mph and shifted down into second gear, the twin pipes made quite a racket!

**1950 Chevy 4 door Fleetline**

Since there was little to do for entertainment around Belmont and Golden, one of our favorite things to do at night was to hang out with Elwood Hallmark, the Belmont Night Watchman. He usually parked his car under the canopy of the Texaco station at the main intersection. About once per hour he would drive around town (which only took about 10 minutes) and check all the businesses. He would shine his spotlight on each business front door to make sure there were no burglaries going on. One night Harold Ginn, Bobby Woods, Billy Taylor and I were sitting with him when we began to hear a very loud car approaching town. Elwood took his clipboard from the dash of his car, shined his flashlight on it and said, "I don't have anybody scheduled to come through here tonight." He then jumped from his car waving his arms and yelling "Stop!" just as the car went speeding by, barely missing him. We were scared to death! What was going on? He explained that the speeding car was a "bootlegger" hauling illegal liquor and that to ensure safe passage through Belmont they were supposed to tell him which night they would be coming through and pay him $5 for safe passage.

For "entertainment", there was the movie theater, the drug store soda fountain, driving up and down the two-block strip between Hobson Tiffin's grocery store and the depot showing off our cars, and the Dixie Queen, which was owned by Noonan and Vera Deaton, parents of my friend Dean who was one year younger. The Dixie Queen was a small version of a Dairy Queen with a few tables inside and a drive through window. They had the best hamburgers and milk shakes I had ever eaten.

A vivid memory of my high school days at Belmont involves shop class. One of the projects in woodworking was to build a cedar chest. This was the first time I had ever done anything like that and I really enjoyed it. I finished the assembly part of the project before anyone else, so it was time to put on the finishing touches. This involved applying crack filler, sanding, and then several coats of varnish. The shop teacher showed me a big container of powder which when mixed with water was used to fill cracks. Not realizing that the container was intended to supply the entire class, I used it all. For several weeks, my nickname at school was "Crack Filler." Daughter Kristi later took the cedar chest, and still has it in her home.

--- --- ---

As I mentioned earlier, by having the best grade average my freshman year in high school, I earned the privilege to serve as a Page in the state legislature. By a stroke of luck, I was assigned to the President of the Senate, Lt. Gov. Carroll Gartin. I lived in the YMCA in Jackson and worked in the Senate for a month. The Lt. Governor and I hit it off extremely well and at the end of my term he asked if I would like to go to Washington and be a Page in the U. S. Congress. I of course said yes, so he said he would see if he could work something out.

I wasn't sure I would ever hear any more about it, but later that year, Congressman Thomas G. Abernethy contacted my parents, asking if I would like to go to Washington for a month and be his Page. Obviously, the Lt. Governor had followed through on his promise and had convinced the Congressman that I should be given a try. After much discussion, my parents said yes, so I was scheduled to go for the month of May 1955. Mr. Abernethy, being a smart politician, scheduled a different boy (sorry, but they were all boys then) from his district each month. That way he made more people happy and got more votes.

This was big time stuff for a little kid from Golden. No one from Tishomingo County had ever done this before. In preparation, I had to buy the prescribed uniform; a navy blue suit, white shirt, and black tie. I also needed some other clothes, so my parents took me to the J. C. Penney store in Tupelo. In addition to the suit, I got some new trousers, a couple of shirts, several pairs of socks and new underwear. The whole bill was almost $100. At age fifteen, I was going alone by train to Washington, D.C., to live in an apartment and be a Page in the US Congress! I had to be the luckiest guy in the world!

The new trousers were "permanent press/wrinkle free," the first I had ever owned, so I chose those to wear on the train ride from Corinth to Washington, an overnight, 18-hour ride. I had been told that Mrs. Abernethy and their daughter Gail would meet me. Gail was my age and I had heard that she was a real knock out. I fantasized during most of the trip that she would greet me with open arms and we would fall madly in love with each other. Upon arrival, sure enough, they were there at Union Station to meet me and sure enough, Gail was the best-looking thing I had ever seen. The only problem was, rather than greet me with open arms she stared at my pants with an obvious distasteful look. They were permanent press all right...crushed almost beyond salvage, but not nearly as bad as my fantasy.

"Mrs. A", as I was told to call her, talked up a storm during the car ride to Capitol Hill. Gail said nothing, and I said mostly "Yes Ma'am" or "No Ma'am." They took me to a townhouse at 212 6th Street SE, which belonged to Mrs. Edith Ridgley, the hostess of the House Restaurant, who also kept Pages for various Congressmen in her spare bedrooms. Once I was alone, I wanted to cry. My new pants had been a fashion disaster, my fantasy girlfriend did not ever speak to me, and here I was alone in a dark room in a dark townhouse, in a dark, strange city, wondering how I ever got there...and why.

The next day, I learned that my duties in the House of Representatives would begin each weekday at 10:00 a.m. Before the House convened at noon, the Pages were to distribute the Congressional Record from the previous day, and respond to any requests that a Congressman or his office staff might have, such as delivering documents. As soon as the House adjourned, which in those days was usually by 2:00 or 3:00 p.m., we were free to leave. Since this seemed like pretty short hours to me and since I felt I was indebted to Congressman Abernethy, I would go to his office each morning at eight o'clock and each afternoon after the House adjourned and ask if there was anything I could do. I later learned that I was the first Page of his to have ever done that. At first, they had to think of things for me to do but pretty soon, I had regular tasks in his office, such as opening and logging incoming mail, hand addressing envelopes for his monthly newsletter, running the mimeograph machine, etc.

One of the other Pages staying at Mrs. Ridgley's was George Gaines from New Iberia, Louisiana. He was a Page for Congressman Edwin Ellis. One of the first things I learned about George was that he also loved R&B music and that he had a 45-RPM record player. Mrs. Ridgley would conspicuously leave her keys to the House Restaurant on a table near her front door, so George and I would frequently go over to the restaurant at night and help ourselves to ice cream. There is no doubt that she knew exactly what we were doing and it made her happy.

Wembley neckties, which were very popular in the '50s, were made in Congressman Edward Hebert's (pronounced A-Bear) district, which included New Orleans, so he gave every other Congressman a tie for Father's Day. He usually asked all the Pages from Louisiana to distribute them. I enjoyed helping George distribute his and managed, with Congressman Hebert's approval, to have a couple of ties left over for my own use.

Being so far away from home for the first time, I was very lucky to have George Gaines as a friend. We were both Southerners, we both loved R&B music and we got along great. He introduced me to Tabasco Sauce, which was made near his hometown. I'm still addicted to it. He also introduced me to pizza! He took me to the Bayou, a live music place on the Potomac River in Georgetown, which served pizza. We sat on the upper balcony listening to jazz and blues and eating pizza. I thought pepperoni pizza was one of the best things I had ever eaten! George was very patient in showing me around Washington. He pointed out a townhouse between our apartment and the Capitol where Senator Joseph McCarthy from Wisconsin lived. Sen. McCarthy dominated the news in those days with his accusations of there being large numbers of Communists within the federal government. He had just recently been censured by the Senate, which passed a resolution condemning McCarthy for abusing his power as a Senator. George also taught me how to ride the trollies, which were operating in Washington at that time. I had never seen anything like that and thought it wonderful that we could just run along beside, jump on and ride all the way to downtown for a dime.

Near the end of my scheduled month, Congressman Abernethy asked if there was any way I could stay until the House adjourned for the year, which was expected in about another month or two. He said that he and his staff had been spoiled by having me around, and he wanted to keep me as long as he could. He explained that his patronage appointments were already committed for the rest of the year but he had spoken to the other Congressmen and Senators from Mississippi and that they could pool their patronage, allowing me to stay. I was thrilled, so after clearing it with my parents, I stayed on until the House adjourned in early August, rotating on a daily basis from one office to the next. Since I was missing school back in Mississippi, the school agreed to continue sending me homework assignments as they had been for the planned one month. Staying in Washington also meant I had to give up my job as projectionist at the Belmont theater. Mr. Mann had been holding it open for the expected one month I would be away, but now it would be two to three months and it was unreasonable to expect him not to want to find a permanent replacement.

To my great surprise, Congressman Abernethy called me in the fall of 1955 and said that if I wanted to return to Washington he could offer me a job as a Doorman in the House of Representatives. That would require me to enroll in the Capitol Page School, which met each weekday from 6:30 to 10:30 a.m. I would have to find my own apartment (he had a list of 3-4 possibilities), mentor his Pages who he would continue to have on a monthly basis, and to work in his office when not on duty as a Doorman. I was thrilled with the offer.

This had to be a tough decision for my parents. Here was their son who had just turned 16 going off to Washington to live unsupervised in an apartment for six months, yet it was a tremendous opportunity. I give them credit for allowing me to go. I don't reminder much discussion about it, but I'm sure they had a lot of soul-searching discussions out of my presence.

The deal was that I would attend the first semester of school at Belmont and the second semester at Capitol Page School in Washington. Page School was an accredited high school of the District of Columbia located on the top floor of the Library of Congress and attended by Pages from the House, Senate, and Supreme Court. Back in those days Congress always adjourned in May or June until the next January, so there was no reason for me to be there during the first semester.

In early January 1956, I left in my 1950 Chevy for the approximately 18-hour drive to Washington. Richard Morrison, a new Page from Daingerfield, Texas, rode with me. "Dickie" and his parents drove from Daingerfield to Golden so that he could ride the rest of the way with me. We got along great on the trip, which was good because we were to be roommates for the next 6 months. Our apartment was at 322 Maryland Avenue SE, just a few blocks from the Capitol, and owned by Mrs. Myrtle Duckett. Dick and I soon discovered that we shared birthdays. We called our moms to find out what time we were born and determined that Dick was thirty minutes older. He never let me forget it.

Being at school by 6:30 a.m. was not a lot of fun but going to a school on the top floor of the Library of Congress was impressive. At the time, it was the only high school in the US with an elevator. A very new experience for me was walking to school in the dark through several inches of snow.

I really enjoyed being a Doorman. It paid more than being a Page (about $350/month as I recall) and was more prestigious. Most of the other Doormen were much older than I, either college students or retired people. The job entailed standing at one of the doors and allowing only Congressmen or Senators onto the floor. This meant I had to know all 435 Congressmen and 100 Senators. Since Senators seldom came over to the House, I concentrated on learning the Congressmen first. I was assigned to the East Door, which was the busiest door, with an experienced and very patient man by the name of Frank DelBalzo who helped me to recognize all the Congressmen. He always had a stick of pepperoni in his coat pocket from which he would frequently take a bite. Another duty of a Doorman was to go onto the floor and get Congressmen for constituents and lobbyist who would come looking for them. Very often, the answer would be "Tell them I'm not here." Sometimes I would have to tell them, "But Sir, they have been up in the gallery and they saw you here."

Over the two years that I was there, I got to know a lot of Congressmen and Senators. Most of them were very nice. Several would stop by each day and chat a while. Some would routinely stop and ask what the upcoming vote was about and who was pro and con, because I had made it a habit of keeping up with such things. A few Congressmen, who could not make a roll call vote, would call me and ask me to vote for them. Congressman Ken Gray of Illinois did this frequently. The House floor sloped upward from the "well" (where speeches are made) to the rear of the chamber, with a walkway below the last row of seats. People in this walkway could not be seen from the front of the chamber, so I would position myself there and when the Congressman's name was called, I would shout out "Yea" or "Nay", according to how he had instructed me to vote. Luckily, I was never caught doing that. Some of the Congressmen even corresponded with my parents to let them know that they were looking out for their little boy.

Lyndon Johnson, who was then the Senate Majority Leader and seeking the Democrat Party nomination for President, came to see House Speaker Sam Rayburn frequently and usually stopped by to say hello. He had the reputation of being tough and gruff, but he was always very nice to me. He even invited me to one of his campaign parties.

Lyndon B. Johnson's triumphal return to Washington after winning the '56 Texas presidential primary. House Speaker Sam Rayburn is to Johnson's right, his daughters, Luci and Lynda Bird, are in the foreground.

**That's me between Luci and Lynda**
**Courtesy UPI**

The East Door was just across the hall from Speaker Rayburn's office, so even though he had his own Page, Ken Smith, the Speaker frequently asked me to do him favors such as giving his constituents and/or friends a tour of the Capitol. Over the two years I was there, this included Red Skelton, Jimmy Durante, Grace Kelly (who soon thereafter became Princess Grace of Monaco), Tippi Hedren and Audie Murphy. Red Skelton's nine-year-old son Richard had just been diagnosed with leukemia and given less than a year to live. I toured the two of them around the Capitol and it was very obvious that Mr. Skelton, although a famous comedian, was not in a humorous mood and just wanted to make sure his son was having a good time. I felt honored just to be with them and tried to give all my attention to his son. Grace Kelly was very gracious and gave me a sweatshirt that said "Kelly for Brickwork," which I still have. Her dad was in the brick business in Philadelphia. I spent several hours alone with Audie Murphy, the most decorated American soldier of all time. I had just recently seen his movie To Hell and Back, in which he played himself, and wanted to talk to him about it, but he seemed reluctant. He did tell me that the movie was pretty accurate, except the scene in France where he single-handedly held off (and killed most of) an entire Germany company. The movie showed him on top of a burning tank firing a 50 caliber machine gun. He told me that he actually was underneath the tank and that is how he survived and killed so many Germans. He said, "The Germans thought that nobody was dumb enough to crawl under a burning tank, so that's why they never saw me."

In addition to my roommate, Dick Morrison, I developed lasting friendships with my fellow Pages and classmates: Stan Armstrong, Charles Bush, George Gaines, Paul McClinton, Billy O'Neal, Robert Parrott, Terry Scanlon, Ken Smith, Roger Williams, and many others. We did a lot of fun things together such as movies and concerts.

Dick Morrison, Billy O'Neal and I went to see Elvis on a cruise down the Potomac. The boat was to go to Mount Vernon and back.

Something was wrong with the engine, so the boat never left the dock. Elvis put on an outstanding performance anyway. After his show Dick, Billy and I went up to meet Elvis and his band. Dick and Elvis had dated the same girl in Shreveport, Louisiana. We all shook hands with Elvis and then kind of split up with Dick spending a long time with Elvis and Billy and I talking to Sonny Moore and Bill Black. I now wish I had spent more time with Elvis. That fall, back in Mississippi, Linda and I went to see Elvis at the Mississippi-Alabama Fair and Dairy Show in Tupelo. His performance was outside (on the back of a flat-bed truck, as I recall) with a ton of screaming young girls. Linda didn't scream, but we both enjoyed him immensely.

Since most of us were really into R&B, we went to a lot of live performances. In my Page School stuff you will find some ID cards which say I was a year or two older than I really was. That was not in order to drink alcohol, but to get into performances where it was served. We saw LaVern Baker, The Platters and Bo Diddley at the DC Armory, and Mickie and Sylvia at a downtown bar.

I even enjoyed the extra work in Congressman Abernethy's office. He must have been pleased, because he asked me to come back for another year and finish high school there. He may not have been so pleased had he known of some of the pranks I was involved in. One of my new best friends was Terry Scanlon, the Documentarian Page. The Documentarian Page gets to sit up front just to the left of the Speaker. (The other Pages sit in the rear corners of the House chamber; Democrats on the left, Republicans on the right). He serves the Parliamentarian and the House Clerks who read all the Bills under consideration. One of his other duties is to raise and lower the U. S. flag over the House side of the Capitol whenever the House is in session. A part of that job was to take up several flags each day and run them up the flagpole for a few seconds so that Congressmen could then give them to constituents, schools or other organizations with a certificate that said the flag had flown over the U. S. Capitol.

I would often go with Terry to help him. One day Terry and I added a Confederate flag to the stack, quickly raising and lowering it. I am pretty sure it is the only Confederate flag which ever flew over the U. S. Capitol! It seemed like fun at the time, but I suppose that is grounds for treason.

Over the Memorial Day weekend in 1956, Terry visited with me in Golden. He and I flew to Jackson, where we were met by my parents. This was an eye opener for Terry, who had never been to the deep south. On Sunday we took him to the Catholic Church in Tupelo for Mass. That was an eye opener for me and my parents. Afterward, we stopped by Elvis Presley's birthplace in Tupelo and Terry, a big Elvis fan, thought that was really neat. While in Golden/Belmont, Linda, Clytee Smith and I showed him all the great tourist attractions such as the cotton gin, the forest fire lookout tower in Dennis, and the Patterson's Chapel bridge!

**Terry Scanlon, Clytee Smith and me on Patterson's Chapel Bridge**

One great benefit of working in my Congressman's office was that one of my duties was to take care of his friends parking tickets. He was on the District of Columbia Committee, which then served as the government of the District. (They now have their own mayor and city council and even a non-voting member of the House of Representatives). Once a week I would get a stack of parking and speeding tickets and stamp them "Void." On occasion I would add one or two of my own parking tickets to the stack. I never got a speeding ticket, but it was nice to be able to park almost anywhere and know that I could get away with it.

Another benefit was that I could help my friends get jobs in Washington. The FBI was hiring a lot of folks in their Identification Division. These were the days when fingerprints were still filed in large cabinets and they were way behind in filing. I mentioned this to my Uncle Charlie Mink, who passed it on to his nephew Edwin. Edwin said he was interested, so I sent him all the application paperwork and once I received it in the Congressman's office, forwarded it to the FBI with a letter of recommendation. Others from the Golden/Belmont followed, including Shirley Yarber, Dexter "Pat" Patterson, Jerry Owens, Moore Hallmark, Catherine Wheeler, and James Richard Sparks. Pat was the only one who stayed very long. He went to FBI school and became an agent.

To witness the National Fireworks Display on July 4, 1956, I invited Pat to watch from the Capitol roof with me and several of my Page friends. I'm pretty sure we couldn't do that now.

A big piece of legislation came before the House in June of 1956, the "Federal Aid Highway Act", which established what we know now as the Interstate Highway System. President Eisenhower, recalling his exposure to the German Autobahn during World War II, conceived the Interstate System which would vastly improve transportation and safety in the U. S. It also was considered as a great stimulus to the economy in that it would employ thousands of people. It passed with little opposition.

Adjournment night in the House of Representatives was a big deal. Adjournment at the end of my junior year in high school is especially memorable. I had done a lot of favors for Helen Thomas, who was a journalist/reporter at the time. She later became a White House correspondent and became the Dean of the White House correspondents during the Clinton Administration, allowing her to be the first to ask a question at presidential press conferences. In celebration of adjournment in 1956 she gave me a pint bottle of

Haig & Haig Scotch whiskey. I had never drank any kind of whiskey before, but since everyone was in such a happy mood, it seemed like the thing to do. The only "mixers" in the Cloak Room were water and orange juice. I should have chosen the water! Among the many festivities on the House floor, Congressman Kenneth Gray of Illinois was doing magic tricks. He was an amateur magician as well as a Chrysler/Plymouth dealer back in his home state. He asked me to help him with one of his tricks. I was already so drunk that I still can't remember the details, but somehow, in the well of the House, he removed my shirt without taking off my suit coat!

After the official adjournment, my roommate Dick Morrison, with whom I had shared my Scotch whiskey, and I went to what was then called the New House Office Building (now named Longworth), climbed the stairs to the fourth floor, finished off the Scotch, and dropped the empty bottle down the stairwell all the way to the basement. It made a big bang. I then apparently passed out. Dick somehow got me to the basement tunnel, put me on a mail cart and pushed me through the tunnel all of the way to the Senate Office Building (now named Russell), which was only about three blocks from our apartment. He did a great job of getting me home, but had failed to notice that while on the mail cart, my hands were dragging the floor and were both bloody.

The following morning I was scheduled to be at Congressman Abernethy's house at 6:00 a.m. to take some of his belongings to Mississippi for the summer in my car. His son Tommy was also going to ride with me. By about 7:00 a.m., since I had not shown up at his house, he called Mrs. Duckett, our landlady, and asked where I was. She tried to wake me but couldn't, so she told the Congressman that I was okay, but apparently still drunk. "Mr. A" showed up soon afterward, drug me out of bed and put me in the shower. Needless to say, we didn't drive to Mississippi that day. By the next day I was fine so we departed on the trip, spending the night on the way with

Congressman Carl Elliott at his home in Jasper, Alabama. Since Congressman Elliott was also a friend of mine, I was worried that "Mr. A" would tell him why we were a day late, but he made up some other excuse and to my knowledge never told him the real reason. I'm pretty sure he did not tell my parents either, because they never said anything about it. Tommy, years later told me that he was amazed at how I could shift gears so fast in my 1950 Chevy! Isn't it strange what people remember?

— — —

During the summer of 1956, I got involved in local politics for the first time. I drove J. P. Coleman, the current Mississippi Attorney General and a candidate for Governor, all over northeast Mississippi to 5-6 campaign stops per day. Late in the afternoons, after 3-4 speeches, he would ride in the back seat and take naps. Occasionally he would practice his campaign speech with his eyes closed. He would say things like "It warms the cockles of my heart to be in this redneck town with all you illiterate farmers." I just prayed that he would never actually say that, although he would often close his eyes during his last couple of speeches. He won the election.

That fall of 1956, when I was back at home, Linda and I started dating again pretty steadily. Since we both worked at the Belmont Theater (Etha Mann had hired me again as projectionist and Linda sold popcorn), we saw each other a lot. We agreed that while I was there, we wouldn't date anyone else, but that when I went back to Washington, we both could date other people. Even though I was only at Belmont High School the first semester of each year, Linda and I each racked up a lot of honors. Linda was on the yearbook staff our Junior year and we both were in our Senior year. We were voted "Most Intelligent" both years. In addition, our Senior year we were "Mr. and Miss Belmont High", Linda was the F.F.A. Sweetheart, and I was voted "Best Dressed", if you can believe that.

One of the most exciting things to happen around Belmont/ Golden was a military jet crash in the fall of 1956 near Phil Campbell, Alabama, about an hour away. It happened during final exams at Belmont High and everyone was talking about it. Cline Harris, the basketball coach, was supervising study hall that day and told us that he would allow us to either stay there or "go home and study." Clytee Smith, Margaret Yarber, Harold "Gabby" Ginn, Bobby "Salty" Woods, Jerry Stephens, and I loaded into my 1950 Fleetline and headed toward the crash site. It occurred in hilly, rocky terrain and created a hole in the ground about 50 feet deep. All we could see was molten metal at the bottom of the big hole. The pilot did not survive. The trip there and back took longer than we had expected, so we had missed our lunch period. The cooks and servers were already cleaning up when we got back to the lunch room. Mr. Harris came in and told the servers to find us something to eat and that he wanted a cup of coffee. As we sat eating our lunch, he came to our table, set his coffee cup down and said "So how big was the hole?" He obviously had known we would go to the crash site rather than home to study for finals.

--- --- ---

Back in Washington, the Abernethy's treated me like a part of their family and I frequently went to their house for dinner. Gail and I went to several functions together, but there was never anything serious between us. Their next-door neighbor was Congressman Hale Boggs from Louisiana. Their daughter Corrine, who was called Cokie, was four years younger than Gale and I but we often took her and Gail's younger brother Tommy along with us. Once we went to an amusement park where we all rode a rather terrifying roller coaster. Gail screamed all during the ride saying she hated me for taking her on the ride but once it stopped, she asked if she could ride again. Cokie was a real brat at that age. Later she married and became quite a TV star as a political analyst, Cokie Roberts.

In January 1957, upon my return to D.C. for my senior year, Dick Guyton of Tupelo, who was to serve for one month as a Page for Congressman Abernethy, rode to Washington with me. His parents brought him to Golden and we left early in the morning, spending the night on this trip in Bristol, Tennessee. I had found an apartment for Dick in the same place where I was to live that year, 123 C Street, only about 2 blocks from the Capitol. Dick was a great guy and we became very good friends. He later became the Director of The Elvis Presley Birthplace Museum in Tupelo.

Speaker Rayburn's chauffeur, George Sullivan, hung out at the East Door a lot and we became friends. In 1957, George drove me and my date (the sister of one of Mr. Abernethy's secretaries) in the Speaker's limousine to my Senior Prom. I doubt if the Speaker ever knew about it, but George volunteered to do it, so I cheerfully accepted. That was the first time I had ever ridden in a limo. Pretty good for a little kid from the cotton patches of Golden, Mississippi!

Times were a lot different then. There was very little security at the Capitol. The Capitol Police force had been beefed up several years earlier after some disgruntled Puerto Ricans had fired shots from the House gallery wounding a number of Congressmen, but compared to what exists today, overall security was minimal. Being employees, Pages and Doormen could go anywhere they desired without challenge. On weekends, several of us would really explore the building from the roof to the basement. This is how I learned that the dome is not structurally attached to the building. It merely sits on granite blocks atop the main building with no bolts or other attachment devises. Only gravity holds it in place. An example of the change in security over the years is that in January, 1957, several other Pages and I sat on top of the House wing of the Capitol with our legs hanging off the side and watched the inauguration of President Dwight D. Eisenhower as it took place below.

Another almost unbelievable example is that a few nights before the inauguration, we took gag photos for the school paper (I was Co-Editor) of each other placing "bombs", actually socks filled with a magazine, under the inaugural stand. Today, I doubt if you could get within a mile of the presidential inaugural stand, even if you were an employee of the Capitol. It is sad that such security is now required.

**Me placing "bomb" in Eisenhower's inaugural stand.**

One of the neat things I remember is that the President was in a Cadillac convertible when they left the Capitol, but his escort cars were Mercury Turnpike Cruiser convertibles with fender skirts like I had never seen before. They not only covered the rear wheels, but went all the way to the back bumper!

Since I was one of the few Pages who had a car, my trusty 1950 Chevy, I was very popular at times, like whenever anybody wanted to go somewhere. Frequently we went to movies or concerts and sometimes we just cruised. One night while out cruising, one of my friends came up with the question of what would happen if you put a bunch of soap in one of the many water fountains that are in the street circles in Washington. This called for some experimenting. It was an easy matter to drive by these fountains and toss objects into them. We discovered that one box of laundry detergent made a few bubbles, but it was hardly noticeable. Obviously, more was better. These experiments led to the scientific conclusion that four boxes of large size detergent combined with eight small boxes of powdered food coloring, each with holes punched in the sides, when tossed into the average fountain would create a beautiful display of multi-colored soap suds flowing into the street within about thirty minutes. That gave us enough time to rush back to my apartment and see it on the local TV news.

These temporary lapses of common sense were infrequent and we spent most of our time either at work, at school or studying. Page School was harder than I had experienced before. I never really had to study much in the past to make good grades, but the pace was definitely faster now and I had to spend a lot of time hitting the books. I was determined that nobody could say I was stupid because I was from a hick town in Mississippi, so I set a personal goal to make nothing but A's. Early in the final semester before graduation I learned that there was a really close race between George Weaver and me for Valedictorian. Although coming in second at such a prestigious school would have been a great honor, I was determined to be number one; for my parents, my home town, my state, and for my Congressman who had so much faith in me. I made it and am still very proud of it. I still wear my Capitol Page School ring rather than my college ring.

Mother, Daddy, sister Mary and Linda came for my graduation. I had spent some time the year before doing an article for the school paper (Appendix 1) about the chandelier in the Vice President's Capitol office. It had been placed there at the direction of President Theodore Roosevelt because it made too much noise from the wind blowing in the open windows of the White House (obviously before the days of air conditioning), and he felt the Vice President needed a little noise to keep him awake. To do the article, I had full access to the Vice President's office "when he's not in." One day VP Richard Nixon came in while I was there and when I started to leave, he insisted that I stay and then spent about half an hour telling me everything he knew about the chandelier and the other historic furniture in the office. When the article was published, I took him a copy, which he seemed to really appreciate. After that, every time he came to the House, he would stop by and say hello. The next year, we talked about the up-coming Page School graduation and about the fact that he would be giving out the diplomas. When he learned that my parents were coming up for the ceremony, he insisted that he would like to meet them and asked his secretary to schedule a thirty-minute meeting with them. When we did go to see him, he was extremely nice to my parents and spent almost an hour with them. As we were leaving the Capitol after the meeting, I asked my parents what they thought of the Vice President, thinking they would be very impressed. My mother, who as I mentioned earlier, never had a bad thought or harsh words to say about anyone, immediately said, "There's just something about that man I don't trust!" This was 17 years before then President Nixon was disgraced and resigned from office over the Watergate scandal!

Being Valedictorian meant that I had to speak at graduation. The president had always handed out the diplomas at Page School graduation, but since he (Eisenhower) was ill, Vice President Richard Nixon would do the honors that year.

Senator Frank Church of Idaho was to be the principle speaker. Senator Church was the most frequently named possible candidate for President in the next election. Others mentioned included Senator John F. Kennedy of Massachusetts, whom I had met my junior year when I was a Doorman on the East Door of the House chamber. Not recognizing him immediately, I stopped him one day when he attempted to enter the House. He was very nice, introduced himself, and told me "That's okay, I'm often mistaken for a Page."

One of my many weaknesses was, and still is, public speaking. How could I get up before the Vice President of the United States, Congressmen, Senators, my parents, my girlfriend Linda (who was Valedictorian at Belmont High), and my classmates and make a speech without making a fool of myself? My answer was practice,

practice, practice. I wrote a speech, typical of most high school speeches, and began to practice every night. For inspiration, I went to the Washington Monument almost every night and practiced out loud. I would stand there, look toward the brightly lit Capitol and practice my Valedictory address, over and over and over. If anyone saw me I guess they just thought I was another crazy person in Washington. When I finally gave the speech on graduation night, my Daddy said, "I didn't know you could do that," and Senator Church liked it so well he asked if he could insert it into the Congressional Record (Appendix 2), which he did. This did not make Congressman Abernethy happy. He wanted to be the one to put it in the Record. Senator Church also invited me to have lunch with him in the Senate Dining room the next week.

**VP Nixon giving me my diploma. CPS Principal Henry DeKeyser looks on.**

(He later signed it with the inscription: "To Jerry Bostick with congratulations and best wishes. From Richard Nixon")

The night before my last day at school, I set my alarm clock for 5:30 a.m. as usual so that I could easily be at school by 6:30. The next morning when the alarm went off, I threw the clock against the wall breaking it into dozens of pieces!

During my last year in Washington, I had several discussions with Congressman Abernethy about where I should go to college, what I should major in, and what career I should pursue. His idea was that I should go to Ole Miss (University of Mississippi), get a law degree, go back to Washington as his Legislative Assistant, then he would retire and I could run for his seat. The problems I had with this plan were: I didn't want to go to Ole Miss; I didn't want to study law; and I had concluded by this time that I didn't want to be a politician! I took an aptitude test offered at Page School, hoping the results would tell me what I should do when I grew up. The results were a little shocking, saying I should be either a funeral director or an engineer. I found a book, "What Engineers Do" and it sounded interesting to me. Therefore, I decided to go to Mississippi State and study Engineering. "Mr. A" was supportive of my decision and never mentioned a law degree again. He only asked that if I wanted to join a fraternity, he would like me to consider his college fraternity, Lambda Chi Alpha.

– – –

## Chapter 3

# COLLEGE

I entered college at Mississippi State College (Starkville, Mississippi) in the fall of 1957. It became a University the following year. That first college year turned out to be the worst in my life! What a change! I felt like I was going from king of the mountain to scum of the earth. From Capitol Page School Valedictorian, headlines in the local papers, congratulatory telegram from the Governor, diploma handed to me by the Vice President of the United States to lowly freshman with a shaved head. It was tradition at Mississippi State that upper classmen could shave freshmen's hair, cut in front of them in lines at the bookstore, cafeteria, movie, or wherever, make them run errands, or anything they felt like requesting. There was nothing on the face of the earth lower than a freshman!

To make things worse, upon enrolling at MSC I discovered that I could not get into the College of Engineering because I had not taken high school Plane Geometry. It was not offered at the time at Belmont and I couldn't fit it in at CPS. Therefore, I had to enroll in Liberal Arts and take Engineering courses. I still had not decided what kind of engineer I wanted to be, Mechanical or Civil, but the first year curriculum was essentially the same for either option.

I lived the first semester of my freshman year in Old Main dormitory, which was built in 1880 as the first building at what was then Mississippi Agriculture and Mechanical College. It was the largest dormitory under one roof in the United States and built of wood with a brick exterior. I had two roommates in a room about 10 by 12 feet. Two bunk beds (we were lucky to only have 3 in the room), no closet and no bathroom. The four story building had two bathrooms on each floor, so with about 1100 guys in the dorm, there were lines waiting to use the bathrooms. People were always setting fires to trash in the hallways, but they did only minor damage. The wood floors and walls were too dirty to burn! Two or three times a month someone would run up and down the hall screaming, "Old Main's on fire". After a while, we would just ignore them and go back to sleep.

A very memorable event occurred soon after I enrolled at MSC. On Friday, October 4, 1957, I left Starkville for a weekend at home. About half way there I heard on the car radio that the Soviet Union had placed an artifical satellite, Sputnik, into earth orbit. It transmitted a beeping signal which we could hear over the radio. This was pretty scary to me. If they could put something like that into orbit, what would keep them from putting bombs in orbit and threatening us with them? When I arrived home my parents were even more alarmed than I.

Tom Carter, a civil engineering student from Tupelo, and I had many classes together and become great friends. We spent a lot of time playing table tennis at the YMCA and pool at the Starkville Pool Hall. We played frequently with Ben Katz, Jr., the son of the owner. We knew he was good because he usually beat us. Later we would learn that he was considered the best pool player in the state and in 1962 challenged Willie Mosconi, the World Straight Pool Champion, to an exhibition match in Starkville. Ben handily won the match, running 150 straight shots.

At the beginning of the second semester of my freshman year I moved into the Lambda Chi Alpha fraternity house, where I was a pledge. Congressman Abernethy had been a Lambda Chi and had written a nice letter of recommendation for me. I had not pledged any fraternity the first semester because I couldn't afford it. In January,

1959, someone came running through the house at night screaming "Old Main's on fire!" We all just said, "Sure. Go back to sleep." Finally, we got up to look and we could see the red sky and black smoke coming from the campus. We drove up there and sure enough, Old Main was really burning. Several students were throwing their ROTC uniforms onto the fire, even though they had escaped the dorm with most of their clothes. Everyone escaped the fire except for one student who was initially declared missing, but whose remains were found the next day. Ironically, he lived in the room directly below the one where I had lived my first semester. His room was where the fire was believed to have started. There remains some mystery as to whether it was an accident, a suicide, or a murder.

**Remains of "Old Main"**
**Courtesy Jackson Clarion Ledger**

Linda had enrolled at Lambuth College in Jackson, Tennessee, for her freshman year. We kept in touch, mostly with letters (phone calls were too expensive) and saw each other at least once a month while visiting home. We decided that she should transfer to MSU her sophomore year, which she did somewhat to the chagrin of her mom. We both worked to help pay our tuition and expenses and we both tried to study enough to make decent grades, so we didn't see each other nearly as much as we had anticipated. Linda worked in the Purchasing Department and for the Dean of Engineering. I delivered newspapers on campus, washed dishes in the cafeteria, and scooped ice cream in the Dairy Products Grill, called the DP.

I also was in Army ROTC, for which I got paid a little. Beginning with my junior year, I was an ROTC Squad Leader for 10 football players. I was never sure how that came about, but it worked out fine because it led to a job tutoring football players. Other than the pay, a great benefit of that job was that the football players usually got a copy of upcoming tests the night before. When I was taking the same course, that meant I also got to see what to expect on the test. Another great benefit was that when tutoring, I could eat in the athletic dorm cafeteria, where they usually had steak; much better than the mystery meat in the college cafeteria! At ROTC drill each Thursday, I was required to inspect my Squad for proper uniform, haircut, etc. The football players decided to wear red socks at drill rather than the prescribed olive-drab ones. They were all huge guys, most with no neck. At least three of my Squad ended up as professional players: Bobby Bethune with the Chicago Bears; Walt Suggs and Tom Goode with the Houston Oilers. After a couple of weeks of the red socks, I would just pull up their pant legs and say "Nice socks!" I wasn't about to give them demerits for not being in uniform.

During the summers of 1957 and 1958 I measured cotton land for the US Department of Agriculture. Farmers were given an acreage allotment for cotton and the government sent people out with aerial photographs to actually measure and make sure the farmer wasn't planting more than his allotment. I was not usually greeted with open arms and even occasionally was forced to leave by farmers with shotguns! However, I enjoyed the job because it involved "technology" I had never been exposed to before: aerial photo maps and a wonderful instrument called a planimeter, which you ran around the perimeter of a field on the map and it automatically calculated the acreage.

My sophomore year in college was better. At least I wasn't a freshman anymore plus having Linda around and living in the fraternity house made life much better. Linda was selected as the Lambda Chi Sweetheart. The fraternity house, which was about a mile off campus, had a basement which we dug out deeper, poured a new concrete floor, added plumbing, and paneled the walls to make it into our party room. We did have some parties but mostly in compliance with college rules. They were all monitored by our House Mother, Mrs. Oakley, whom we called Mother Nan. She also owned a ranch not far from town, so we would occasionally go out there with a keg of beer (which we had to buy at the "Crossroads" in Lowndes County because Oktibbeha County was a "dry" county, meaning no alcohol sales), build a campfire and have a great time. For Homecoming each year we would build a float for the parade. I don't think we ever placed any higher than fifth in the competition, but we had a lot of fun working on them.

At the beginning of my sophomore year, Rex Kelly and I attended the Lambda Chi General Assembly in Montreal, Canada. We drove to Indianapolis, Indiana, the LXA headquarters, stopping in Evansville, Indiana to see me Capitol Page School friend, Roger Williams. From Indianapolis we rode to Montreal with George Spasyk, the Traveling Secretary who visited our chapter frequently. George would later become the Executive Director of LXA. On our return trip George took us to Stowe, Vermont to visit his brother and then to visit with his mother in Pittsfield, Massachusetts. His mom made Ukrainian dumplings, very much like gnocchi, that were the best ever!

A few weeks before Christmas 1958, I purchased a Lionel train set to give to Robert for Christmas. After a few days, I decided that I should make sure it worked so we set up the track around the Lambda Chi Christmas tree. It worked fine, but drew the attention of everyone in the house. They all wanted to play with it. By late that night, we had burned out the motor and I had to go buy Robert a new train set.

I made many life-long friends in Lambda Chi. Dean Deaton, my friend from Belmont pledged a year after I did and we continued our close friendship. Gary Briggs, Leroy Cooper, Rex Kelly, Charlie Parker, and Pat Scott were the ones with whom I spent the most time. In thinking back, there was not one of the 25-30 members who I didn't like and get along with well.

During the spring of our sophomore year (1959), Linda and I started talking about getting married. The only drawback we could come up with was money. Being college students, any money we made went toward our education. We discussed the idea with our parents and they were not too happy with that prospect but said if that's what we really wanted to do, they would back us. So we set a date of August 30, 1959, and started planning for the wedding.

That summer before we were married I worked for the Mississippi Highway Department on a surveying team headed by Joe Vaughn from Belmont. He and his wife Inez owned a little store just across the street from Belmont High School where we would go to get Cokes and snacks (there were no vending machines on campus), so I was familiar with him. We worked out of the Booneville office and did the surveys for improving (widening, straightening) State Highway 30 from Dennis to Booneville. I really enjoyed the work and was excited about earning a little money for the future.

I still owned my trusty 1950 Chevrolet Fleetline. Daddy had given us his 1954 Chevy Bel Air as a wedding gift but I knew that my fraternity brothers would decorate the car we would use for our honeymoon, so I didn't tell anyone. We parked my Fleetline in front of the church before the wedding and sure enough, when we came out it was covered with crepe paper and cans tied to the back bumper. I found out later that Dean Deaton, Gary Briggs and others had also attached a Mississippi State cow bell to the rear axle! What they didn't know was that we had made other arrangements. Just as we were leaving the church, Zeke Clark, the local Mississippi Highway Patrolman pulled up in his patrol car and Linda and I piled in the back seat. He drove us to Tishomingo, with his siren blaring, where Daddy had stored the Bel Air in a friend's garage. That was the car in which we went on our honeymoon to Gatlinburg, Tennessee, in the Smoky Mountains. A sad memory of our wedding day was that Mary would not allow Robert to attend because his shirt was not properly ironed. I was furious!

When we returned to MSU we moved into a furnished apartment we had rented in a little community called "Cooterville" after the owner Cooter Owens. The monthly rent was $50 which Cooter collected the last day of each month, always with a hammer in his hand. When I asked him why he always carried the hammer when he collected rent, his reply was "If somebody refuses to pay, I hit them over the head with the hammer." My friend Tom Carter had also married that summer, so he and wife Doris had the apartment just to the rear of ours. The apartment was somewhat old and very small but better than dorm or fraternity house rooms. We didn't have a washer and dryer so a chore every weekend was to go to the laundry mat. We also did not have a TV, but soon bought a used one at Allen's Hardware in Belmont for $35.

Not very long after we were married, I woke up one morning with white splotches on my hands and feet. A few days later, I went to the college infirmary where I was told that it was vitiligo, a very rare skin disease resulting in loss of pigment. They sent me to a dermatologist in Tupelo who had very dark spots on his hands. He too, had vitiligo and had attempted to treat it with some sort of dye, which obviously did not work. He discovered several more spots on my forehead and shoulders. I was not too happy to learn that there was no known cause or cure and that it would likely spread further. There still is no known cure but mine has not spread and really only shows up in the summer when I get a sun tan. I don't worry about it and hardly ever even notice it. It's just a part of me now.

In the summer of 1960, I was required to attend Army ROTC summer camp for two weeks at Fort Benning, Georgia. This was quite an experience. We were treated like draftees and pushed to the limit. We had inspections in the barracks at least once a day, had to pull KP (Kitchen Patrol) duty, which involved everything from peeling potatoes to washing dishes, guard duty at night, and exhausting training each day. The last week there I had KP duty one night, then immediately left before daylight the next morning on a 20 mile hike. I had to carry a 50-caliber machine gun, which must have weighed 50 pounds. Small airplanes would frequently fly over us and drop flour sacks. If you got any flour on you, you were declared dead and given demerits for not finding a place to hide. When we finally arrived at our campsite, it was pouring rain. I was assigned guard duty that night, stood on the top of one mountain, and talked by radio with my counterpart on the top of an adjoining mountain. Lightening was flashing all around us. I saw a lightening flash on the adjoining mountain and lost radio contact with the guy I had been talking to. I assumed that the lightening had knocked his radio out. The next day I learned that he had suffered a direct hit with lightening and was killed. Needless to say, ROTC summer camp was not my favorite summer vacation!

After ROTC camp, I again worked for the Mississippi Highway Department overseeing construction of a new bridge on Highway 30 at Bay Springs. The bridge was in anticipation of a dam that would be built nearby for the Tennessee-Tombigbee Waterway which would flood the existing bridge. I loved that job also because it involved real construction and many things new to me. My favorite task was testing concrete samples (pigs, they were called) in the lab. When each truck delivered concrete, a sample was taken. I thought it was really neat to put pressure on a concrete cylinder until it cracked.

In the fall of 1960, my very generous parents asked if we would like to have a new Chevy Impala convertible, which was on display at Moore Chevrolet in Belmont. Apparently, Mr. Moore was having a hard time selling it, so he gave my parents a good deal on a trade-in. Of course we said yes, so Tom Carter and drove to Belmont to make the swap. It was a beautiful white car with a black convertible top and red interior. On the way back to Starkville, we stopped and let the top down even though it was dark and cold. After a while, Tom begged me to put the top up, but I insisted on driving all the way to Starkville with it down. Why have a convertible it you aren't going to use it?

Linda graduated after only 3 ½ years, so in January 1960, she started working full time in the University Purchasing Department. That added income really made it possible for me to stay in school. I had decided by then that I wanted to be a Civil Engineer, with a minor in structures. I still could not be admitted to the College of Engineering because of the lack of high school Plane Geometry. Finally, after completing every college math course required for an Engineering degree, I had to enroll in a correspondence course from the University of Mississippi (Ole Miss) to take high school Plane Geometry! Thankfully, I passed the course and was finally admitted to the College of Engineering. With all my indecision about what kind of Engineer I wished to be and the confusion over my being in the College of Liberal Arts, but taking Engineering courses, it took me 4 ½ years to graduate.

My senior project was to design a café-gym-itorium, a facility which could be used as a cafeteria, a gymnasium or an auditorium. I really enjoyed that project and received an A grade. Our senior Structures class also assisted the professor in designing and building a roof for a storage building beside the Engineering building. The roof was in the shape of a hyperbolic paraboloid. That sounds very sophisticated, and it is mathematically complex, but it also is the shape of a Pringle potato chip. The hardest part was building the forms for the concrete roof. Years later, when I returned to the campus, the building and roof were still there.

When interviewing for jobs before graduation, I had choices between several state highway departments, oil and gas refineries, and a couple of aircraft companies. I decided to accept an offer from Boeing in Seattle in the weights and balances department. I would be doing things I had never dreamed of, like reviewing the design of aircraft structures and calculating the center of gravity. Seattle was a long way from Mississippi, but I was excited about going to a part of the United States to which I had never been.

Soon after accepting Boeing's offer, I was walking across the campus one day with a friend who needed to go by the Placement Office, so I went with him. The Placement Director saw me and said, "I know you've already accepted a job with Boeing in Seattle, but I've been trying to get NASA to come here for interviews and they have now agreed to come, but I don't have any good people for them to talk to. Would you please sign up for an interview and act interested?" As a favor to him, I signed up. I unfortunately cannot remember the name of the NASA person who did the interview, but he convinced me that there was no better place for a Civil/Structural Engineer than the Structures Division at the NASA Langley Research Center in Hampton, Virginia. I received a firm offer from NASA the next week (GS-7 at about $5300/year), so I called Boeing and told them I wasn't coming.

In my last semester at Mississippi State, I had a GPA which exempted me from final exams. This meant I could leave early and start working at Langley. However, the ROTC commissioning date was after final exams, so I was faced with hanging around for two weeks just to be sworn into the Army. I visited with the Professor of Military Science and Tactics, (PMS&T), the head Army guy on campus, to discuss my dilemma. He pulled out Army regulations and read to me; "ROTC cadets must be commissioned on the campus where they received instruction, except by permission of the Commander in Chief."

Therefore, it appeared I was doomed to delay the beginning of my NASA career in order to receive my Army commission. When I told Linda about what the PMS&T said, she asked, "Who is the Commander in Chief?" While explaining to her that he was the president of the United States, it occurred to me that while working in my congressman's office, I had dealt with many requests for favors from constituents. There was a network of people in Washington who handled such special requests without ever getting the principals involved. So, I called my Congressman's secretary and explained my situation. The next day she called to tell me she had a letter signed by the Commander in Chief saying that any officer at any U.S. military base could commission me, and that she had already spoken to the Base Commander at Langley Air Force Base and that he would be happy to swear me into the Army. This meant we could leave immediately for Virginia and start to work.

# Chapter 4

# NASA THROUGH APOLLO 11

We were excited about finally finishing college and getting a real job. I told Linda, "We will get the finest apartment we can find, even if it costs $100/month!" We rented a 5'x 8' U-Haul trailer for all our possessions, which only amounted to clothes, a few dishes, a TV set and baby furniture for our first child, due in March. We had the trailer weighed empty so that NASA could reimburse us for the weight which we transported. We stopped enroute in Suffolk, Virginia, at a peanut factory to have it weighed loaded. The attendant told me he could make it weigh more if I wanted, just by placing his cigarette lighter on the balance beam. I declined that offer.

On the way to Virginia, we spent the night in Knoxville, Tennessee, with our friends Tom and Doris Carter. Tom had graduated in the summer of '61 and accepted a job with the Tennessee Valley Authority there. It was good to see them and to see that if you had a good job you could afford a decent apartment.

We arrived in Hampton/Newport News in time for me to report to work at the Langley Research Center (LRC) on Monday, January 29, 1962. We checked into a motel, parked the U-Haul and began looking for apartments. The apartment situation was very depressing. There were few decent ones available and they were priced way over our budget. It was very clear that my anticipated $100/month wasn't going to be enough. We found a group of apartments on Elizabeth Road, which we liked and could afford, but none were available. For the next week, I almost camped out at the front door of the manager, who was from Mississippi, until she finally put us at the top of her waiting list. Soon afterward she told us that a two bedroom furnished apartment would be available on March 1 for $150/month. We immediately signed a contract. This meant that we would have to live in the motel for several weeks, but that was okay with us as long as we had locked in a decent apartment. Rather than pay for renting furniture, we went to the local Sears store and bought furniture for which the payments would be $35/month, the same as we would have to pay extra for a furnished apartment. Since we had no established credit, I had to get Daddy to sign the note at Sears.

On February 20, we watched the launch of John Glenn in our motel room. How exciting! Little did I realize then that within a few weeks I would be working for the NASA Operations group and within a few months be working in the Mercury Control Center we were seeing on TV.

At LRC, I was assigned to the Erectable Structures Section, Space Structures Branch, Structures Division. I was assigned a research project to design, build and test an antenna that could be folded up into a very small package, launched into space and then unfurled to be used as a communications satellite antenna. The antenna would be an elliptic paraboloid.

At first, I was really excited. What a challenge and what an opportunity! I would have use of all the wonderful facilities at Langley: test stands, vacuum chambers, etc. However, I soon began questioning my Section Head about who needed such an antenna, to what specific use it would be put, and what would become of my project after the one year in which I was expected to complete it. He could not give me answers to my satisfaction, so he sent me to the Branch Chief. Same result. I ended up visiting with the Division Chief, Mr. Heldenfels. His answer was that I would write a NASA Tech Note, which would go out to all NASA libraries. Then "people will call you and ask questions, and most likely, ask you to help them build one." My question then was "What if nobody calls?" The answer was that I would be assigned to another research project.

This made me very uncomfortable and led me to the conclusion that I was not a research person. I would much rather work on solving known problems.

At about this time I noticed that my office mate, Ed Martin, was disappearing at lunchtime almost every day without explanation. At Langley, everyone usually "brown bagged" and ate at their desk. After a few days of this, I asked him what was going on. He whispered for me to follow him out into the lab. There he told me that the Space Task Group, on the other side of Langley field, was interviewing for people to work on the manned space program, and he was trying to get a job with them. This really excited me. Here was a group that probably really had some problems needing a solution. Some of my college friends had gone to work for NASA, most in Huntsville, Alabama, but they all had degrees in Aeronautical Engineering, so I never had considered that as an option. I asked my friend if he could set up an interview for me. Anything other than research was attractive, and it was rumored that they were moving to Houston, Texas, which I thought would be a much better place to live than Hampton, Virginia.

My interview at the Space Task Group was with Chris Critzos, who was an Executive Assistant to Chris Kraft. Just the association with Chris Kraft excited me. I had read about him and seen him on TV several times, and he had become a hero of mine. He was so articulate and always very nicely dressed. He was the Flight Director of the early Mercury missions. How much more important can one get?

When Critzos explained to me that they were looking primarily for Aeronautical, Mechanical and Electrical Engineers, not Civil

Engineers, I felt instantly as if I were doomed to research at Langley for the rest of my life. As I was dejectedly leaving his office, in walks the man himself, Chris Kraft! Critzos introduced me to him saying, "This young man is a Civil Engineer now working in the Structures Division at Langley. I explained to him that we aren't looking for Civil Engineers." Kraft looked at me and asked why I wanted to come to work on the manned space program. I explained my dissatisfaction with research and that I really wanted to work on solving specific, more immediate problems. Without any more questions or comments, Kraft turned to Critzos and said, "Hell, hire him. We may need somebody to survey the moon."

So, in late March 1962, after only doing research at Langley for 6-7 weeks, I was hired by the new NASA Manned Spacecraft Center. The first people I met were Glynn Lunney and Lyn Dunseith. They were both very nice and receptive. I knew immediately that I was going to like this new job a lot. Little did I realize at the time how intertwined with Lunney and Dunseith my future would be.

In the middle of all this, Linda was expecting our first child. Son Michael Tiffin Bostick was born March 26, 1962, in Hampton, Virginia. We did not know ahead of time if it was to be a boy or girl, but were very happy that it was a boy and that he was healthy. If it had been a girl, her name would have been Katherine Elizabeth.

Linda knew I was trying to get a job with the manned space program and that it would require a move, but she was a little surprised when she was still in the hospital and I asked how soon she would be able to move to Houston, Texas. Her reply was, "I can leave as soon as you need." She knew that I really wanted this new job, and neither of us really liked living in Hampton/Newport News, so she was as ready to go as I was.

There was only one small problem. As I mentioned before, while in college I was in Army ROTC, which meant I was facing a two-year commitment in the Army. I was a little nervous about explaining this to Chris Critzos, afraid that it might blow the whole deal. However, he said that was no problem and that I needed to talk to Bob Ernull, who worked there and was serving out his Army time. Ernull explained to me the entire process: "When called to active duty by the Army you will have to go to Army school for 6-9 weeks, but upon completion of that, you will be assigned back to NASA. You will continue to be officially in the Army and receive Army pay, but will work at NASA, just like all the regular NASA employees." What a relief. I really was going to have a job as a "Steely Eyed Space Scientist!" Not bad for a kid from the cotton fields of Mississippi.

My assignment was to the Trajectory Analysis Section in the Mission Analysis Branch. My immediate boss was Carl Huss, who also served as the Retrofire Controller in the Mercury Control Center at Cape Canaveral. Pretty exciting stuff! Carl was already heavily involved in preparations for Scott Carpenter's flight and was at the Cape most of the time.

He told me to follow Clay Hicks and Charlie Allen around for a few days and they would train me to do the trajectory design for upcoming missions. I had to learn Fortran computer programming quickly. They taught me how to use a computer that used punched cards as input. I would punch the cards myself and then submit them to the computer operators and get the results the next day. This was entirely new to me. (I had operated a computer my senior year in college as a part-time job for my structures instructor who was working on his doctoral dissertation. The "computer" was a 12 x 12 room, which had plug-in sockets on three of the walls. Using a diagram the instructor had given me, I would string cords from plug-in to plug-in, making sure that I didn't get wired up in the room.) Within a week, I was doing analysis of reentry trajectories, varying the time and spacecraft attitude of retrofire, to determine the change in landing point. If retrofire is late by 1, 2, 3, etc. seconds, how far downrange does the spacecraft land? If the spacecraft is out of the correct attitude in yaw, pitch, and roll by X degrees, how does that affect the landing point? The plots I generated from these trajectory runs ended up in Carpenter's on-board Flight Plan! Something I had created was actually going to fly in space and if the astronaut used the data, he would land closer to his intended splashdown point. How much better can life get than this?

In early April Linda, Mike and I were headed to Houston via Mississippi. I dropped Linda and Mike off with her parents, which was hard to do, but I had a job to do and was excited about it. In the meantime, I had received my call to active duty and would be required to report to Fort Bliss in El Paso for nine weeks of Artillery training, beginning in early May. Specifics would come later.

What was then called the Manned Spacecraft Center was spread all over Houston in temporary offices while the new facilities were being built in Clear Lake. The Flight Operations people were in the Houston Petroleum Center (HPC) on the Gulf Freeway. I got a room in a motel on South Main, where several other Flight Ops people were staying. Marty Jenness, an MPAD co-worker, was staying there, so we carpooled to work. We passed by the Astrodome construction site each day. It was the first domed sports arena and after completion in 1965 was called the "Eighth Wonder of the World." I continued to work with Clay Hicks and Charlie Allen, mostly in planning the MA-8 mission of Wally Schirra. Carl Huss, by phone from the Cape, still had us doing some special studies for Carpenter's MA-7 flight, but I spent most of my time on MA-8 launch abort studies, which would end up in a formal publication prior to the flight. I still had a hard time believing I was doing stuff that Flight Controllers and astronauts would actually use. What an exciting job!

Just after arriving in Houston, I learned that my Army report date would be May 5, 1962. I would be going to Fort Bliss in El Paso, Texas, for Artillery School. I really wanted to see Mike before leaving, but I had not worked at NASA long enough to accumulate any leave time. I told Carl Huss about my situation, and he said that I should just take time off without pay and go see my son. Since Kraft was at the Cape, Huss suggested that I go see Sig Sjoberg, Kraft's Deputy, and tell him I needed to take leave without pay. Huss said he would call Sjoberg and tell him I was going to make such a request and he didn't think there would be any problem. When I saw Sjoberg, he seemed to understand fully and said to give him a day or so to work on it and he would let me know.

The next day I got a call asking me to come to his office. I wondered why the secretary couldn't just tell me yes or no over the phone, but if Sjoberg wanted to see me, I would surely go to his office. He asked me again where in Mississippi I was going and how far it was from the Marshall Space Flight Center in Huntsville, Alabama. I told him it was only 1 ½ hours away. He said that he was supposed to go to a meeting in Huntsville, but couldn't make it, so could I go and sit in for him? I said sure, so travel orders were cut for me to fly to Huntsville for a meeting on a Friday morning, but not return to Houston until the following Monday. Sig explained that he would expect a written report of the meeting and that if I were to use my rental car for any personal business, I would have to pay for it myself.

If I had ever doubted that I was now working with a bunch of wonderful people, this proved that I certainly was. Sig had not only allowed me to go see my newborn son, but had arranged it so that I didn't have to take time off without pay and NASA would pay for my travel. I did write a report of the meeting that I attended on his behalf in Huntsville, and sent it to him. He called and said he would like to talk to me about it. I figured he had more questions about the meeting, but when we met, he only had questions about how my son was doing.

– – –

In early May, I reported to Fort Bliss for the beginning of my Army tour. The drive from Houston to El Paso was a long, desolate one. It was pretty hot for that time of year, and my Chevy convertible did not have air conditioning! I drove most of the way with the windows down and my arm up on the sill. The new Interstate 10 was great to drive on, but from Kerrville to Fort Stockton, it was barren. I started counting how much time elapsed between seeing people. That became so long that I changed to how long it took to see <u>any</u> form of life. Just before getting to Fort Stockton, I saw smoke on the horizon ahead; first thinking it was a brush fire. Soon I realized it was a diesel truck coming in my direction with a lot of "dust" flying out of the trailer. As it passed, I saw that it was an empty cattle truck, and instantly felt pain in my upper left arm. I quickly pulled onto the shoulder of the road and got out of the car. Blood was all over my upper arm and after cleaning it with my handkerchief, I could see that there was a bad cut. When I started getting back into the car, I saw a big clump of something in the rear seat. Upon further inspection, I could see that it was a big dried cow patty! The cut was so bad that I stopped at an emergency room in Fort Stockton and had it sewn up. When the doctor looked at it, he said, "That's a pretty nasty cut. How did you get that?" My reply was "Would you believe it if I told you I was hit by a flying turd?"

El Paso/Fort Bliss was very hot and dry. The humidity was so low that helicopters were grounded. Quite a change from Houston! At least the barracks were air-conditioned, albeit with evaporative cooling (we called them "swamp coolers") and not very effective.

For nine weeks, I attended Artillery school, learning about Nike Ajax and Nike Hercules missiles. The last week of school involved going to the White Sands New Mexico Missile Range and actually firing a couple of each. My last Hercules actually hit and destroyed a drone target. This was not planned, as a proximity fuse was supposed to explode the warhead a "safe" distance from the drone and only knock it down, not destroy it. I figured I would get into trouble, but it was determined that the fuse was set properly but had malfunctioned. I graduated number one in the class of about 30.

**NIKE AJAX**
**Courtesy US Army**

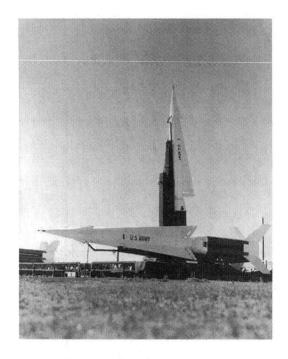

**NIKE HERCULES**
**Courtesy US Army**

**US Army Artillery School, Ft. Bliss, TX, 1962**
**Courtesy US Army**

Later I found out that I had been used in ROTC classes at Mississippi State as an example of how one does not do things in the military. "You do not pull strings to get around regulations. This guy has done an unpardonable thing. He got the Commander in Chief to allow him to receive his Army commission at an Air Force Base, of all places." However, after I graduated from Artillery School as number one in the class, they put my picture up in the ROTC building, since I was the first cadet from Mississippi State to have ever done that. I went from goat to hero in only a few months!

While at Fort Bliss, Scott Carpenter's Mercury Atlas Seven flight took place. I listened on the radio and was dismayed that he was not in the proper attitude at retrofire and landed several hundred miles long. I said aloud to the radio, "Why didn't you use my charts? They were in your Flight Plan!" It turned out he got carried away with the scenery and did not pay attention to his attitude. He just wanted to enjoy the view from space!

Also, while there, several of us went to Juarez, Mexico, on the weekends. It was safe back then and we could get Carta Blanca beer for a dime a can. I saw Johnny Cash there at the La Cuca Racha (The Cock Roach) nightclub. Years later, I discovered that my Meadowlakes friend Lloyd Dalton played guitar for Johnny that night. It is a small world!

Upon completion of Artillery School, I was assigned back to NASA in Houston. I drove the desolate miles back to Houston, and then flew to Mississippi so that I could see Linda and Mike. Mike seemed to have grown a lot in the almost three months since I had seen him. Boy, was I proud to have such a fine son!

**Lieutenant Bostick**

– – –

The welcome that NASA received in Houston was unbelievable. There was a lavish welcome party almost every week in places like the Shamrock Hilton hotel, Glenn McCarthy's Cork Club which served exotic wild game, the Music Hall and, when finished in 1965, the Astrodome. At the grand opening of the Astrodome, they conducted a drawing for unbelievable prizes. I won a TV, which was presented to me by Loretta Swit, "Hot Lips' on the TV show M*A*S*H. Free tickets to Houston Astros baseball and Oilers football games, usually box seats were always available. Judge Roy Hofheinz, majority owner of the Astros and the major person behind the building of the

Astrodome, had private living quarters and a huge guest box high above center field. He often invited us to sit in his box. Private clubs waived their membership fee for NASA employees. Almost every department store in town gave us credit cards. What a difference from Hampton, Virginia, where Linda and I could not get credit from Sears to buy some furniture. There was only one problem. The Houston radio and TV people pronounced NASA as a word, not the individual letters N-A-S-A. Since NASA had replaced NACA, the National Advisory Committee for Aeronautics, which was always pronounced N-A-C-A, it was offensive to the old NACA folks like Center Director Bob Gilruth and Kraft. We finally gave up.

When I returned to Houston, I started looking for an apartment into which we could move. I located a new complex called "Royal Palms", just across the street from the Palm Center Shopping Center, which was nice back in those days. A few weeks later, we moved in. The complex had a swimming pool that Mike loved. He wasn't afraid of the water and never was ready to get out.

I would return to the same job I left nine weeks before, but I would receive Army pay. It was a struggle for the next two years living on $228/month (about ½ of what I had been making as a NASA employee) with no overtime pay and no Army Commissary closer than Fort Sam Houston in San Antonio, which was my official base. My Branch Chief, Carl Huss, did allow me to keep track of the overtime I worked (which routinely was 3-4 hours per day) and use it as compensatory time off rather than use any of my Army leave. The plan was that by not taking any of my leave, I would be reimbursed for it upon completion of my two-year tour. In 1963, Linda also went to work at NASA for my friend Lyn Dunseith, a Branch Chief in the Flight Support Division. As a secretary, she made more money than I was making and it sure did help!

Upon returning to Houston, I heard from my good Mississippi State friend Tom Carter, who was then working for the Tennessee Valley Authority. He called to ask if there was any chance I could help him get a job in Houston with NASA. He sent in an application, and I recommended to Carl Huss that he be hired. So within a few weeks, old friend Tom and I were sharing an office in HPC, both doing trajectory planning for the Mercury missions. Our computers were located on the University of Houston campus in what had once been the PBS studios (KUHT). Tom and I spent a lot of time after normal work hours in the computer room. We made friends with the night shift operator who would let us make changes and re-run our programs if there was a problem with the first try. They also had huge plotting machines there that we were allowed to operate in order to make the plots for the Mission Plans, Flight Plans, and the Mission Control Center plot boards.

Tom and Doris rented an apartment near us at the Royal Palms. After living there for a while, Doris became the assistant manager and was later asked to be the manager of the new Park Place apartments, owned by the same people, so we moved there with the Carters. (Doris gave us a cut on the rent!)

Mike was a happy camper at the new apartment because it also had a pool. He loved being in the water. Near his first birthday, in March 1963, I took him for his first haircut. I had worried that he wouldn't like that, but he thought it was fun!

**Mike's First Haircut, March 1963**

– – –

John "Shorty" Powers was the Public Affairs Officer at the new Manned Spacecraft Center, and had called himself the "Voice of Mercury Control" and sometimes "The 8th Astronaut." After the last Mercury flight, NASA had enough of his arrogance and terminated him in September of 1963. He was replaced by his former NASA Headquarters boss, Paul Haney. Shorty then purchased a radio frequency and formed KMSC, broadcasting from Clear Lake. At a press conference after one of the early Gemini flights, at which I was a participant, after all of us had spoken, Haney opened the floor for questions. The rule was that the reporters would only ask questions after being recognized. Paul allowed every other reporter to ask at least one question, totally ignoring Shorty, who was in a front row seat, jumping up and down, wanting to ask a question. Finally Paul said, "The little short guy on the front.", pointing to Shorty. Shorty then just slammed his notebook shut and left the room. The guys in the Trench liked Paul a lot because he did his homework and subscribed to a policy of complete openness. We later made him an honorary member of the Trench, only the second one, after Chris Kraft.

Thursday, November 21, 1963, was an exciting day. President Kennedy was making a trip to Texas, with his first stop in Houston. He landed at Ellington Field and paraded up the Gulf Freeway to downtown Houston. We all went outside to watch and wave as his motorcade passed the HPC. There he was, the proponent of landing men on the moon passing by in his convertible with the top down. Later that evening several of us took our families and watched from the Foley's Department Store parking garage as he paraded toward the Rice Hotel where he would stay that night. Early in the afternoon of the next day at work, Homer Scott, an aide to Chris Kraft, came running into our office screaming, "The president has been shot in Dallas!" We listened to the radio to try to learn more. Finally, I left work and went home to see if I could hear more on TV. As I pulled into the parking lot of our apartment, I heard the announcement on the radio that President Kennedy was dead! To say that was a sad day would be a gross understatement. The loss of the great man who had so concisely laid out the lunar landing challenge was indeed discouraging. However, we looked upon that challenge now as a crusade. We were even more determined to meet his goal.

At about this time Linda and I started thinking about where we would live in the Clear Lake area once NASA finished the facility there, planned for mid-1964. We looked at all the available subdivisions and purchased a cul-de-sac lot in Nassau Bay, directly across the street from NASA. We agreed on a floor plan and I drew the architectural plans. We selected a builder (Doyle Stucky), but when he submitted the plans, the Property Owners Association (POA) would not approve them because they were not signed by a licensed architect. I had to pay an architect $250 to look at the plans and sign them! The POA then approved the plans with one minor change (it looked too much like another house already in Nassau Bay, so we had to change the brick color) and construction soon began. We had a lot of fun selecting materials and colors, but usually had to settle for the least expensive options.

About six weeks before the end of my tour of duty, the Army pulled one of its favorite tricks and reassigned me to Fort Polk, Louisiana, which was the nearest Army base to my "Home of Record" in Mississippi. The Army pays you for returning to your home upon tour completion, so by the reassignment, they would have to pay me less money for the trip.

In the notification of the change, I was ordered to report for duty at Fort Polk, Louisiana. I reported as ordered, but in civilian clothes rather than Army uniform. That caused a bit of an uproar at Fort Polk. "Where is your uniform?" I explained that I wasn't required to wear one at NASA and that the only one I had was left over from my ROTC days. They started asking me about my MOS...Military Occupational Specialty. What was I qualified to do? They told me I would have to buy a new uniform and return for duty for the next month before my dismissal date. I wasn't about to do that, so I ended up having to use all my military leave in order to return to Houston to work! So much for the plan for getting paid for my unused military leave.

During my two years as a military detailee at NASA, I worked on mission planning for Wally Schirra and Gordon Cooper's flights. For both of these missions I got to go to the Cape for simulations and the actual missions. For Schirra's flight, MA-8, I had the duty, under the close supervision of Charlie Allen, of releasing balloons during the pre-launch phase, tracking them, and then calculating where the spacecraft would land in case of an abort during various times of the launch phase. I started releasing the balloons at four hours prior to the scheduled launch and then every half hour up to 30 minutes prior to launch. I released them from the parking lot in front of Hangar S at Cape Canaveral that was the spacecraft final assembly and checkout facility, as well as the astronaut crew quarters. I tracked the balloons with skin-track C-Band radar that fed into a small computer inside the hangar. Once I had calculated the spacecraft landing points, assuming aborts at various times, using the actual winds, I called Bob Thompson, Chief of Recovery, in the Mercury Control Center with the results. Any predicted landings on land were a No-Go for launch. For MA-9, I was the lead guy doing this with Tom Carter as my assistant. Thank goodness, we didn't have to call a launch No-Go on either flight. I don't think I was ever happier. Here I was in the middle of the most exciting thing going on in the world (or at least I thought so). After launch, along with Charlie Allen and Tom Carter, I worked in a "back room" supporting Huss, the Retrofire Controller and Glynn Lunney, the Flight Dynamics

Officer. This concept later became the Staff Support Room (SSR) activity we had in the new Houston MCC.

On my first trip to Cape Canaveral, I went to see the Redstone pad from which Alan Shepard was launched in 1961 to become America's first man in space. It was an impressive site. Rather than

a launch pad with a big gantry like we are now familiar with, there was this huge concrete pad with railroad tracks on which his Redstone rocket was rolled out. The umbilical cords were lying out on the concrete leading to a true "block house." There was no elevator. Shepard was inserted into the Mercury capsule with a cherry picker crane. I thought anyone would have to be really brave to get on top of that rocket and say, "Okay, light the fuse."

**Redstone Pad at Cape Canaveral**
**Courtesy NASA**

Cooper's was the last Mercury flight scheduled, but I did a lot of work on a possible MA-10 flight, which would conduct a water ejection experiment from the rim of the heat shield during entry and hopefully alleviate "blackout." The blackout period during entry is caused by ionization of the atmosphere, which blocks out communications for a few minutes. The water ejection was believed to be a solution to this problem, in that it would break up the ionization.

I prepared a presentation on the proposed mission and went over to the Farnsworth/Chambers building to present it to Walt Williams, who was the Deputy Director at the time. This was my first presentation to such a high-up official and I was a little nervous about it. None of my bosses, Huss, John Mayer, or Kraft went along (which was typical of their management style), so I really was on my own. A couple of minutes into the presentation, Williams closed his eyes and I would have sworn that he was sound asleep! This made me even more nervous. I didn't know whether to continue the presentation or stop and try to wake him. I continued. Once I had concluded, he opened his eyes and asked several questions, which revealed that he had not been asleep, but in fact, had heard every word. He thanked me, said it was a good presentation and said he thought the water injection scheme would work. Unfortunately, the mission was not approved, so we never found out.

Shortly after MA-9, the last Mercury flight, Carl Huss suffered a heart attack. It was not life threatening, but he would not be able to continue as a RETRO. John Llewellyn moved up to the prime RETRO position and I was asked to be his understudy. Now I was going to be a FLIGHT CONTROLLER, not just a "back room" guy!! How good can life get?? I continued mission planning work for the upcoming Gemini missions, but beginning with GT-1, an unmanned test flight in April, 1964, I was a Retrofire Officer. Llewellyn had questioned why the RETRO was only a "Controller" while everyone else was an "Officer," so the name was changed. Soon thereafter, Tom Carter became the third RETRO. There were now two flight controllers with Civil Engineering degrees from Mississippi State.

**Cape MCC Gemini 1, April 1964**
**Courtesy NASA**

The office wing of Building 30 at NASA Clear Lake, which would also house the new Mission Control Center, was completed in late June 1964. We had tried to coordinate the completion of our new house in Nassau Bay for about the same time to minimize the drive to work. That worked out well, so by early July we were ready to make the moves. We closed on our house the same day that Gerry and Sandy Griffin closed on theirs. Gerry had transferred to NASA from General Dynamics and they had purchased a new home just down the street from ours. Ironically, our professional and personal lives would be intertwined for many years. Gerry and Sandy's kids, Gwen and Kirk, were like my own kids. One of my fondest memories is waiting at a stop light on the way to work. I looked over at a school bus, which was waiting beside me. There I saw Gwen, only from the eyes up, giving me a wave. The final cost of our house was $20,280, $280 over our tight budget! It was the smallest (approximately 1700 square feet) and least expensive house in Nassau Bay, but we were extremely proud of it. I lay awake at night worried about how we were going to be able to make the $165/month mortgage payments.

While I was on active Army duty, my Branch Chief Carl Huss, with Chris Kraft's concurrence, had given me two promotions "in absentia." So much to my surprise, I went back on the NASA payroll upon my Army discharge as a GS-11. From Army pay to a GS-11 level at NASA was one of the biggest raises I ever received, and I could now be paid for overtime. Maybe we could make those house payments after all, and maybe even buy a little more furniture.

In early October 1964, I was at an American Institute of Aeronautics and Astronautics (AIAA) conference in New Orleans with Astronauts Ted Freeman and C. C. Williams. The last night there, we went to Pete Fountain's club in the French Quarter and got to meet him. (Astronauts got to meet *everybody*). Ted, who also lived in Nassau Bay, said he had seen the climbing ivy on the lamppost in our front yard and really liked it. I told him that I would be happy to give him a sprig. We agreed that on Saturday, October 31, he would come by and get a cutting. He had to be in St. Louis the week before, training on the simulation facilities at McDonnell Aircraft. He would return on Saturday morning. I was in our driveway washing the car with the radio on. I heard that a NASA T-38 had crashed at Ellington Field, killing the pilot. I instantly had a sick feeling that it was Ted. Unfortunately, that turned out to be the case. He crashed and was killed during final approach to landing after hitting a goose.

We continued to fly missions from the Cape through Gemini 3, the first manned Gemini flight. One of the changes in the Cape control center between Mercury and Gemini was the addition of a Guidance Officer position. The "GUIDO" was the third member of the Flight Dynamics team. I did not fully understand the specific contributions of the Guidance Officer until we began simulations. Charley Parker, the original GUIDO, had developed all the displays to monitor and compare the on-board and ground based launch guidance systems. It immediately became clear why the Guidance Officer was there and how valuable he could be to the Flight

Dynamics team. During the first day of simulations, Charley would tell us things during the launch phase like, "You may see a little deviation in flight path angle coming up in about 10 seconds, but don't be alarmed. The on-board guidance system is just taking a long time to converge." To the amazement of both the RETRO and FIDO, the launch plot boards would reflect exactly what Charley had said. Lunney, Cliff Charlesworth, Llewellyn and I would just look at each other and say, "How does he know all this?" Early on, Cliff started calling Charley "The Fox," not because he was sly or conniving, but because he was so quick, clever, skillful and shrewd! I began to wonder how we had ever flown the Mercury missions without a GUIDO.

GT-3 was the first manned Gemini flight, with Gus Grissom and John Young as the crewmen. After two unmanned flights and a weeklong Network Simulation, I was beginning to feel comfortable as a RETRO. Of course, I fully realized the difference in having two humans on-board. This was the real thing. Actions, or inactions, by the Flight Controllers could have severe consequences.

The crew simulator was in the same building at the Cape as the control center, so this made simulation de-briefings much more realistic. The crew would come into the control room and we debriefed eye-to-eye. After a long day of sims with the crew, at the conclusion of the last debriefing, I heard Grissom say, "Okay, I'm headed for the Mousetrap. Anyone want to ride with me?" Nobody else said anything, so I finally said, "Yea, I would like to." Gus had the coolest Corvette I had ever seen, so I was excited about getting to ride in it. Little did I know that the more experienced Flight Controllers had ridden with him before and didn't really care to ever do it again. Once we got in his car, he did a couple of tailspins in the parking lot and then headed for the main road to the gate. I looked at the speedometer as we passed the Air Force gate and we were doing over 100 mph! The guard had apparently experienced this before, because he only saluted as we passed by. Gus turned into the parking lot at the Mousetrap, one of our favorite watering holes, doing about 80 mph and began doing tailspins again. Somehow, he ended up parked by the front door, with the front of the Corvette pointed toward the street, just as if he had easily backed into the spot. When we got out, I could hardly stand, much less walk. Gus just looked at me and said, "You okay?" Never again did I volunteer to ride with him.

Staying at the Cape during Mercury and early Gemini flights was an experience. We scrubbed missions a lot, so we usually ended up staying there much longer than planned. This was hard on our families back in Houston, who in general thought we were off just having a good time. We did have some pretty good meals. Chris had some favorite steak houses and Glynn liked an Italian place in Merritt Island, which is where I learned to like Chianti. My favorite was Ramon's, which had wonderful prime rib. It was there that I had my first margarita. Across the street from Ramon's was Jack Bishop's Gulf station, where a guy by the name of Chuck Miller worked. We usually gassed up our GSA cars there. When Chuck found out that the Mission Control Center was going to move to Clear Lake, Texas, he loaded up his whole family and everything they owned in an old station wagon and went to Clear Lake. He bought a corner lot in Nassau Bay and put in the first service station, a Texaco. He ran the first wrecker service from there also and made enough money to later become the local Ford dealer.

If we had any spare time in the daylight, we played volleyball at the motel. Carl Huss was given the name "Dancing Bear" for the way he continually jumped around on the court (before he had his heart attack). Almost every night we would play some kind of card game, usually poker. Never being any good at the game, I usually just watched. Mostly, however, it was long days and hard work. We didn't complain, but it was not a vacation.

Between GT-3 and GT-4, Cliff and Glynn came to me and asked if I would like to switch from RETRO to FIDO. Cliff was going to leave the FIDO position and join Glynn as a Flight Director. They pointed out that if I chose to do so, I would have to move from the Mission Planning and Analysis Division to the Flight Control Division. I said yes, I would like to do that. John Mayer, my Division Chief at the time, had a fit. He said he would not consent to the transfer. Lyn Dunseith, a Branch Chief in MPAD, advised me not to do it, his rationale being that "the real work takes place in MPAD". That's the only time in my career that I did not follow Lyn's advice. I respected him greatly, but I knew what I wanted to do. Mayer, John Hodge (Flight Control Division Chief) and I ended up in Kraft's office to resolve the issue. Chris started the meeting by asking me if I wanted to transfer and why. He must have liked my answer because he immediately said, "So be it, the transfer is approved."

Several months after the transfer, Mayer offered me a job as Section Head in MPAD if I would transfer back. It would be a promotion to a supervisory job and a pay increase, so after thinking about it for a couple of days, I said yes. Mayer said he would start the paperwork. Soon thereafter, Kraft showed up in the control center during a simulation. He came to my console and asked why I wanted to transfer back to MPAD. I explained the supervisory aspect and the pay increase. He asked how many people I supervised as a FIDO. When I said none, he pointed out that the FIDO position was the lead position in the Trench* and that I not only supervised the RETRO and GUIDO, but also the Flight Dynamics people in the Real Time Computer Complex (RTCC) and the MPAD people in the SSR. Then he shifted to the pay increase. He said that he understood that, but that in his experience, "Your needs always grow to meet your income." He departed by saying that he would not interfere either way, it was entirely up to me. Within a few seconds after he left, I concluded that he thought I should stay, so that was my final decision. If Chris Kraft took the time to talk to me about it and really gave the impression that I should stay, I wasn't about to do otherwise.

- *The term "Trench" began to be applied to the first row of consoles in the Houston MCC, occupied by the Flight Dynamics team, RETRO, FIDO and GUIDO. RETRO John Llewellyn, a decorated Korean War veteran, observed that all the pneumatic tube carriers lying by his console reminded him of the empty 105 mm Howitzer shells that filled his trenches in Korea. We were, as Chris Kraft later said, "the first line of defense against any and all assaults on the safety and success of the mission."*

― ― ―

In the spring of 1965, we went to Mississippi to visit with parents. We traded cars at Moore Chevrolet in Belmont. The 1960 Impala convertible was a wonderful car, but with no air conditioning, it was almost unbearable in the Houston climate. We got a 1965 Impala Super Sport, silver with a black vinyl top. It had everything on it, including air conditioning, and was the most expensive car that the dealer had ever sold: $3600.

― ― ―

GT-4 was to be the first flight controlled from Houston. Because the control center there was brand new and we didn't want to take any chances, a skeleton crew of Flight Controllers was deployed to the Cape for the launch phase. Glynn was the Flight Director, Arnie Aldrich was the combined EECOM and GNC, and I was the combined RETRO, FIDO, and GUIDO. Alan Shepard was the assigned CAPCOM, but he didn't show up for the 3-4 days of simulations we had prior to launch. At the Cape, all the switches that controlled the ground computers were on the CAPCOM console, so for the launch phase sims, I had to serve as CAPCOM as well as all three Flight Dynamics positions. On launch day, Shepard showed up. As he was unpacking his head set, I went over to him and started explaining the changes in the switches on his console from what they were during the Mercury program. He never even looked up at me, but finally said, "Do you know who I am?" I replied, "Yes sir, I know who you are and I know you have worked this console during the Mercury program, but there have been a lot of changes for Gemini and if you don't do it right, you'll screw the whole thing up." He looked shocked and said, "Well in that case I guess you had better show me what I'm supposed to do."

During the launch phase, the Houston MCC lost power but did not hand over to us at the Cape. Thankfully, they came back up after less than a minute, but we gave John Hodge, the Houston Flight Director, and Cliff, the FIDO, a hard time for not handing control over to the Cape like they were supposed to. Shepard operated the computer switches on his console just as I had instructed. When we built the MCC in Houston, this problem was solved by putting all the computer switches and the Abort switch on the FIDO console, where they should have been all along. After launch, Glynn, Arnie and I went to the Cape Skid Strip and boarded the Gulfstream for Houston, where we would pull shifts during the rest of the mission.

— — —

Between Gemini 4 and 5, I made another trip to North American Aviation to discuss Apollo launch aborts. I arrived at LAX at just about sundown, picked up my GSA car and headed for Downey, as I had done many times before. When I got to a section of Los Angeles known as Watts, I began to see buildings on fire, people all over the streets and dozens of police officers. I had no idea what was going on but was soon stopped by a policeman and told to get out of there as fast as I could. It turned out to be the beginning of a civil rights riot, in which several dozen people were killed and lasted for almost a week. Needless to say, when I left Downey a couple of days later I didn't go back through Watts. On future trips, I continued to avoid the area.

— — —

At about this time, Chris Kraft made his prediction come true. When he told Chris Critzos in 1962, "Hell hire him. We may need somebody to survey the moon." I don't think either of us thought it would ever happen. But in the fall of 1965, he assigned me and Neil Hutchinson to work with the U.S. Air Force and their contractor, Aerospace Corporation, on camera systems that could be used to map the moon and aid in the selection of landing sites. Our task was so classified that we couldn't tell our bosses what we were doing. We each had a security clearance several levels above Top Secret. The fact that those clearances even existed was classified Top Secret. When I initially got my clearance, it was delayed for about six months because the FBI, which did the clearance investigation, could not pinpoint where I was for two weeks one summer when I was in college. I had worked for Lambert Construction in Belmont and went to Oxford for two weeks to work on a schoolhouse there. The work crew stayed in a rent house in Oxford and I had forgotten to put that on my application, so my clearance was held up until they could verify where I was for that two weeks. Chris signed all of our travel orders and he was the only one at JSC that we could talk to about the project. A similar camera was already being used in geo-synchronous orbit (about 22,300 miles altitude) for earth surveillance but the pointing system algorithms would require major changes to work on lunar targets.

Neil and I traveled a lot to the Los Angeles area and to Palo Alto/Sunnyvale, California, just south of San Francisco. The systems involved were so highly classified that it scared both of us. We spent many hours in security vaults poring over systems drawings and software code. We were shown a photo of Rice Stadium taken by the geo-sync camera during a football game. You could easily see the yard markers on the field and even read the numbers on the player's uniforms. The "Black Vault" at TRW, where we spent hours upon hours, is the same one used by the Falcon and the Snowman, two young TRW employees who were turning over secret documents to the Russians. They were eventually caught and featured in a book and movie.

The system flew as the unmanned Lunar Orbiter Program with five missions in 1966-67 and provided very detailed maps of the lunar surface. When people marveled at the resolution of the pictures and wondered what kind of camera had been used, Neil and I would just look at each other and grin. Since retirement, I have asked Chris why he gave that assignment to us. He said, "I couldn't think of two more qualified and dedicated people who would get the job done and keep their mouths shut." Just another example of how great it was to work for a guy like Chris who gave great challenges to the people he trusted.

When in LA, we always stayed at the Holiday Inn near the airport. The bar there had a piano player named Raul Bianca. We kept asking him to play *Cast Your Fate to the Wind*, which was popular then. He would just shake his head, indicating that he didn't know it. Several months later, on another trip to the vaults, we walked into the bar one night and Raul stopped playing whatever he was playing and went into *Cast Your Fate to the Wind*. He had a huge smile on his face because he had learned it just for us. I think that is the first time I ever gave a tip to a piano player in a bar. We also managed to take in some good entertainment. We attended both a Roger Miller and a Neil Diamond concert and saw Johnny Rivers (I couldn't believe how small he was) at the Whiskey a Go Go on Sunset Strip.

We also went to see a UCLA basketball game at the new Pauley Pavilion, where freshman Lew Alcindor (before he changed his name to Kareem Abdul-Jabbar) was creating quite a stir. I was not overly impressed, thinking he was slow. When the team ran up the court, he was always the last one to arrive. The next morning I read in the paper however, that he had scored 32 points, so I guess I had underestimated him. A couple of years later I saw Alcindor and the Bruins play the University of Houston Cougars and Elvin Hayes in the Astrodome. It was a close game but Houston won by two points, in what became known as the game of the century.

While at Palo Alto, we went to San Francisco as often as possible. I was overwhelmed with all the great seafood. We spent a lot of time in the North Beach area at the hungry-I and the Purple Onion, where we saw such groups as the Righteous Brothers and the Kingston Trio.

— — —

We were flying Gemini missions about once every two months, so these were busy times. We also had to get used to the new control center in Houston. The capability existed to display a lot more data than we had at the Cape. We had console call-up displays, a huge rear-projection screen in the center of the room, and large TV displays on either side of the big screen. One new thing was the pneumatic tube system which allowed us to send messages to the RTCC, our staff support room and to all the other controllers in the MOCR. For the first two flights, we brought in the old style plot boards, like we had at the Cape, and placed them in front of the big center screen, because we were not sure the new-fangled digital displays would work. For those of us who had worked at the Cape, the whirring noise of the plot boards make us feel more comfortable.

During the launch phase of Gemini 5, Dr. Chuck Berry, the chief doctor, or "Surgeon" as he was called in the MOCR, wired Chris Kraft, himself, and me with ECG monitors. He wanted to compare our heart rates with Cooper and Conrad in the spacecraft. When he reported that Cooper had gone to sleep during the pre-launch countdown, I knew that I probably would not win the $10 bet for who would have the lowest heart rate. About three minutes into the launch, doctors from the Surgeon's staff support room came running into the MOCR to see if I was all right. Once the crew got into orbit, they removed my monitors and told me that I had a highly irregular heartbeat, which I should have checked out.

I was diagnosed with Wolff-Parkinson-White syndrome, which was described to me as "a perfectly normal abnormality." In a normal heart, there is only one path for electrical signals to flow from the atria to the ventricles, causing the heart to beat. With W-P-W, there are two paths, causing the signal to get to the ventricles too soon, resulting in irregular and high heart rates. It doesn't happen all the time and I am not even aware when it is occurring. I just considered it as having redundant paths and never did worry about it. It did cost me $40: $10 each to Conrad, Cooper, Kraft and Berry.

Since 1964 I had been a participant in the Longitudinal Study of Astronaut Health (LSAH) program where the doctors compared astronaut health to that of mere mortals. Of course, I was in the latter category. The benefit to me was that I got very extensive physical examinations twice a year at no charge. The W-P-W had not shown up in those physicals.

**MCC Houston with old style plot boards, Gemini 5**
**Courtesy NASA**

— — —

We began having splashdown parties at either the Nassau Bay Hilton or the Flintlock Inn, both on NASA Road 1. Soon we were overcome with outsiders, so we shifted to private parties at our homes or to the Singing Wheel in Webster, where John Llewellyn's wife, Olga, was the bartender, or the Hofbraugarten German Village Restaurant in Dickinson. Both would close and allow us to have private parties. It was at the Hofbraugarten that Jack Schmitt, Dick Thorson and I had a chug-a-lug contest. Schmitt came out the clear winner and I was a distant third. Some of the best splashdown parties where at Gerry and Sandy Griffin's house. Gerry had an old refrigerator with a beer keg inside and the spout on the outside, and Sandy always had outstanding hors d' oeuvres. We had one party at our house, which went well until Llewellyn went into the back yard to relieve himself. He didn't realize that our backdoor neighbors, the Highs, were sitting on their back porch and were shocked to see someone urinating on the chain link fence between us.

— — —

During the fall of 1965, Glynn Lunney and I spent some time in the rendezvous simulator at the McDonnell Aircraft facility in St. Louis with the recently assigned prime crew for Gemini 9, Elliott See and Charlie Bassett. We accomplished a lot of good training for us and the flight crew. The simulators in Houston were booked solid in preparation for Gemini 6, so this was a great opportunity for us. On two different occasions while there, See and Bassett offered to let us ride back to Houston in the back seat of their T-38s. For one reason or another, it didn't work out so we just flew back home commercially. The next year, on February 28, Elliott and Charlie were headed back to do some more training, this time in a single T-38. The runway at the McDonnell facility had low visibility and Elliott aborted the first attempt to land. On the second try, he hit the corner of Building

101, where their spacecraft was being manufactured. They both were killed instantly. About a year and a half later, C. C. Williams was killed when his T-38 crashed shortly after take-off from Patrick Air Force Base. After these two crashes, and that of Ted Freeman in 1964, untrained passengers were no longer allowed, so I never got to fulfill my dream of riding in a T-38.

– – –

The next Gemini flight was even more eventful. We were to launch an Agena target vehicle and then launch the Gemini spacecraft, which would rendezvous, and dock with the Agena. However, the Agena exploded during launch, so an alternate plan was developed to go ahead and launch Gemini 7, with me as the prime FIDO, on its planned date, then launch Gemini 6, which would perform the planned rendezvous, but no docking.

Cliff was the prime FIDO and did the launch and rendezvous on Gemini 6. Of course, I was there to watch it all because I knew that if we did rendezvous, it would be a first in space flight history. The Russians had beaten us on first satellite, first person in orbit, and first EVA. If we could successfully pull off the rendezvous, it would mean we finally had beaten the Russians on something! Feeling that we should somehow celebrate this accomplishment, I asked Kraft if it would be okay if I could get some American flags, hand them out at the end of the rendezvous and ask everyone to wave them. He said he thought that was a wonderful idea, so I called Ginny Engle, the FDB secretary and asked her to find as many small American flags as she could. It turned out that her husband worked at a funeral home where they had several such flags on hand which they put on vehicles for military funerals. So, at the conclusion of the first space rendezvous, everyone in the control center waved their flags and showed how proud we were to be Americans. I believe this was the first, and last, time we ever celebrated during a mission. Tradition was that we would only celebrate once the mission was successfully concluded, demonstrated by the astronauts being safe on the recovery ship. We did continue to fly our flags on each subsequent mission.

Another flag-waving event during this mission was the birth of my daughter, Kristi Anne, on December 17, 1965. As with the birth of Mike, 3 1/2 years earlier, we did not know ahead of time if it would be a boy or girl, but were extremely happy that it was a girl. Now we had one of each.

The Mission Control Public Affairs Officer read the following as a press release early the next morning after her birth. I actually was a Flight Dynamics Officer at that time, but had previously been a Retrofire Officer, so it really didn't matter. I was just thrilled.

## GEMINI 7 MISSION COMMENTARY TRANSCRIPT
### 12/18/65, 6:28 a.m., Tape 609, Page 1

This is Gemini Control, Houston. The update is continuing at Canaries. One other piece of information, one of the happier people in this room this morning is one of our Retrofire Officers, Jerry Bostick, whose wife presented him with a baby yesterday afternoon. Mr. Bostick is quoting the time of the birth, of course, in retrofire language. He calls it 22 hours 18 minutes 18 seconds Greenwich Mean Time, he also has it worked out in ground elapsed time into the mission, 314 hours 48 minutes and 57 seconds. The name of the baby is Kristi Anne. This is Gemini Control.

## END OF TAPE

— — —

During simulations for Gemini 8, Prince Philip of the United Kingdom visited the Manned Spacecraft Center and I was asked to brief him in the control center. He was very nice but didn't seem to be all that interested or to understand anything I told him.

**Briefing Prince Philip**
**Courtesy NASA**

— — —

Gemini 8 was the first time we rendezvoused and docked. I was the prime FIDO, Tom Carter was the prime RETRO, and "The Fox", Charley Parker, was the GUIDO. The launch phase went well, until Charley said to me, "FIDO, you're looking good coming onto the third scale, but it's going to be a little noisier than you have ever seen before." When the Velocity vs. Flight Path Angle did go to the third scale (approaching the final couple of minutes of powered flight), the Titan onboard guidance system was all over the place. When Charley first warned me, I thought, "Why the hell is he telling me that?", but when it happened, I probably would have had a heart attack if he had not warned me. Once again, I felt it sure was a nice thing to have a Guidance Officer sitting next to me.

We made it into orbit just fine and the rendezvous phase went great. We were pretty happy upon completion of the successful docking and were thinking about going to have a cool one. Then the crew came over a tracking station and reported that they were spinning out of control and had to undock from the Agena, thinking it was the culprit. My first thought was "Damn Agena! What a sorry piece of trash!" In order to stop the spinning, the crew had to use one of the spacecraft backup attitude control rings. The Mission Rules said that if this happened, we had to reenter at the next opportunity. Therefore, Tom and I did not hand over to the oncoming shift but started planning for a contingency area landing, which was in the North Pacific, in the dark. As far as the retrofire, entry and landing, everything went fine. Once the recovery helicopter got there and dropped two swimmers, we heard almost immediately that a third swimmer was being dropped into the water. This usually meant that something was wrong with the crew, because the third swimmer was a doctor. It turned out that the doctor was dropped because the first two swimmers were sick and throwing up. The flight crew, Neil Armstrong and Dave Scott, were fine. The contingency recovery forces had been in a bar, drinking more than they should, when called to duty for crew rescue in the North Pacific. They thought it was just another simulation and didn't take it seriously until they were over the spacecraft. Somehow, they got the astronauts onboard the helicopter just fine and then headed for the recovery ship. Armstrong told me years later that on the helicopter ride, all the recovery forces were passed out on the floor. He woke up one of the guys and said, "I think you're supposed to be checking us out medically. Didn't NASA send you a big box with thermometers, blood pressure cuffs, etc.?" So they found the box, opened it and started reading the instructions. Neil and Dave finally told them what to do and how to do it. Dave verified this story and added that once they were in the Admiral's quarters on the ship, a recovery guy came to him and whispered, "Sir, do you know how to open the hatch and get into the capsule?" Dave replied that he did and asked why they needed to get into it. Turns out that after they got the capsule on deck, they had closed the hatch not realizing that one of their guys was still inside!

**Celebrating Gemini 8 successful recovery**
**Courtesy NASA**

— — —

For Easter, 1966, Linda, the kids and I went to Mississippi. Kristi was less than 4 months old. While there, we were visiting Ruth and Etha Mann when Jenny's husband Jerry Reed mentioned that he had submitted an application to NASA but had not heard from them. When we got back to Clear Lake, I went to the Personnel Office, found his application and took it to Lyn Dunseith who was working on flight software for the Apollo program. I figured that since Jerry was a mathematician, he would fit right in. Lyn agreed and sent him an offer. It didn't hurt that Linda was Lyn's secretary! By June, Jenny and Jerry had moved to Clear Lake and he started working for Tom Gibson, a Section Head under Lyn, who was developing navigation software. We really enjoyed having them near us, especially when we needed a baby sitter! Their first son Jay was born in August 1967. Jerry had decided that he wanted to get his doctorate, so shortly thereafter they moved back to Mississippi where he had accepted a teaching job in the MSU math department. We hated to see them leave.

– – –

When the Agena target vehicle for Gemini 9 was lost in another Agena launch failure, the Augmented Target Docking Adapter (ATDA) was launched on an Atlas booster to serve as a docking target. Once again, anything having to do with Gemini docking targets had a problem. One of the lanyards on the shroud enclosing the docking adapter got hung up, not fully exposing the docking port. Telemetry signals indicated that the shroud had separated, but not jettisoned. A couple of days later when Tom Stafford and Gene Cernan completed the rendezvous, the telemetry was confirmed. Stafford said it looked like "an angry alligator." So, not being able to dock, the Gemini 9 crew conducted two more rendezvous exercises with the ATDA. Cernan set an EVA time record of over 2 hours, but his visor became fogged, and he was therefore unable to test the astronaut maneuvering unit. We were getting the rendezvous down, but successful demonstration of docking and EVA seemed to be problematic.

On Gemini 10, with John Young and Mike Collins aboard, we finally had a good rendezvous and docking. The rendezvous, due to some on-board navigation problems used a lot more fuel than planned, so rather than separating and practicing more docking maneuvers, they stayed with the Agena until it was fired to take them up to over 400 miles to rendezvous with the Agena from Gemini 8. So, we set an altitude record and rendezvoused with two different targets. The EVA experience was better than Gemini 9, but still had problems. Collins, like Cernan on 9, found it difficult and tiring to move around. He got tangled in the umbilical several times.

Gemini 11 was a challenge for the Trench. We were to attempt a first orbit rendezvous (M=1, we called it), which took a lot of precision in target vehicle launch time, chase vehicle launch time and maneuver execution. This was a demonstration of the capability needed on Apollo for Lunar Module launch from the moon and rendezvous with the CSM. Ed Pavelka and Steve Bales as the Prime FIDO and Guido, respectively, spent many months in preparation for this dicey rendezvous and (with a little help from Pete Conrad and Dick Gordon) pulled it off perfectly.

In between Gemini 11 and 12, we conducted a Network Simulation, NS-2, to work out the kinks in the Apollo network. Phil Shaffer had done most of the work in preparation for this exercise. I sat in most of the time just to learn more about Apollo, since I had spent most of my time on Gemini, plus Grady Meyer had left and I was the new Flight Dynamics Officer Section Head.

With only one more Gemini flight to go, we still had some EVA procedures to perfect. As far as the Trench was concerned,

MCC During Gemini 12
Will Fenner, John Llewellyn,
me, John Aaron, Pete Conrad,
Bill Anders, and Gene Cernan
Courtesy NASA

rendezvous and docking was becoming routine, and that part of the Gemini 12 mission went off without a hitch. Much to the pleasure of everyone involved, the EVAs also went very well. Hand and foot restraints had been added to the outside of the spacecraft to facilitate moving around and a new water tank had been used for the EVA pre-flight training. I have to give Buzz Aldrin a lot of credit for recommending these changes and working so hard in the Water Emersion Training Facility (WETF) to perfect the procedures.

So now the lead-in programs, Mercury and Gemini, were complete and it was time to get on with our new National objective... landing a man on the moon by the end of the decade. We only had three years remaining, so that goal seemed like a big challenge, but one we were more than willing to take on. We felt like we were finally catching up to the USSR, if not ahead of them. We rarely talked about it, but we all wanted to "beat the Commies"!

By the end of Gemini, we had already completed three unmanned Saturn 1B/Apollo test flights, so most of the Trench Apollo guys felt pretty comfortable with the vehicle, the network and the control center. Now it was time for the good stuff...manned flights!

At the conclusion of the Gemini program, my good friend Tom Carter left NASA and went to work in California for TRW. He soon ended up in Hawaii, living on a sailboat, helping design an underwater control center for nuclear submarines.

– – –

If Mike had been our only child, Linda and I would have thought that other parents just didn't know how to raise their kids. Mike was the "perfect" child. He minded perfectly and really never did anything wrong. His only "problem" was actually caused by me and not of his own doing. I had the habit of putting him to bed and then reading him a book. At the end of the book, he would lie down and I would stay with him, sitting on the floor by his crib, and patting him on the back. While patting, I would sing to him, singing the only songs I knew at the time: The Righteous Brothers, The Beach Boys, Mamas and Papas, and Neil Diamond. Unchained Melody by the Righteous Brothers seemed to be his favorite. If I stopped singing and tried to leave, he would immediately start crying. Kristi was another story. She slept all night long the first night she was home from the hospital. We had learned our lesson...just put the baby down and leave the room! She was sweet and beautiful. We thought we again had the "perfect" child. However, when she started crawling and pulling up on the coffee table, we saw a very determined, almost defiant, child. She would push all magazines/books off the coffee table, sending them tumbling to the floor. When we put them back and told her "No, no, don't do that", she would stare at us with glaring eyes, purse her lips and swipe them off again. We had quickly learned a lesson: all kids are different. Their differences continued throughout their lives. When faced with a test in school, Mike would stay up until after midnight studying so that he could make an A. Kristi, on the other hand, would study for a couple of hours at most and say, "I can make a B on the test and that's good enough." When they were teenagers, I gave them each a $20 bill to keep as emergency money. At least 20 years later, after Mike was married and living in Los Angeles, he and Andrea went to a restaurant and discovered that they didn't take credit cards and that they didn't have enough cash to pay the bill without using his emergency money. He told the cashier to hold that same $20 bill and that he would be back within an hour to retrieve it. He probably still has it. When I asked Kristi about her $20 bill, she said she remembered it but spent it within a week or two of receiving it.

One nice thing about living in Nassau Bay was that we had our own TV channel. Mostly they showed ads for shops in our shopping center but during space flights, they showed a live picture from the MOCR. One evening Mike reported to Linda, "I don't think Dad will be coming home for dinner tonight because I can see him eating a hot dog at his console."

— — —

In January 1967, Joe Shea, the Apollo Program Manager; Mel Brooks, the Lunar Module Systems Branch Chief, Arnie Aldrich, the CSM Systems Branch Chief, Gerry Griffin, Neil Hutchinson and I went to North American Aviation (NAA) in Los Angeles to review progress on the Apollo hardware. The NAA managers told us that if we could come a day earlier, they would take us to the AFL-NFL Championship game to be played on the Sunday before our meetings were to begin. The six of us flew out on the NASA Gulfstream and landed at the Ontario Airport where we were met and taken to the game at the LA Coliseum. Later, such a gratuity was declared illegal, but at that time, such "favors" were common practice. The game, later named Super Bowl I, was between the Green Bay Packers and the Kansas City Chiefs. Mel was from Green Bay and a huge Packer fan, so that's who I cheered for. They won by the score 35-10. I especially liked the halftime show, which featured Al Hirt, the jazz trumpeter from New Orleans, and a man with a rocket backpack who flew over the spectators. He flew directly over us at an altitude of about 100 feet and we could definitely feel the jet blast. The stadium was not full, so at halftime, we moved to seats near the 50-yard line, only 3-4 rows up. We went to the meetings on Monday with NAA and concluded that they were behind schedule and over budget. The following week the AS-204 pad test was scheduled.

— — —

AS-204 was to be the first manned flight of Apollo. Most people now refer to it as Apollo 1, which it later was named, but at the time, to us it was AS-204. "AS", of course stood for Apollo Saturn. The number 204 meant that the booster was a Saturn 1B and it was the 4th flight of the Apollo hardware. The January 27, 1967 pad test, officially considered not hazardous because the Saturn 1B was not loaded with fuel, was a "plugs-out" test to determine whether the spacecraft would operate nominally on internal power while detached from all ground cables and umbilicals. There previously had been a lot of problems with the Block 1 CSM and Gus Grissom, the flight Commander, had even hung a lemon inside the spacecraft.

There wasn't much for people in the Trench to do on such a pad test, other than make sure all of our countdown procedures were correct and carry out our usual interface with the Range Safety Officer at the Cape. I had been in the control center during the day and it seemed the test was going fairly well, even with a long list of technical problems. So, at around 4:30 p.m., I left for home. Linda and I were scheduled to have dinner that night with Glynn and Marilyn Lunney and Bill and Valerie Anders. While showering, I got a call from Glynn. Linda said that he wanted to talk to me even though he realized I was in the shower. He told me that dinner was off and that he would meet me in the control center. "Something has happened." was all he said. Figuring that it must be something pretty big to call off dinner, I hurriedly dressed and drove to the control center.

As soon as I got out of my car, I saw Dutch VonEhrenfried, who had been on duty as the Guidance Officer, walking toward me and openly weeping. "They're all dead," he said. That's all I could get out of him, so I dashed upstairs to the MOCR. Not much time had elapsed since "something" had happened, so the room was not yet sealed. I quickly learned that there had been a fire inside the Command Module and that all three crewmen, Gus Grissom, Ed White and Roger Chaffee, were dead. It was one of the lowest moments of my life. The astronauts were not only co-workers, they were friends.

I had a general acquaintance with Gus and knew his wife Betty and their kids. Ed White and I attended Seabrook Methodist Church together and our wives and children were friends. He and I served as co-lectors a couple of times, where we read alternating verses of the

Psalm for that Sunday. The Chaffees lived in Nassau Bay where we lived and we had a good relationship with both Roger and Martha. That was my first thought, "I have lost my friends." It was made even worse by learning that they had been trapped inside the spacecraft and had burned. The whole thing had been recorded on the voice loops and several console auxiliary recorders, but I refused to listen. It took me years to get that vision out of my mind.

This was NASA's lowest point. Many years later, people referred to Apollo 13 as "NASA's finest hour" because we were able to snatch success out of the jaws of defeat, and it is hard for me to argue against that characterization, but I firmly believe that the NASA response to the AS-204 fire was its finest hour. Before the end of the day of the accident, NASA appointed an investigation committee, called the Apollo 204 Review Board, headed by Langley Research Center Director, Dr. Floyd Thompson. The Board met the very next day at the Kennedy Space Center. Within two days, the Flight Dynamics Branch, which was then located in JSC Building 45, had vacated our office space to make room for the Board when they came there. Frank Borman, who had flown on Gemini 7 with Jim Lovell, played a key role in the investigation.

One event that has received a lot of attention after the accident, was the assembly of all Flight Controllers, by the then Head of the Flight Director's Office, Gene Kranz. In the Building 30 auditorium he told us all that the accident was our fault because we had observed all the problems with the Block 1 CSM, but had not adequately spoken out. We accepted that. Near the end of his speech however, he directed all of us to go back to our offices and write "Tough and Competent" on our blackboards, because that's what we were going to be from that day forward. Some of us from the Trench just kind of looked at each other and frowned. On the way out of the auditorium Cliff Charlesworth remarked, "If you are really tough and competent, you don't need to advertise it." I did not write those words on my blackboard and I don't think anyone else in the Flight Dynamics Branch did. We mostly all agreed with Cliff.

I know Gene was sincere in his remarks and agreed with his assessment that we could all do more; but most of us, if not all, did not agree that we should adopt some new public relations campaign to show the world we would do better.

George Low, who was Deputy Center Director at the time, took over management of the Apollo program. He instituted a lot of new controls including a change management system. No changes to the spacecraft could be made without taking the proposed change to his change control board (CCB) and getting approval.

Within 21 months, NASA and North American Aviation determined the cause of the fire, redesigned the CSM to hopefully preclude a recurrence, and launched the first manned Apollo mission, Apollo 7.

In the meantime, we flew three unmanned test flights, AS-501, AS-204, and AS-502. AS-501 (Apollo 4) was the first flight of the Saturn V and the first flight of its S-IC and S-II stages, as well as the first restart of the S-IVB stage. It was an "all up" test, a bold philosophy developed by Dr. George Mueller, the NASA Associate Administrator for Manned Space Flight.

This cut down the total number of tests, as needed to accomplish President Kennedy's stated goal of a manned lunar landing by 1970, but it meant that everything had to work properly the first time. This was also the first time that the Apollo spacecraft reentered the Earth's atmosphere at speeds approaching those of a lunar return trajectory. To a lot of people's surprise, the mission went very well, achieving most major objectives.

— — —

When we moved to Nassau Bay, we met Bob and Colette Sheets, who also lived in Nassau Bay, just a block away. Their daughter Andrea and Mike were the same age and become good friends, frequently playing in the Baptist church parking lot, accessible from both of our back yards. They both attended kindergarten at Webster Elementary. From then through high school they were in the same classes.

**Mike and Andrea in Kindergarten at Webster Elementary**
**(Mike on the left end of the 3rd row, Andrea on right**
**end of 1st row next to the teacher, Ms. Pell)**

There was a lake in Nassau Bay which had quite a few fish in it. The first time I took Mike there he caught a full stringer of bream, which spoiled him with fishing. From then on, if he didn't catch anything in about 15 minutes, he was ready to leave.

We switched to the new Clear Lake Methodist Church in Clear Lake City, which was then meeting in a temporary trailer while the sanctuary was under construction. Bob and Colette were already there and we made new friends, Jerry and Betty Woodfill, Roy and Sue Day, Milo and Mary Keathley and many others. Astronaut Alan Bean and wife Sue were also members there.

— — —

**Mike's first fishing experience**

Travel to and from the North American Aviation facility in Downey, California, increased after the Apollo 1 fire. The airline companies, all with representatives in Clear Lake, were in heated completion to get their share of these trips. Continental airlines was one of the first to give us free upgrades to first class if room was available. I was returning to Houston on Friday, March 24, 1967, just two days before Mike's birthday, which would coincide with Easter Sunday for the first time. I was upgraded to first class and ended up sitting next to Don Knotts, who played Barney Fife on the very popular Andy Griffith show. Not wanting to disturb him, I said nothing other than "Hello" when I took my seat. He soon introduced himself and asked questions about where I was headed and what I did for a living. When I mentioned that I was anxious to get home for my son's 5th birthday, he asked a million questions about Mike. It turned out to be a very pleasant ride and I was left with a very favorable impression of Don Knotts.

— — —

AS-204 (Apollo 5) was the first flight carrying a real Lunar Module, although as I recall, they left the landing legs off to save weight! The primary goal of the mission was to test the ascent and descent engines and to perform a "fire-in-the-hole" test, where the ascent stage of the LM would initiate firing while still attached to the descent stage. This would simulate a lunar descent abort and a normal launch from the lunar surface. All did not go well in the first attempt to fire the descent engine. After about four seconds of firing, the guidance computer shut off the engine, thinking that the thrust was not building up fast enough. Dave Reed, the Prime FIDO, and other controllers came up with a technique to start the burn manually, which worked without a hitch. The descent engine was ignited twice in this fashion and performed as planned. Then the "fire-in-the hole" burn also worked like a charm. After one more burn of the ascent engine, all major test objectives were met. This crazy looking Lunar Module, the first true spacecraft, because it could only operate in a vacuum, really did look like it would work. Dave, who had spent most of his NASA career on the Lunar Module, had a good day.

SA-502 (Apollo 6) was the final unmanned Apollo/Saturn flight and only the second test of the Saturn V. Since AS-501 had gone so well, we figured this flight to be a piece of cake. Not so. During the first stage of launch, the S-IC experienced "pogo," a severe oscillating up and down movement of the whole stack. Once we got through the first stage, we figured that the worst was over and we could press on with no more anomalies. Not so, again. One of the five S-II stage engines developed performance problems and finally shut down. A few seconds later, a second engine also shut down. The Saturn Instrumentation Unit computer was able to compensate and burn the remaining three engines much longer than usual. After S-II shutdown however, the S-IVB stage also experienced thrust problems, and realizing the altitude was too high, started pitching down, approaching the abort limit lines. Jay Greene, the Prime FIDO, earned his money that day, keeping his hand close to the abort switch, but remaining calm and never touching it.

We finally got into orbit, albeit a rather peculiar elliptical one. Then, the S-IVB stage failed to restart, which was to be a test of the Translunar Injection. That planned burn would also have allowed another test of reentry, achieving a velocity approximating that of a lunar return. It was finally decided to burn the Service Propulsion System engine to achieve an altitude and an entry speed as high as possible. It was a good unplanned test of the SPS, but most mission objectives were not met. It was always interesting to me that even with all the Saturn V problems on this final test flight, the system was certified for manned flight without any further tests.

– – –

In 1968, I was appointed to be the JSC Range Safety Representative, responsible for coordinating the launch range safety aspects of the Apollo, Skylab, and Space Shuttle Programs with other NASA Centers and the Range Safety Office of the U.S. Air Force Eastern Test Range. Glynn Lunney had been the Rep up until then, but he and Chris Kraft felt it appropriate that an active FIDO, who had the primary interface with Range Safety, be made the official Rep. The Range Safety Officer monitored the launch phase much as the FIDO did, but had different limit lines. His responsibility was to protect people and facilities on the ground, and he had the capability to terminate thrust and initiate destruction of the launch vehicle if his limit lines showed that an impact was going to be over land in the Cape area. Obviously, all FIDOs and Range Safety Officers coordinated very closely and had procedures to be used during launch to ensure that each knew what the other was thinking and doing.

This close coordination became even more important on Apollo, because the Lunar Modules destined to land on the moon would each carry a Radioisotope Thermoelectric Generator (RTG) containing plutonium-238, which would power various experiments to be left on the moon. In case of an Apollo launch abort, the Range Safety

Officer was concerned that the radioactive plutonium could cause a lot of damage in the launch area, so we had to conduct several drop tests of the containment device for the RTG to ensure that it would survive, without breaking open, in such an abort. It passed all tests with no damage. For each launch we established a code word to let the other know we were going to abort. The code word was always two syllables, such as "Baseball", "Aardvark' or "Pineapple." The document in which we agreed upon and recorded the code word was classified Top Secret. I would never even write it down, afraid that I might accidently say it.

On Apollo 13, I had not even thought about the RTG until about two hours before we were planning to jettison the LM. Glynn Lunney came to me and said that the Atomic Energy Commission (AEC) had called saying that we must make sure that the RTG would land in a safe place in the ocean. My response was "You've got to be kidding! We have a lot more to worry about than that!" Glynn said, "I know, but just double check and give me something I can tell them to make them happy." Reluctantly, I got Chuck Deiterich, the RETRO on duty, and the FIDO, Dave Reed, and told them about the AEC input. Their response was the same as mine… "You've got to be kidding!" They called on Bob McAdams in our SSR to see what could be done. Of course we were going to put the LM down in the ocean, but maybe we could make some small change to the LM separation attitude to ensure that the LM, with the RTG, would impact in one of the deepest spots in the South Pacific, the Tonga Trench off the coast of New Zealand. He quickly figured out that we could. I reported that to Glynn, who in turn reported it to the AEC. Now everyone was happy. I just shook my head. The AEC should have known that the thing was indestructible and that we would not plan for anything to hit land. I don't think the containment device was ever tested for salt water corrosion over several decades, but hopefully it is still safe.

— — —

For Easter, 1968, we gave Mike and Kristi a rabbit. What a mistake! I built an elaborate raised cage for it behind the garage. Mike named it "Sweetie Pie" which turned out to be ironic because it was a very mean rabbit and bit Kristi one day as she was trying to feed it. After a few months of this meanness, it "disappeared." Someone left the cage door open and it ran away. Imagine that!

**Mike with Sweetie Pie**
**Mother in background**

Another project for the kids turned out much better. Using cedar posts and fencing material, I built an 8' x 8' clubhouse in the back yard. It had interchangeable plaques, one with "Mike's Mansion" and the other with "Kristi's Kastle." They got a lot of use of it and even had sleepovers in it with their friends. They kept it for 6-7 years, even moving it to Virginia when I went to NASA Headquarters in 1973. When we returned to Clear Lake in 1975 the folks who purchased our Virginia house wanted the clubhouse, so we left it there.

**Kristi charging from her Kastle**

– – –

For several years, I had my hair cut by Pete Miller, husband of Suzanne, one of the Flight Control Division secretaries. Pete had a barbershop in the Nassau Bay Hotel and several of my NASA friends also got their hair cut there. In 1968, Pete announced that he was signing up with a new hair styling franchise called Sebring. It involved a special way to cut men's hair and a complete line of hair products like shampoo, conditioner and hair spray. To kick off the new franchise, he needed two volunteers for the franchise owner, Jay Sebring, to demonstrate his cutting style to Pete and two other barbers who worked for him. I volunteered and Pete selected me and Chris Kraft as the two "guinea pigs." So, for about two hours on a Sunday afternoon, Chris and I sat patiently while Jay Sebring showed the others how to cut and style hair using his technique. The Sebring franchise was a huge success for Pete and his business increased dramatically. About a year later, the man who had cut our hair that day, was murdered, along with his girlfriend Sharon Tate, by the Manson family in Los Angeles.

— — —

Progress was being made at North American Aviation on the redesigned Command and Service Modules and the Trench turned its attention to the critical first manned Apollo flight, Apollo 7. The computers in the RTCC had now been upgraded to IBM 360-75s, giving us much more computer power and display capability than we previously had. There were five of these computers, each with the unheard of memory capacity of 1 megabyte! These were the latest and greatest computers that Government money could buy. We got serial numbers 1-5. Only one was used for real time support, with another serving as a back up. The other three were used for software development and off-line telemetry processing.

In the fall of 1967, NASA formed the "Science and Technology Advisory Committee" and asked them to come to Houston and review our planning for the first lunar landing. The Committee included Dr. William Shockley, the co-inventer of the transistor, for which he was awarded the Nobel Prize in Physics. He also was an atheist and a racist. Presenters included me, Buzz Aldrin, T. K. Mattingly, Jack Schmitt, Deke Slayton, and Dr. Chuck Berry. My presentation was "Transearth Injection Through Earth Landing." For some reason, Dr. Shockley was very interested in the trajectory and guidance aspects of the mission, so I ended up spending a lot of time with him. On the last night they were in town, a farewell dinner was held at the MSC (later changed to Gilruth) Recreation Center and I ended up being seated next to Dr. Shockley. Somehow the conversation turned to the theory of evolution. Knowing that he was an atheist, I tried not to provoke him, but did tell him that I was a firm believer in God and believed in the Genesis version of creation. He said "Jerry, you seem to be a pretty smart fellow. I just can't understand how you could not believe in evolution." My answer was, "Well sir, I don't know exactly <u>how</u> we all got here. I just know who did it." The subject changed after that.

– – –

I enjoyed playing golf in those days, but never was good at it. Glynn Lunney, Charley Parker, Wiley Beal, Chuck Pace and I played well together, because we played about the same. When I first started playing, my goal was double par. When I finally achieved that, I lowered my goal to 100 on an 18-hole course. I achieved that only once. Occasionally I would play with Cliff Charlesworth, Phil Shaffer, Bob Regelbrugge and John Zarcaro. I could not keep up with them, but that didn't bother me. It did bother them, because they were always having to wait for me. When Tom Carter started playing with us, he took it very seriously and would get furious when he made a bad shot. One day he became so furious that he threw a brand-new set of clubs, bag and all, into a lake. I went home that day and told Linda she could put my clubs in a garage sale. It wasn't fun anymore.

– – –

When I became Chief of the Flight Dynamics Branch, Gene Kranz, the then Acting Flight Control Division Chief, called me into his office to explain his new rules for how the FDB would submit their requirements to the Flight Support Division (FSD) for implementation in the control center. Historically, all Flight Control Division requirements were collected by Dick Hoover's Branch, packaged into Flight Control Data Acquisition Requirements (FCDAR), and then submitted to FSD. The one exception was the Flight Dynamics Branch. Much to the dismay of John Hodge, Gene Kranz and the other Branch Chiefs, we always worked directly with MPAD and FSD to implement our requirements. This was a tradition established by Glynn Lunney, going back to the Mercury days, when the computers and the implementers were at the Goddard Space Flight Center.

MPAD developed most of the trajectory processors, and the FSD personnel liked working directly with us to develop displays. Others in FCD, especially John Hodge and Gene Kranz, always felt we got more than our share of RTCC computer capability with this arrangement, and now Gene was going to put an end to that. He told me that if I would not submit FDB requirements through Hoover, he would find a new Branch Chief who would. My answer was that we could not operate that way and that he might as well start looking for a new Branch Chief. When I got back to my office, I called Jim Stokes, the FSD Chief, and told him about my conversation with Gene. He immediately called Gene and told him that he would not accept any FDB requirements through Hoover, so if he wanted any trajectory and guidance capability in the control center, he had better leave it the way it was. I didn't hear any more from Gene and I got to keep my job.

– – –

Phil Shaffer was the lead FIDO for Apollo 7 and took much of the load in FDB preparation. It was a jam-packed timeline. Many spacecraft systems and flight techniques had to be tested on this flight if there was any hope in maintaining the goal of landing on the moon by the end of the decade.

On Friday, August 9, 1968, only a month prior to the planned Apollo 7 launch, things got a little more hectic. I received a call from Gene Kranz, now the Flight Control Division Chief, asking me to join him in a meeting with Chris Kraft. Arnie Aldrich and Cliff Charlesworth were also invited; so the four of us showed up in Chris's office.

Chris, as usual, was brief and succinct. He said that George Low, the Apollo Program Manager since the fire, wanted to go to the moon before the end of the year. Assuming that the Apollo 7 flight went well, the very next one would be a lunar orbit flight, without the Lunar Module. The LM was still behind schedule, and Low saw this as the only way to maintain the lunar landing schedule. Chris said that he would need an answer as to whether we could support such a flight by the following Monday morning.

Chris said that he and Low were going to Huntsville that afternoon to see if they could have the Saturn V ready by December, and that he would let us know that night how the meeting went. He called me, and I assume Gene and Arnie, that night and said that the Huntsville folks thought he and Low were crazy, but would take a serious look at it. I then told Chris that in order to do a thorough assessment of our capability, I needed to bring in Bob Ernull from Mission Planning, and Jim Stokes from the Flight Support Division. There were just too many questions about the mission planning and the MOCR/RTCC for me to answer alone by Monday morning. Chris said he understood and would call them himself, just to make sure they understood that this was an important exercise. He said he wanted to have another meeting the next morning, Saturday, with me, Gene, Cliff and Arnie and that he would invite Ernull and Stokes to that meeting. It turned out that they had already been asked by Chris to take a preliminary look at such a mission.

In the Saturday morning meeting, Chris expanded a little on the Huntsville meeting, and said he thought they would give a "go" because they didn't want to be the Center that said no. Ernull said that he would need complete access to both the Building 12 and the MCC computers 24 hours a day between then and Monday morning. Jim Stokes said he would need to bring in some IBM and Philco guys to help him access the readiness. Chris okayed both, but told Stokes to not tell the IBM and Philco people any more than he had to. "Bring in whomever you need, but you don't have to explain the details of the plan." I asked Chris if I could bring in Chuck Deiterich, Ed Pavelka, and Charley Parker. He said, "Okay, but make sure they know this is not to be revealed to anyone else." Almost as an afterthought, Chris then said that since this would be the first time we would be using the Return to Earth software in the control center, and since I used to be a RETRO, he wanted me to be a RETRO again if the mission was approved. I just responded, "Whatever you say."

When I got back to my office, I called Deiterich, Pavelka, and Parker and asked them to come in as soon as they could. They all showed up within a half hour. I explained to them what was going on, who was involved, and what I needed them to do. Ernull was doing the basic mission planning, Stokes was assessing the ability to implement all the MCC software and displays required. What I needed each of them to do was look at the minimum software and displays they could live with, assess the console procedures and come up with the training requirements. I told each of them that they would be the lead operators at their positions, but explained to Chuck that Chris had asked that I be a RETRO once again. This came as a shock to Chuck because he had not been a lead operator on a manned flight, and he realized that the team he would be leading consisted of his Section Head, John Llewellyn, and me, his Branch Chief. He did not hesitate, however, to take the assignment.

By Monday morning we were able to report to Chris that there was no valid reason we could not fly the mission in December. We could have all our procedures ready and get in the training time needed. We still had some work to do with Jim Stokes on the minimum MOCR displays we could live with, but were confident we could work that out.

Stokes said he could have the essential software ready (Translunar Injection, mid-course corrections, Lunar Orbit Insertion, Transearth

Injection, etc.) and the telemetry data that Arnie said the systems controllers would need. Ernull recommended a December 20 launch date. He also said that MPAD could support the mission with the Auxiliary Computing Room (ACR) to back up the MCC calculations as required.

Chris told all of us that a final decision would not be made for another few days, but for us to proceed as if the mission would happen, just continue to keep it under wraps. About a week later it was announced that the December mission, Apollo 8, would be commanded by Frank Borman and that it would be an earth orbit mission with a "lunar option." It did not take long for people to figure out that something strange was going on, and most suspected it was a lunar flyby, without going into lunar orbit. It was not until after the successful completion of the Apollo 7 mission that the full Apollo 8 plans could be revealed.

But before we could embark on this bold mission, we had to fly the first earth orbit flight. Apollo 7 was launched October 11, 1968. Commander Wally Schirra was a very close friend of Gus Grissom and felt a deep personal responsibility to make sure the necessary spacecraft changes were made after the fire, and then fully tested during the mission. This, plus the NASA management's desire to test the hardware as quickly as possible, resulted in probably the most ambitious flight plan we had ever flown. Each day was jam-packed with tests, with very little, if any, free time. One of the activities that Schirra did not want in the flight plan was live TV. He thought this was unnecessary and took up valuable test time. He lost that argument, but never liked the idea of doing "public relations stunts" on a hardware test flight. This attitude of Schirra's, along with a very full flight plan, plus a head cold he contracted in orbit, led to some tension between the flight crew and Mission Control.

I was not personally involved in this tension during the flight, so am not qualified to talk about it. I do know that after the flight, both Don Eisele, the CM Pilot, and Walt Cunningham, the LM Pilot, told me they were sorry if they caused us any problems, but they were just following the lead of their Commander, Wally. Unfortunately, neither of them ever flew again.

From a technical point, the flight was a huge success. The newly redesigned CSM worked really well, and everyone involved was pleased with the results. It cleared the way for the bold Apollo 8 flight to the moon, which was officially announced soon afterward. One interesting note about this flight: after clearing the launch tower, Eisele said, "I vonder vere Guenter Wendt?" referring to Guenter Wendt, the longtime Pad Leader, who was the last person the flight crews saw before launch. This line was later used in the movie Apollo 13.

With the successful completion of Apollo 7, the Apollo 8 lunar orbit flight was officially announced, and we began an intense preparation period to get ready for this bold and exciting flight. This would be one of the toughest missions we had ever flown. The prep time was short and we would not have all the MOCR computing capability and displays we had originally planned for, but nobody complained. Finally, we are going to the moon! The Flight Directors would be Cliff Charlesworth, Glynn Lunney and Milt Windler, with Cliff as lead. Obviously, everyone in the Trench was very happy to have two ex-FIDOs being the FDs on all the critical phases.

During the simulations for Apollo 8 George Low showed up in the Trench one day and stayed for a couple of hours. He said that Chris Kraft had grown tired of answering all his questions, so he wanted to join us and find out for himself if we were really prepared. He must have been satisfied.

The crew assigned to Apollo 8 was one we all liked and respected; Frank Borman as Commander, Jim Lovell as Command Module Pilot, and Bill Anders as Lunar Module Pilot (even though there would be no LM on this flight). Borman had done an outstanding job in overseeing the changes to the CSM after the fire, Lovell was considered by most people in the Trench as the best rendezvous pilot you could have, and Anders, although he had not flown before, had proven to be a very smart and easy guy with whom to work. As a CAPCOM, he had gone out of his way to learn as much as he could about the Trench and had picked it up quickly. A dream mission with a dream team as the crew. The launch phase went smoothly, even though we had experienced all the problems with the last unmanned Saturn V flight, AS-502. There was a little "pogo" during the second stage, but nothing like before.

We spent a couple of revolutions in earth orbit and then gave a "Go" for TLI, Translunar Injection. Even though we had done this numerous times in simulations, this one was for real. In the Trench, we all kind of looked at each other and without words said, "We're really going to the moon!"

TLI, transposition and docking all went well also. On the way to the moon, Charley Parker and I entertained each other with a discussion about how much we could speed up computer processing if we could come up with a decimal based time system. Pretty crazy, but a reflection of how well things were going. Early in the third mission day, we entertained ourselves with discussions of what would happen when we got to the lunar sphere of influence, a point at which the gravitational pull of the earth and moon would be equal on the spacecraft. Of course, we knew that nothing would happen, but it was entertaining to have this discussion. This would be the first time that a manned spacecraft had ever escaped the gravitational pull of the earth.

Targeting for the moon is somewhat like duck hunting. You don't shoot at the duck, you shoot ahead of its flight path and let it fly into the shot. So we were shooting (targeting) for a spot out in front of the moon's path (left side as you look up at the moon) and trusting God that the moon would get there at the right time. We wanted to miss the moon by about 60 miles, which seems like a lot, but when compared to how far we were from Earth, almost a quarter million miles, it was minuscule.

Now it was time to get ready for the Lunar Orbit Insertion (LOI) burn. We did one more small mid-course correction burn and then started running the final calculations. I remember thinking, "Okay, this is serious business!" Everything we did in the control center was serious, but we were getting ready to pass a maneuver to the flight crew that would put them in an orbit about the moon. Ed Pavelka, who was the FIDO on duty for this, calculated the final LOI burn numbers, wrote them on the PAD (Pre Advisory Data) to be given to CAPCOM for his read-up to the flight crew, and then went over them about three times to make sure he had written them down correctly. Without saying anything, I knew Ed was having the same thought: "This is serious business."

Once the maneuver numbers were passed up to the crew, I really felt helpless. There was nothing else we could do. We would soon have loss of signal with the crew as they went behind the moon, where the LOI maneuver would be performed. For about 20 minutes we would have no contact with them. Never before had I experienced such a "hand wringing" time. We set the clocks on the RETRO console, one to count down to spacecraft acquisition time if no burn occurred, and one for a nominal burn. There were too many options for partial burns, so these two times would frame the situation.

Just after loss of signal, Lunney, who was the FD on duty then, said over his loop, "Okay, all Flight Controllers, this is a good time to take a break." My initial reaction was, "Has he lost his mind? We have astronauts behind the moon and he wants us to take a break?" I quickly realized, however, that he was, as Glynn usually was, exactly right. There was nothing we could do for the next 15-20 minutes to help the crew and this was an excellent opportunity to go to the restroom and then come back to wait for acquisition of signal from the spacecraft.

We all got back into the MOCR well before the time of spacecraft acquisition if no LOI burn had occurred. That time came with no signal, which was somewhat comforting, yet we still could have had a partial burn, which would have not been good. Finally, the time of acquisition reflecting a nominal burn came, and almost exactly on time, we heard the crew report, "Houston, this is Apollo 8. Burn complete." What a relief and what an experience.

For me it was an assurance that, indeed, there was a God and He was, among other things, a good navigator. He had gotten the moon to exactly the right spot at exactly the right time! I said a short "Thank You" prayer. We actually had American men in orbit around the moon! About four hours later, we had the crew do a small burn to put them into a circular lunar orbit.

On Christmas Eve, the crew caught all of us by surprise by reading from the Book of Genesis about the creation of Heaven and Earth. I was totally overwhelmed, and tears came to my eyes. What could be more appropriate than a Bible reading about creation, coming from the first people to ever leave the influence of Earth, on Christmas Eve?

**Earthrise as seen from Apollo 8**
**Courtesy NASA**

But now it was time to get ready for another critical burn, Transearth Injection, TEI. The Service Module engine, SPS, would have to do another perfect burn to start the crew on their way back home. We were all apprehensive once again when the spacecraft went behind the moon for the last time before the burn.

Waiting, when there is absolutely nothing you can do, is a helpless feeling. When we heard Lovell report, "Houston, there is a Santa Clause," the MOCR let out another collective sigh of relief.

Apollo 8 was certainly my favorite flight up until then, and still is. It was bold, it was exciting, it was historical, and it was successful. It was even more special for me because Charles Lindbergh, who made his historic solo non-stop flight across the Atlantic Ocean in 1927, came to the MOCR Viewing Room during the flight and Chris Kraft took several of us to meet him. We had finally demonstrated that we had the hardware, the techniques and the people to pull off such an awesome adventure. We also demonstrated that we were clearly ahead of the Soviets. President Kennedy's goal now really felt achievable. Of course, we had not landed, but I felt like Apollo 8 had "baked the cake," and the landing would just be putting the icing on that cake.

After the flight, I took Mike to the control center, thinking he would be awed by what his dad was doing. When we got back home, he told his friend Tommy Stapp about his tour of NASA. Tommy asked, "What does your dad do there?" Mike's answer was "He watches TV."

The next flight, Apollo 9, would start applying that icing. The Lunar Module was finally declared ready and we would test it thoroughly in earth orbit. In my mind, Apollo 9 was Dave Reed's flight. Dave had been working on the LM since he first arrived at NASA. He had made many trips to Grumman, the manufacturer, in Bethpage, New York, and to the MIT Draper Labs, and made a lot of inputs into the propulsion and guidance systems. We all kidded him about "his" flimsy, funny looking spacecraft, and he became very defensive of the LM. "It will work great. Just wait and see." Of course, many others on the Flight Dynamics team had invested a lot of time and effort in the LM, but Dave was the easiest target for our "ridicule" of the LM.

As I stated earlier, Apollo 7 had been a very ambitious test flight with a jam-packed flight plan. Apollo 9 was even more jam-packed. This would be the first manned LM flight. Not only did we have to completely test the LM propulsion and guidance systems, but also a few little things like rendezvous and docking with the new Apollo hardware, and EVA. We had done all this during Gemini, but not with the much different, and hopefully better, Apollo systems. The Apollo 5 unmanned LM flight had been a pretty good test of the propulsion systems, but now we had to test them the way they would be used on a lunar landing mission, with astronauts aboard. One of the big differences was that the LM would separate from the CSM, with rendezvous and docking absolutely critical to the survival of the LM astronauts, because that was their only way of getting back to earth. The mission went very well, and all of us felt better about being able to reach President Kennedy's goal, now only nine months away.

A more extensive test of the entire Apollo system, including the LM, was scheduled for a couple of months later. Apollo 10 would be a manned simulation of the real thing, a "dry run" of the lunar landing mission with everything except an actual landing on the moon. They would even target a landing at the site planned for the upcoming Apollo 11 flight. This flight crew was another one in which all the guys in the Trench had a lot of confidence and trust. Tom Stafford was Commander, with Gene Cernan, LM Pilot, and John Young, CM Pilot.

The Apollo 10 flight was another huge success. All the hardware, the Manned Space Flight Network (MSFN) and flight and ground crews performed as designed and expected, with few problems. Stafford and Cernan came within about eight miles of the lunar surface, causing Stafford to say, "We're down here amongst 'em." The total system, including the Trench, was now ready for the real thing, Apollo 11, which was scheduled for July, only two months away.

The crew for Apollo 11 was another one with which the Trench was familiar and very comfortable. Neil Armstrong, the Commander, was "Mr. Cool." None of us had ever seen him get ruffled. On Gemini 8, when his spacecraft went into a wild tumbling mode, he was as calm and casual as a test pilot can get, and by all accounts, did exactly the right thing. Buzz Aldrin, the LM Pilot, was a rendezvous expert and had been the guy to show that EVA was easy if you prepare right and have the right body support, like hand and foot holds. Mike

Collins, the CM Pilot, was in the "cool" class with Armstrong. He just always did a great job and took everything in stride. The Trench assignments came about by pure rotation. I would have been comfortable with a number of controllers, and we had at least two or three people who could have been lead for the new critical phases: powered descent/landing and ascent/lunar orbit rendezvous.

Prior to lift-off on July 16, I think most of us had a similar feeling to that which we had prior to Apollo 8.... "Okay, this is real. This is what we and the Country have been waiting for." The Trench approached the flight with confidence. Even though we were confident, and this was the third time we had gone through things like translunar injection and lunar orbit insertion, we all realized that this was not a test flight. It was not a dry run. This was the mission that most of us had spent our entire careers preparing for.

The mission went extremely well until we got to powered descent. About 5 minutes into descent, the LM guidance computer started issuing a series of 1202 and 1201 alarms. Computer alarms are not what you want to get during such a critical phase. After Armstrong reported the first one, I immediately looked at Steve Bales, the GUIDO on duty. Steve, with confirmation from our SSR, reported to Flight that we were "go" with that alarm. Shortly thereafter, the second alarm was reported by Armstrong. Again, Steve told Flight, "We are go on that one. Same thing." We determined later that the alarms were just a report that the primary computer was getting behind on its tasks and needed to terminate some non-essential calculations. A few years before, a Draper Lab software programmer had written a program that prioritized the calculations the computer had to do and would terminate the one at the end of the list if the computer became overloaded. This was somewhat revolutionary in computer programming. It turns out that the alarms were occurring because both the rendezvous radar and the landing radar were operating. The rendezvous radar, which was tracking the CSM in lunar orbit so that it would be ready if we had to abort the landing, was obviously at that point less important than the landing radar, so the computer was just announcing that it was becoming overloaded and was going to terminate the lowest priority job.

Then it became obvious from crew reports that they were going long and could not find a nice smooth spot to land. The last few seconds before landing were very tense, as we were approaching running out of fuel. We all started breathing again when Aldrin reported they were "kicking up dust," indicating they were low enough that the descent engine exhaust was impinging on the lunar surface. Then came Armstrong's report: "Houston, Tranquility Base here. The Eagle has landed." WE HAD DONE IT!

It came as no great surprise that Armstrong and Aldrin decided they would start preparations for the first EVA, rather than waiting until after their scheduled sleep period. Every astronaut and flight controller descended on the MOCR. Everyone wanted to be there and witness the first step on the moon.

Each console had four places (jacks) to plug in earphones, and these places soon filled up. Pete Conrad, who was scheduled to be Commander on the next lunar flight, could not find an open jack at the CAPCOM console, so I invited him to plug in to the last jack available at the FIDO console.

Pete and I were sitting on the small ledge behind the FIDO console when Neil stepped onto the lunar surface and said, "That's one small step for man, one giant leap for mankind."

Pete turned to me and asked, "What did he say?" I told him that Neil had said something about "a giant leap for mankind." Pete thought about that for a couple of seconds and said, "That's just like

Armstrong to say something profound like that. If it had been me I probably would have said 'Jesus Christ, that shit is slippery!'"

When I left the control center, I went to a local liquor store, bought a bottle of Scotch for Steve Bales, and left it in his car in the Building 30 parking lot. I was convinced then, and still am now, that had it not been for Steve's knowledge and skill, we would not have been successful in landing on the moon that day. Unfortunately, I found out years later that the bottle was not there when Steve headed for home. I still owe him one.

The rest of the Apollo 11 mission went very well. After splashdown, I left for Mississippi to see my parents. When I arrived, my dad said that I had received a call from Phil Shaffer and that I was to call him back, no matter what time of day or night. When I called, Phil said that President Nixon was going to issue the Presidential Medal of Freedom to the Apollo 11 Flight Operations Team, and Kraft thought someone from the Trench should receive it. Phil's question to me was, "Who should it be?" My answer was Steve Bales, whereupon Phil said, "Good. That's what I already told Chris."

A few months after the Apollo 11 flight Neil Armstrong came by our house and Mike told him I was taking a nap so he couldn't come in. I saw Neil later and apologized. He said that was okay, he just wanted to thank me for helping to get him back home safely.

One of my most prized "souvenirs" of the space program is a lapel pin which Grumman Aerospace, the Lunar Module manufacturer, gave out after the Apollo 11 mission. It is a very elegant pin of the moon with the U.S. flag superimposed on it. Jack Buxton, the Grumman representative in Houston, handed them out to all the flight controllers. Although I have not been able to verify exactly how many were made, Jack's wife Vicki tells me she thinks there were 500 brass/bronze pins and 50 gold ones. After being made, the mold was broken. The brass ones were distributed to NASA Flight Operations and Apollo Program Office personnel as well as Grumman employees who worked on the LM. The gold ones were given to the flight crew, Flight Directors, and Grumman and North American Aviation managers. I actually received two of the bronze ones immediately after the flight, one from Buxton and one from Chris Kraft. After I went to work for Grumman in 1985, I was able to pick up a few more and then afterward I have purchased several on eBay. It is sad to see them for sale, but I have been able to get enough for all my kids and grandkids. I will come back from my grave to haunt them if they ever sell them!

**Apollo 11 Lunar Landing Lapel Pin**
**Distributed by Grumman Aerospace**

— — —

# Chapter 5

# NASA AFTER APOLLO 11

I have divided this book at Apollo 11, because in many respects, my life was divided at that time. Even until today, every time I hear a date; someone's birthday, death date, or date of some event, my first thought is "That was before (or after) we first landed on the moon." In my mind, that was a turning point in world history. It was indeed "A giant leap for mankind."

It was also a turning point in my life. Professionally, I felt at the peak of a mountain. Personally, I felt as if I were a failure as a husband and a father. I had been so absorbed in my job that even though I tried to be there for what I considered important family events, I had missed a lot, including Christmas in 1968. Even professionally, somewhere in the back of my mind, I kept hearing the Peggy Lee song *Is That All There Is?* What were we going to do for an encore? We had already achieved the impossible. The only direction from a peak is downward. My priorities became; work (yes, still at the top, but I didn't know how to give it anything other than my best), family, and finding a future career outside the control center.

I thought about what I had given up over the past 7-8 years. I felt as if I had missed a big part of my youth. I was so busy at work that I vaguely knew about the Civil Rights movement and the Vietnam War, but I really had missed all of that. More importantly, I had missed a big part of Mike and Kristi's childhood. How could I make up for all that I had missed?

I knew we had several more lunar landings planned (nine more were on the books then) and there were many challenges and things we had to improve upon. There was a lot of talk about space stations and reusable space vehicles, but those didn't excite me like the challenge of landing men on the moon for the first time. I resolved to work as hard as ever to make sure we were ready for the continuing challenges at work, but also to not be so absorbed in my work that I overlooked other obligations.

**Hippie Grandpa Jerry
Courtesy NASA**

I let my hair grow long (I had a crew cut for as long as I could remember) and experimented with beards and mustaches. I started wearing what I had considered "Hippie" clothes; bell-bottom pants, paisley shirts and wide white belts. I bought a Mustang convertible.

— — —

Apollo 12 was coming up quickly and we had a lot of work to do. We had to figure out why we had landed long (overshot the target by about four miles) on Apollo 11 and make the changes necessary to achieve a pin-point landing next to the unmanned Surveyor spacecraft which had landed in a lunar crater some three years earlier. The mission started out with a bang. A bang of lightening! Less than a minute into the launch, the spacecraft and the ground lost all data. When telemetry data returned, John Aaron, the Electrical, Environmental and Communications (EECOM) flight controller, saw that it was scrambled in a fashion that he remembered from a pad test a year before. He immediately asked the Flight Director, Gerry Griffin, to have the crew "take the SCE (Signal Conditioning Equipment) switch to Aux (Auxiliary)." Gerry didn't understand exactly what the switch was and what it would do, but he trusted John so he relayed the request to CAPCOM Jerry Carr, who passed the request on to the flight crew. LM pilot Alan Bean threw the switch and data was restored, both in the spacecraft and on the ground. Once we got into earth orbit, there was concern throughout the control center about whether we should proceed to the moon after such an incident. Sig Sjoberg, came to me and said "Jerry, if you feel uncomfortable in any way about the TLI, speak out. I will support you if you give a No Go today." He repeated that message to the BOOSTER Controller. After reviewing all the data that we had, and conferring with the BOOSTER, GNC, and EECOM, we gave a Go to proceed.

The solution to the pin-point landing, developed by Emil Scheisser of MPAD and Bill Lear of MIT, and refined in the Data Priority meetings led by Bill Tindall, was to monitor the radial rate of descent with Doppler radar from three MSFN tracking sites, and update the distance to the landing site in real time. Dave Reed, the descent phase FIDO for this mission had asked Pete Conrad, the Commander, where he wanted to land. Pete told Dave to target him for the center of the Surveyor crater. Dave's response was, "You got it, babe." Pete didn't believe Dave could do it, but that's exactly where he landed. The mission that had started out with a bang was a banging success!

Soon after the 12 flight, Apollo 20, the last one in the planning stages, was cancelled for budgetary reasons.

— — —

We were still traveling a lot and the airline representatives at NASA did everything they could legally do to get us to fly their airline. The main carriers at that time between Houston and Los Angeles were Continental and National. The National rep gave me a pass to get into the "Executive Club" at Houston Hobby Airport, which was normally reserved for first class passengers. At least you could get free drinks and snacks while waiting for your flight. I was in the lounge in early 1970 when Cheryl Tiegs, a super model who had recently appeared on the cover of Sports Illustrated magazine, walked in. I watched her go to the coffee bar where, after getting a cup for herself, she turned to me and asked "Would you like a cup of coffee?" Without hesitation I said "Yes, please." When she brought it to me she sat down beside me and we had a nice 20-30 minute conversation.

– – –

It is difficult for me to write much about Apollo 13 here. So many books and several movies have expounded on what some called "A successful failure." Of course, the unquestionably best book was *Lost Moon* and the only movie worth seeing was *Apollo 13*. I say that without prejudice, even though Mike was the one who convinced Ron Howard to make the movie. I will say more later about the movie and my experience in serving as a technical advisor. In planning for the mission, the Flight Control team was very happy about the crew assignments. We were very familiar with Jim Lovell from working with him on Gemini missions 7 and 12 and Apollo 8. Most of us considered Fred Haise to be the best Lunar Module pilot we had worked with and T. K. Mattingly was a good friend of several of us. Even though T. K. could sometimes drive us crazy with details, we were all sad when he was removed from the flight because he had been exposed to measles. His replacement, Jack Swigert, was not as well known to us, but after a few days of simulations, we saw that he was more than adequate.

By the time Apollo 13 launched, the media coverage of lunar flights had dropped off drastically. They seemed to be taking the attitude, "Ho-hum, it's another lunar landing flight. How boring!" This is a good place to comment on media coverage in general. Most of the time when I read anything in the newspapers or magazines about a flight, it was full of errors. Unfortunately, the same was true of radio and television coverage. The reporters just didn't seem to put forth the effort to get things right. Walter Cronkite of CBS TV received a lot of attention and praise for his coverage, highlighted by his coverage of the first lunar landing. I only met him once, in the Mercury Control Center at the Cape. He was there to interview Chris Kraft. In my humble opinion, he did not do his homework. As far as I observed, he never called or came to see any flight controllers below Flight Directors. Jim Hartz, from NBC, became a good friend of Gerry Griffin, and was much better, in my opinion. He even came to a couple of our splashdown parties. Cronkite's primary competitors, Jim Hartz and Roy Neal of NBC and Jules Bergman of ABC, did a lot of homework. Roy and Jules called regularly and Roy came to my office several times to get background information. He spent an entire day with me in the MOCR during Gemini rendezvous simulations. Obviously, I think he was the best.

When the explosion occurred on Apollo 13, it caught us completely by surprise. In fact, we didn't know that there had been an explosion. All we really knew was that the CSM was rapidly losing electrical power and oxygen, so we needed to figure out how to save the astronauts. All of us in the Trench starting immediately working on how to get them back to Earth, trajectory wise, while the systems guys worked on getting them into the LM and assessing how long they could survive on the available consumables like electrical power, food, water, and oxygen. Gene Kranz was the Flight Director on duty when the accident occurred. About an hour later, after starting the LM power-up, Glynn Lunney replaced him. An immediate calm came over the MOCR. Glynn was calm, cool and methodical, just as he always was. He didn't try to lead the team to an immediate solution to the problem at hand, but rather focused on "first things first"….a very methodical step-by-step approach. "Let's take care of the biggest problem that is facing us now, then we'll work on solving the next step." I am not the only one who observed this attitude change when Glynn took over. T. K. Mattingly, who was there at the time, has commented on this several times.

**Mission Control during Apollo 13**
**Courtesy NASA**

What most people find hard to believe is that none of us ever thought that we would not be able to get the astronauts back home safely. We didn't know exactly how, but we never thought that we couldn't do it. Fortunately, we <u>were</u> able to get them back safely. It was the finest example of teamwork that I had ever seen. I will have more to say about the movie in Appendix 3.

— — —

On the home front, Mike and I purchased a go-cart, powered by a Briggs and Stratton lawn mower engine. I paid 51% of the cost of the cart so that I could have controlling interest. We soon determined that it was not powerful enough, so I switched the motor from my

3.5 horsepower lawn edger and then it would go plenty fast. Since we lived on a cul-de-sac, we felt safe letting him ride it in front of our house, but he was required to always wear a helmet. We even let Kristi drive it!

**Mike cleaning "our" go-cart**

**Mike ready to race**

When Kristi was 5 years old, she got her first bicycle. We tried to help her learn to ride it but she refused any assistance. She was determined that she could learn all on her own. I watched out the kitchen window as she repeatedly got on, tried to ride, then fell. She did this five or six times, then rode off as if she had always known how to do it. She finally came in the house with a big smile and several scrapes and bruises. She refused any first aid even though at that age her favorite thing was band-aides.

– – –

At about that time in late 1970, NASA cancelled Apollo 18 and 19 due to Congressional budget cuts in the 1971 manned space flight appropriations. This came as somewhat of a shock to most of us and meant that we only had four more approved lunar landings. Since the hardware for those flights was already built, the dollar savings were minuscule! Were we losing the support of the public, the media, the president, and Congress? Did they consider Apollo 13 to be a failure? Some looked at it that way, including Fred Haise, who was obviously happy to be alive but considered the mission a failure because they were not able to land on the moon. I don't know of any flight controllers who felt that way. We saw the mission as proof that we could solve almost any problems thrown at us. We didn't brag about it, we just felt very satisfied.

Alan Shepard, who had been grounded from space flight because of an inner ear problem, was returned to flight status in early 1969. He was originally scheduled for the Apollo 13 flight, but the 13 and 14 crews were switched because it was felt he needed more training time. Even though Al and I had not been on the best of terms since the Gemini 4 incident at the Cape, as soon as his assignment to Apollo 14 was announced, he appeared in my office one day. He said, "As you know, I have been assigned to be the Commander of Apollo 14 and I have a really steep learning curve. Can you tell me everything I need to know about flight dynamics?" We spent the next two hours going over the essential stuff and had a good relationship throughout the training for that mission. The mission went very smoothly, mostly remembered by Al's golf shot from the lunar surface.

– – –

Dave Reed had told me during the Apollo 12 mission that he and his wife were getting a divorce and that he had accepted a job in Cambridge, Massachusetts, with the U.S. Department of Transportation and would be leaving after Apollo 13. This saddened me on several fronts. I hated to see anyone go through a divorce and I sure hated to lose Dave as a FIDO. Away from work, we had become very good friends. We were members of the local Bay Area Lions Club and spent many weekends together selling firewood and Christmas trees. However, I understood his reasoning and wished him the best. He had many of the same feelings that I had; we accomplished President Kennedy's goal and now the public and the Congress seemed to be losing interest; bureaucracy was slowly but surely creeping into NASA; did we want to spend the rest of our careers as a flight controller? He decided after Apollo 13 that he didn't want that to be his last flight. He felt like most pilots who crash-land an aircraft. Tradition dictates that they go up again just as soon as they are able, so he stayed on through Apollo 14.

– – –

In June 1971, Linda, Mike, Kristi and I went on a vacation to New Mexico and Colorado. After spending the first night in Wichita Falls, we drove to Santa Fe, New Mexico. I loved it there! It felt like something out of true Western movie and the food was great. Then we went to Taos and I liked it even more. The pueblo village there was unbelievable. It was hard to image Native Americans actually living there. It must have been a hard life. We visited the Rio Grande Bridge, just a few miles from Taos. I thought it was spectacular, but later when we say the Royal Gorge Bridge in Colorado it was even more spectacular. We rode the incline railway (the world's steepest) to the bottom of the gorge. Thrilling and frightening at the same time! While in New Mexico, I wanted to go by Philmont Scout Ranch, where I went as a Boy Scout in 1954 but I was outvoted.

Our next stop was Durango, Colorado and I liked it even better than Santa Fe and Taos. Stu Roosa, the LM Pilot on Apollo 9, which we had just completed, was born in Durango. The Mesa Verde National Park was breath taking! If I had thought that living in Taos pueblos was tough, it must have been a lot tougher at Mesa Verde.

**Mesa Verde National Park**

I was surprised that they allowed us to crawl all over the place. I bet they don't allow that now.

**Mike at Mesa Verde**

One of my great thrills while in Durango was a ride on the narrow gauge railroad to Silverton. When we boarded the train, there was John Yardley and his wife Phyllis. John was a project engineer and Launch Operations Manager for McDonnell Aircraft on the Mercury program and Technical Director for what had become the McDonnell Douglas Corporation on Gemini. He was then leading the McDonnell Douglas team preparing for the Space Shuttle program. The first thing he said to me was, "Bostick, why aren't you back in Houston getting ready for Apollo 15? I'm going to tell Dave Scott that you're up here goofing off." It seemed as if I was having a hard time getting away from work. The train ride to Silverton was through some beautiful, but treacherous terrain.

One of my cousins had taught school in Silverton for many years and her husband was a pharmacist and drug store owner there. They had since moved away, but I looked forward to seeing if anyone there still remembered them. We went to the drug store and sure enough, all of the locals there remembered them well. She had told me that for several months in the winter, they would be snowed in. The train didn't run and the roads were impassable, so they had to stock up each year in preparation for winter. Silverton was a nice little town (looked like a movie set) but I surely wouldn't want to live there!

Leaving the Durango area, we headed for Central City. We drove through Loveland Pass where there was a lot of snow. Mike and Kristi had seen only limited amounts of snow before, so they had a great time playing in it.

**Kristi & Mike in snow at Loveland Pass**

We stopped in Leadville, an old silver mining town, once the second largest city in Colorado. One of the early silver miners and founder of the town was Horace Tabor. He became the richest man in Colorado. The Opera House there is named for him. He later married Elizabeth Doe a much younger divorcee called "Baby Doe." When her husband lost all of his money and died, Baby Doe moved into a small shack on one of the mine properties where she lived in poverty for over 30 years, wearing rags and newspaper for clothing. We visited the shack and couldn't believe that someone actually lived there in solitude.

Central City was like another town out of a movie set, very picturesque. One of my favorite things there was the famous "Face on the bar room floor", in the Teller House tavern. While there, we called Tommy Stapp, a neighbor and friend of Mike's to see how his Little League baseball team had fared in a championship game. They won! Mike was thrilled and a little regretful that he had missed playing in the game. We found a gift shop and had them print a headline for a fake newspaper: "BEARS ARE CHAMPS! BEAT PHILLIES 12-5."

**Newspaper "Headline" in Central City, CO**

From Central City we drove to Estes Park. It was pretty there and we had a nice chalet. One of my favorite things to do was the go-cart track. What fun! We had made reservations to go horseback riding early one morning and then have a "Cowboy Breakfast" out in the foothills. We all saddled up and started out. Kristi turned loose of her horse's rein, so it started running ahead, with Kristi scared to death. I took out after them and got close enough to shout, "Grab the reins" several times before realizing that Kristi probably didn't know what reins were, so I shouted, "Grab the rope and pull on it." She immediately did that and the horse behaved afterward. We arrived at the campsite where a wonderful breakfast of bacon, ham, sausage, eggs, biscuits and coffee was ready. I vowed to return to Estes Park someday, but have not lived up to that vow.

I wanted to go on to Fort Collins to the National Bureau of Standards that then kept the official time based on atomic clocks. I had worked with them over the years to make sure that the control center and spacecraft clocks were accurate. They were planning to add a "leap second" in June 1972 to account for the slowing of the Earth's rotation. Such a change was of concern to us and we were already in the process of making software changes so that at midnight on June 30, 1972 all of our clocks would go from 11:59:59 to 11:59:60 and then to 12:00:00. My contact there carried the title of "Director of Time." I thought that with a title like that, he must be right after God, Jesus and the Holy Spirit! Once again, I was outvoted, so we headed south for the Colorado Springs area.

There seemed to be dozens of interesting things to see and do around Colorado Springs. High on my list was the Air Force Academy, especially the Chapel, an architectural marvel. My Capitol Page School friend Chuck Bush was the first African American (He detested that term. He said that he had never been to Africa so he was Black American) to graduate from the Academy, in 1963. We also went to Santa's Workshop in North Pole, Colorado, where Mike and Kristi got to visit with Santa and pet real reindeer.

**Mike & Kristi with Reindeer at Santa's Workshop**

Of course you can't go to Colorado Springs without going to the top of Pike's Peak. The drive up to the peak was a little frightening for me. Very narrow, twisting road with no guard rails in places. The car started coughing because of the decrease in atmospheric pressure and I wasn't sure we would make it, but we did. It was a fantastic view, but I wasn't sure it was worth all the tension involved in getting up there.

**Dad, Kristi & Mike atop Pike's Peak**

The drive through Garden of the Gods was wonderful, with all the red sandstone rocks. I had never seen anything like that before.

When we departed the Colorado Springs area, we were headed back to Texas but stopped in Penrose, Colorado to see the Estes model rocket factory, the largest in the world. I'm sure I enjoyed it more than the rest of the family.

After the rocket factory, the only major stop on the way back home was to buy a case of Coors beer. It was sold only in Colorado at that time.

– – –

Shortly after returning home, Mother and Daddy (Grand Bostick and Daddy Bostick to the kids) came to Houston. Daddy was then working for Deaton Funeral Home in Belmont and volunteered to deliver a body to Houston in a hearse. Mike and Kristi reluctantly agreed to ride back to Mississippi with them, so we put sleeping bags and lots of toys and books inside and off they went, riding in the only place there was for passengers, in the back where the casket usually goes. Linda and I didn't know that as soon as they left our house, Kristi started crying and begging to go back home. I think she cried most of the way to Mississippi, a 14-hour drive. Mike said it was the creepiest thing he had ever done. Nevertheless, they survived and we drove to Mississippi to get them as soon as the Apollo 15 mission landed.

– – –

Apollo 15, with Dave Scott as Commander, was to be the longest stay on the lunar surface to date and included the Lunar Rover for the first time. The mission goals were more scientific than any of the previous missions. For the geology to be conducted, we could not have had a more enthusiastic test pilot astronaut. Dave had a genuine interest in geology and took his preparation very seriously. With the eager assistance of Jack Schmitt, he learned more about geology than any of the previous lunar astronauts. For us trajectory types, the only really new challenge was the lunar descent required to fly over higher mountains to get to the desired landing site at Hadley Rill in the Apennine mountains. Just having returned from Colorado, I imagined we were flying over Pike's Peak. It all worked great.

– – –

When we drove to Mississippi after Apollo 15 to get Mike and Kristi, I went to visit my great aunt Emma Berry, the sister of Ma-Ma Bostick. She still lived in the same house, about halfway between Red Bay and Vina, Alabama, and was about 90 years old. I remembered her as a short, plump feisty little lady who was always cleaning, cooking and talking. She now was confined to her reclining chair but her mind was as active as ever and she was still talking a blue streak. She asked me a hundred questions about NASA and was totally convinced that the lunar landing would not have been successful without her "favorite grandnephew." She was watching the Summer Olympics from Munich and marveled at how technology had advanced over her lifetime. She asked if I remembered visiting her in a horse drawn wagon when there were few roads and it took over two hours to travel from Golden to her house. I did remember visiting her, but not the wagon ride. She said, "Now I'm sitting here with my grandnephew who put people on the moon, watching the Olympics on TV from Germany as they happen!" As for her age, she gave me some wonderful advice. She said that when she turned 60 she started wondering about how much longer she had to live. Then when she turned 80, she decided that she had wasted 20 years of her life and didn't worry about her age any more. She said, "Since then, I just go to bed at night, say my prayers and tell God that if I wake up tomorrow that will be fine, and if I don't, that also will be fine."

— — —

After the 1971 season, the Washington Senators baseball team announced that they would be moving to the Dallas/Fort Worth area and sponsored a contest to name the new team. I submitted the name "Texas Rangers" which seemed somewhat logical. I guess it was, because over 50 other people suggested the same name. They held a drawing to determine the ultimate winner, and my name wasn't drawn. I still tell people that I suggested the name for the new team.

— — —

In 1971, the San Diego Rockets moved to Houston, becoming the Houston Rockets. They had some great players including Elvin Hayes, Calvin Murphy and Rudy Tomjanovich, but had a losing record. Ten of us from NASA went as a group and bought season tickets, paying cash. We made such an impression on the ticket office that we were invited to special Rocket functions which normally only box seat holders and local dignitaries were invited. We had wonderful seats about 10 rows up at midcourt. The seats were only $5.80 each! Initially, they played all over town at almost any arena they could book; Hofheinz Pavilion at the University of Houston, the Astrodome, the Sam Houston Coliseum, etc. When they played at the Astrodome, they placed the court in one corner of the arena floor. We attended one game there when the total attendance was only about 250. It was so quiet that we could talk to the referees. When I left to move to Washington, I gave up my seat. Upon my return to Houston a couple of years later, I called the Rocket office to see if I could get my seat back. I started the conversation; "Hello, my name is Bostick. I used to have season tickets..." That's as far as I got until the lady asked, "Jerry, is that you?" It was the same lady from whom we had purchased our tickets four years earlier. I did get my seat back along with Jay Greene, Ed Fendell, Will Presley, Floyd Bennett and several others. By this time, they were considerably more than $5.80.

The Rockets were then playing in the new Summit, which was much nicer than moving all over town. I kept my season ticket for another 2-3 years, but then gave it up because it was getting too expensive. Ed Fendell still has tickets, making him the longest/oldest ticket holder, but in the "cheap seats"...$80 per game. He tells me that the seats we originally had are several hundred dollars each now.

– – –

For Apollo 16, the scientists wanted to land in the mountains, not just in the valleys. Personally, we could not have a better flight crew; John Young as Commander, Charlie Duke as LM Pilot, and T. K. Mattingly as CSM Pilot. I had worked with each of them for many years and highly respected their abilities. From my perspective, the flight went very well. The only downer was that now we only had one more lunar landing in the program.

Soon after Apollo 16, Pete Conrad was returning from ILC, the space suit manufacturer, in Dover, Delaware with intent to land at Ellington Field. When he arrived, the airport was fogged in, so he was diverted to Houston Hobby Airport. By the time he got there, it also was closed due to thunderstorms. He was then diverted to Bergstrom AFB in Austin, but was running out of fuel. When he saw that he wasn't going to make it, he pointed the T-38 toward an open field just beyond the airport and ejected. He landed safely on the lawn of the Officer's Club at Bergstrom, gathered up his parachute and went inside to call his wife Jane to tell her he was okay. While on the pay phone just inside the Officer's Club, someone came running by screaming, "There's been a plane crash about 2 miles away!" Pete calmly raised his hand and said, "Yea, I'm the pilot." After a routine check at the Air Force hospital, he returned home to Clear Lake later that night.

– – –

In 1972 my frustration, both professionally and personally, led me to move out of our house and into an apartment in Seabrook on NASA Road 1. It makes no sense now and it didn't help anything then. I bought a 1968 Corvette, something I had always wanted, but that didn't help either. The water pump failed on it and I couldn't afford to have someone fix it, so I tried myself. Taking the old one off resulted in breaking a bolt head. I tried drilling it out but all that did was wear out a large quantity of drill bits. I then called my friend and co-worker Ron Epps, who owned a Corvette, and we tried a bolt extractor called an "easy out." That didn't work out too well because we broke the "easy out" in the small hole I had drilled inside the bolt we were trying to remove. I finally went to the NASA manufacturing shop and they loaned me a diamond drill bit, which was successful. Mike and Kristi visited me there but I deeply missed being with them at home. The hardest part was spending Christmas alone. I didn't know what the answer was, but being separated from Linda and the kids wasn't it.

– – –

Apollo 17, the last flight of the program, was one we really wanted to get right. Gene Cernan, Ron Evans, and Joe Engle were the backup crew on Apollo 14 and, following the usual rotation, would have flown Apollo 17. Harrison "Jack" Schmitt had served on the backup crew of Apollo 15 and was slated to fly as Lunar Module Pilot on 18. However, after that flight was cancelled, the scientific community pressured NASA to assign a geologist to the last lunar landing, as opposed to a pilot trained in geology. Yielding to this pressure, Jack, a professional geologist, was assigned to replace Joe. We all thought Joe had gotten a raw deal and hated to see him replaced, but at the same time, were happy that our friend Jack would get to fly. We knew him as one who was an expert geologist (we called him "Dr. Rock"), a more than capable LM pilot and a beer drinking friend of all flight controllers. He came to most of our private parties and I learned early on not to challenge him to a "chug-a-lug." The crew called their flight "The End of the Beginning", implying that it should not be the beginning of the end of America's lunar landing program. The flight went well and all the scientists were very happy with Jack's performance, as we were with his piloting skills. My thoughts were that the fun was really over now and I wasn't at all excited about boring holes in the sky with Skylab, the next program on the books.

The Flight Dynamics Branch had been assigned responsibility for managing the development of the software for the Apollo Telescope Mount Digital Computer (ATMDC), the primary attitude control and pointing system for Skylab. Some of the guys in the Branch, mostly new employees who had not been heavily involved in Apollo, were excited about the challenge, but I certainly wasn't. To me, it was a big let down after landing on the moon six times. Other than the launch, rendezvous and entry phases, there was not much for a trajectory guy to do during a Skylab mission. Just track it, confirm the orbit, and occasionally compute an orbital adjustment to counteract the orbital decay. I had even argued that the orbital part of the job could be done from the office and there was no need to have trajectory and guidance people in the control center 24 hours a day. Unfortunately, I lost that battle. I think the Flight Directors wanted the comfort of having a FIDO to talk to in person.

Near the end of the Apollo program, I was asked if I wanted to be considered for Flight Director beginning on Skylab. Almost any flight controller would aspire to one day becoming a Flight Director, but at this point, I was becoming tired of being in the control center, so I said no. I learned years later, when John Aaron, Arnie Aldrich, John O'Neill and I were voted by all the retired Flight Directors to be honorary members of the "Old and Ancient Flight Directors" that we were the only four people who ever turned down the job.

Over the years, starting with Charles Murray, co-author of *Apollo: The Race To The Moon*, several interviewers have asked me why I didn't assign myself to more of the critical phases of the lunar landing missions. As Chief of the Flight Dynamics Branch, I made the mission assignments for the Retrofire Officer, the Flight Dynamics Officer, and the Guidance Officer for each phase of each mission and could easily have assigned myself to any shift in the control center. My first thought when asked that question is always "You obviously don't understand the job that I had." I felt, with no hesitation, that it was my job to ensure that 15-20 fully qualified controllers were available for each flight and that I was responsible for their preparedness and their performance. While I felt that I should be knowledgeable enough to fill any of the three positions for any mission phase, I could never have enough time to participate in the necessary training and simulations for the critical phases of lunar landing and launch. It was my job to make sure that qualified people were available for assignment and to oversee their performance, not to fill the positions myself.

— — —

In 1971 the Request For Proposal (RFP) for the Space Shuttle Program was released by NASA. I was assigned as the "book manager" for the horizontal flight test portion of the RFP. That responsibility included evaluation of the proposals received from the potential contractors explaining how they would conduct that activity. All of the bidders proposed doing the tests at Dryden Flight Research Center, but left the question open about who would control them. Lee Scherer, Director of Dryden, wanted to control the tests from his facility. Of course, the flight operations people in Houston wanted to control them from our MCC. Dr. Kraft agreed that some of us should go out to Dryden and let them demonstrate to us their "superior capability" for conducting/controlling such tests. Chris, Milt Windler, Carl Peterson (Manager of the Shuttle Carrier

Aircraft, from which the Orbiter would be dropped for the approach and landing tests) and I, along with a few others, loaded up on our

Gulfstream and flew to Dryden for their demonstration, which was to be an SR-71 Blackbird flight up to the Canadian border and back.

The Blackbird was being fueled on the runway, but we could only get to within about 100 yards of it. I was shocked at how much fuel was pouring out on the runway. The fuel

**SR-71 Blackbird (with engine spikes forward) Courtesy NASA**

tanks, although sealed as best as could be with silicon, are not 100% tight until the plane gets into the air and the titanium expands as it heats up. Thankfully, the fuel, JP-7, does not present a fire hazard. We then went inside to stand in a hallway and watch through a window into their control room. Everything went fine until the plane started making its turn over Montana. One of the engine spikes failed to the forward position. The spikes are usually full forward (out) for takeoff and landing, below Mach 1.6, and then start to move back in until fully open at about Mach 3.2, the nominal top cruise speed. One forward and one rearward spike causes severe yaw on the plane, and makes supersonic flight impossible, so the pilot commanded the remaining good spike to the out/forward position, and dropped the speed to subsonic, about Mach 0.9. In this configuration, the plane consumes huge quantities of fuel, so the pilot radioed that he could not make it back to Dryden and asked for the nearest field where he could land. The Dryden controllers went into panic mode. They were looking for a telephone directory so they could call an airfield and request permission to land. One controller even went to his car and got a road map looking for possible places to land. Finally, the pilot said, "Forget it! I'm going into Nellis. I know where it is and I know how to get there." Nellis is an Air Force base in southern Nevada with runways over 10,000 feet long, plenty of length to land the SR-71.

While the Dryden controllers were then trying to find the telephone number for Nellis, the pilot reported that he had already talked to the tower and was beginning his descent. He landed just fine, but then another big problem arose. It takes special tools to get the pilot out of his suit, and they didn't have those at Nellis. There was a brief discussion about using a chain saw to cut him out, but Nellis reported that they had plenty of oxygen to feed the suit if Dryden would just fly over with the proper tools. Scherer then had to ask Dr. Kraft if they could borrow our Gulfstream to fly the tools to Nellis, get the pilot out of his suit and bring him back.

There wasn't much discussion between us and the Dryden folks in the meantime and we departed for Houston as soon as our plane arrived back from its rescue mission. When we all got on our plane, Chris just said "Any questions about which control center we're going to use?"

- - -

After Apollo 17, my good friend Gerry Griffin had been reassigned to NASA Headquarters in Washington as Assistant Administrator for Congressional Affairs. I talked to him by phone frequently and told him I would be willing to also move to Washington and take almost any job that might be available. I was just really tired of being a flight controller and needed a change of pace. In early 1973, he called to ask if I would be interested in being an Executive Secretary in the NASA Administrator's office. I had no idea what it entailed, but after a brief explanation, I told him that I would like to be considered for the job. Pete Clements, who had been Chief of the Flight Support Division at JSC, was then the Executive Secretary to the Administrator. He came to JSC and interviewed me for the job. The Administrator's Office consisted of the Administrator, Jim Fletcher, the Deputy Administrator, George Low (who had been the Apollo Program Manager), and

Willis Shapley, the Associate Deputy Administrator. The overly simplified jobs of each was that Low ran the NASA Centers, Shapley ran Washington (budget, legislative affairs and international relations), and Fletcher was the boss. Each had their own Executive Secretary, who was responsible for reviewing all incoming and outgoing mail, scheduling, attending all meetings, writing minutes of such meetings, and following up on any assigned action items. The Executive Secretaries were "horse holders", holding the boss's horse while he saddled up to ride off to the latest challenge. I would primarily work with Shapley. Pete also explained that Fletcher traveled a lot and that he, Pete, didn't like to travel, so I would also accompany Fletcher on most of his trips.

I told Pete that I definitely was interested in the job. A few days later he called to make the official offer. I called Linda to tell her that I was considering moving to Washington and that I would like for her and the kids to go with me. We ended up having a "date" where we discussed my general frustration with life over the past three years and concluded that moving into a new community with a new job would probably be good for us all. So I called Pete and accepted the offer. Shortly thereafter, I was on my way to Washington. I would live in an apartment until school was out in Texas, we could sell the Nassau Bay house, and buy one near where I would be working.

In the meantime, I called my college and RETRO friend Tom Carter, who then was working for TRW at the Pentagon, to tell him we were heading that way and asked for suggestions on where we might buy a home. A few days later he called to tell me that he was tired of going to work each day and "trying to figure out how to kill people", so had purchased a furniture factory in North Carolina and would be moving there. He said that we could rent his house in Vienna, Virginia, while we looked for one to purchase. It was near where Gerry and Sandy Griffin lived, so it sounded like a good idea. After looking at the house, I agreed to rent it for at least six months.

— — —

In early 1973, before moving to the Washington area, we took the kids to Disney World. On the way there, we stopped by the Cape. I had arranged for us to drive out to the Apollo launch complex and to go inside the old Mercury Control Center. I was really excited about the MCC because I hadn't been there in several years. I thought Mike and Kristi would be excited also to see the historic building where their dad once worked. We did a quick tour and then went outside to get into the car whereupon Mike said, "Can we go to Disney World now?" To say that the kids were not impressed with the Cape would be an understatement. We stayed at the big fancy hotel and rode the monorail, which I thought was neat. I really wanted to see the underground tunnels where the supplies are brought in, the trash is dumped, and the employees have their dressing rooms, but they wouldn't let me go there. My lingering remembrance of Disney World is that Kristi got a stomach ailment and we had to take her to the nurses station.

— — —

Soon after returning to Clear Lake from the Disney World trip, I headed for DC. I discovered that a 1968 Corvette is not the most comfortable vehicle to travel in for long distances. The right front tire blew out while going about 80 MPH on Interstate 40 near Knoxville, Tennessee. Getting the spare out from underneath the car was a big chore and getting the flat tire into the spare location turned out to be impossible because it was an oversize tire. The car was packed to overflowing but I somehow managed to get the flat tire and wheel into the passenger seat. I bought a new tire in Knoxville and made it okay on to the DC area where I had rented an apartment on Washington Boulevard for one month until Tom and Doris moved out of their house so that we could move in.

On my first day of work at NASA Headquarters I learned that my duties would be even more extensive than expected. Because I had experience in the control center, I was tasked with being the interface between Headquarters and MCC for the ongoing Skylab missions. I had to write a report each morning outlining the previous day's accomplishments/problems and the current day plans. I knew George Low from his days as Apollo Program Manager, had met Jim Fletcher several times, but knew nothing about my immediate boss Willis Shapley. He turned out to be very nice and one of the smartest people I ever met. He had previously served as Special Assistant to the Director of the Bureau of the Budget for Space Program Coordination, and had actually argued against undertaking a lunar landing mission, based purely on the cost. Thankfully, he lost the argument, but was so articulate and persuasive that the then NASA Administrator, James Webb, asked him to transfer to NASA, which he did in 1965 as Associate Deputy Administrator, the number three person in the agency.

At first, my duties seemed overwhelming. I was supposed to review all correspondence addressed to Dr. Fletcher or Mr. Shapley and attach a simple one paragraph summary of what it said and what action was required. I also was required to attend all of Mr. Shapley's meetings and most of Dr. Fletcher's and then write a one page or less summary of each meeting. I found a nice green pen in the supply cabinet so I started using it to write the summaries of correspondence. One morning George Low came into my office and asked if I had a green pen. When I showed it to him he took it and said "I am the only one in this office that can use green pens."

The meetings that Fletcher, Low and Shapley had were somewhat mind-boggling, not only in content, but also in frequency. Each was booked for some type meeting almost every minute of the day. George Low let me know right off the bat that his meetings should only be scheduled to last for 45 minutes because he needed time between meetings to answer/make phone calls and to read/sign correspondence. That made perfect sense to me especially since I had always felt that most meetings last too long. When the three of them were attending the same meeting, I was usually tasked as the minute taker.

The meetings of the center directors with the Administrator's Office were always interesting. It was very obvious that the research and un-manned flight center directors were very jealous of the manned flight centers. They felt that they weren't getting their fair share of the NASA budget and that their programs were not getting enough attention from NASA management and from the public. This was especially true of Dr. Hans Mark, the Director of the Ames Research Center. If George Low would have allowed him, he would have gone on for hours about how his center was not getting its fair share. A decade later, Dr. Mark and I would become "good friends", but never agreed on the importance and criticality of manned spaceflight.

After a month on the new job, I flew back to Houston where the family piled into our station wagon (I still can't believe I let Linda talk me into buying a station wagon!) and headed for Washington. At each gas refueling stop along the way, Mike and I would ask for STP stickers. He had started collecting them to put on his go-cart. In Nashville, we stopped at the Opryland amusement park. Mike and I rode a corkscrew roller coaster that killed my back, but we rode it twice. For the rest of the trip, I was in severe pain, but who could pass up the opportunity to have so much fun with their son? We also visited the Hermitage, home of President Andrew Jackson. I really enjoyed it, but I think Mike and Kristi were a little bored. After a four-day drive, we finally made it to our new home in Lakevale, Vienna, Virginia.

The house we rented from Tom and Doris was very nice and had a two car enclosed garage, which was rare in the neighborhood. The main drawback was the steepness of the driveway. When we had the first big snow, I discovered what a drawback the driveway really was. I decided that I would take the station wagon to work because it had snow tires and the Corvette did not. (Who would put snow tires on a Corvette?) I started backing out of the garage, went into a 180 degree skid on the driveway and hit the street going forward. I tried for a few minutes to continue on to work, but couldn't make it up the hill leading out of Lakevale. I abandoned the station wagon, walked back home and called the office to say I would not be able to make it. I was told to not worry because Fletcher and Low were not able to make it in either (and they both had chauffeurs!). Later that day I was able to retrieve the station wagon and go to the hardware store to buy my first snow shovel. It looked a lot like the scoop that my daddy used to scoop corn, but was made of plastic.

At about the same time that we moved to the Washington area, my friend Ed Smylie who also was a Mississippi State graduate and Chief of the Crew Systems Division at JSC during Gemini and Apollo, moved there to become the Deputy Associate Administrator for Aeronautics and Space Technology. He parked his boat in our driveway until he could find a house to buy. This began a long lasting friendship for the rest of my NASA career and picked up again when we both went to work for Grumman.

We enjoyed living in Lakevale despite the drastic change in weather. Living across the street from us was U. S. Attorney General John Mitchell and his wife Martha. We rarely saw the Attorney General but Martha was everywhere and always very friendly. If you had any conversation with her, it usually got around to the innocence of her husband in the ongoing Watergate affair. I guess she was wrong because later he was sentenced to prison for his involvement. We had a nice community pool, in which Kristi became the original "Tadpole." She was a member of the swim team and showed the same determination she had when first learning to ride a bicycle! Another girl on her team was the daughter of Jack Pardee who played for the Washington Redskins at that time and went on to be the Head Coach of a number of teams including the Chicago Bears, the Houston Gamblers and the Houston Oilers. I was impressed that despite his obvious busy schedule, he never missed a swim meet.

Gerry Griffin and I car-pooled to work each day. It was about an hour's drive depending on what time we left. Griffin usually complained about how rough riding the Corvette was. One night going home after work, it completely flamed out on the George Washington Parkway, so we had to have it towed to a garage. They told me that it needed ignition points, spark plugs and spark plug wires. The cost for that was astronomical in my mind, so I had it towed home where I would attempt to do the work myself. I changed the points without any trouble, but had to use four different wrenches to change all eight spark plugs. Chevrolet did their best to make the plugs almost impossible to access. The spark plug wires were another story. The car had headers for the dual exhaust system and the wires were only accessible if the headers were removed. The big problem with that was that there was no way I could get the headers off without raising the engine a couple of inches. I thought about that for a few days and concluded that the task was beyond my ability and I couldn't afford to have someone else do it. The car ran with the new points and plugs, but not very well, so my decision was, sadly, to sell it. I looked up the wholesale, trade-in and retail prices in a Kelley Blue Book at the Headquarters Credit Union (this was long before the internet!), added $100 to the retail price and advertised it in a local Vienna newspaper that was published every weekend. The paper was put on newsstands at all the local convenience stores on Friday night. At about 9:00 p.m. that night I got a call from a potential buyer who only asked two questions: does it run, and does it have any body damage. He said he would be there in 30 minutes to pick it up and would pay my asking price in cash, which he did. Over the next two days, Mike and Kristi kept count of how many calls we got asking about the car...24! I obviously should have asked for more. I replaced it with a used Mercury Cougar which actually costs less than what I had received for the Corvette. Griffin liked riding in it much better than the Corvette.

– – –

Dr. Fletcher was a devout Mormon and did not smoke, curse or drink any beverages which contained alcohol or caffeine. He let it be known that he was not to be disturbed at home on Monday nights unless there was a real emergency. Each Monday night he and his family observed "Family Home Evening", during which they studied the Bible, prayed and played card and board games. Once I began traveling with him, I learned that he was a wizard at all card games, including poker. He soundly beat me every time!

He had what I thought was a very good policy of traveling around the country and talking to various groups (bankers, college presidents, lawyers, etc.). He would open with a brief summary of what was going on at NASA, and then ask what suggestions the group had to make NASA a better agency. My first trip with him was to New York City to talk to telecommunications company executives. Upon arrival at LaGuardia, we were picked up in the longest limousine I had ever seen. Our first visit was to AT&T where his brother Steven was Vice President and General Counsel.

Our next such tour (he tried to do one a month) was to Boston to visit college/university presidents. Dr. Donald Monan, President of Boston College had volunteered to host the meeting at his college. Dr. Fletcher and I were checking into the Ritz Carlton when I noticed a big sign over the desk which read "No checks or credit cards accepted. CASH ONLY!" As we were riding the elevator up to our rooms, he asked me if had seen the sign and wondered what I was going to do about it. I told him not to worry…I would take care of it. Once my luggage was in my room, I went back down to the registration desk and explained who Dr. Fletcher was, and that we didn't have enough cash with us to pay for our rooms. I got nowhere with the desk clerk so I asked to speak to the manager. After listening to my sob story he said, "Young man, John Wayne is staying here tonight and he's paying cash." Not knowing what to do, I called Dr. Monan and explained our situation. He asked to speak to the manager, but I could tell he was also getting nowhere. Dr. Monan ended up driving into the Ritz Carlton, arriving after midnight, and paying cash for our rooms. He also gave me a $50 bill to pay for breakfast the next day. When I met Dr. Fletcher for breakfast he asked what I had done to solve the cash problem. I just told him I had taken care of it and he asked no more questions. As we were eating, over in the corner of the restaurant was the Duke himself, John Wayne. It turned out that he was in town for the Harvard University Hasty Pudding award show. After all of that, the meeting went very well and I reimbursed Dr. Monan with a NASA check which he freely accepted.

At this time I was still wearing very long hair and a big mustache. One day Dr. Fletcher introduced me to Art Buchwald, humorist and columnist in the Washington Post, as "My hippy assistant." Realizing that my appearance bothered him, I shaved my mustache and gradually got my hair back to "normal" length.

**Dr. Fletcher presenting the NASA Exceptional
Service Medal to his "Hippy Assistant"
Courtesy NASA**

One very interesting trip that we took was to the CIA Headquarters, at Langley, Virginia between Washington and McLean. Dr. Fletcher and Mr. Shapley wanted to talk to them about using the Space Shuttle to launch their spy satellites. I was surprised that I was asked to go with them. John Stumpf, Dr. Fletcher's chauffeur, drove down the George Washington Parkway and turned left onto Highway 123 toward McLean. After a few miles, he stopped to ask directions at a gas station. He told the attendant that he was trying to find the Virginia Highway Department, which at that time, was how the entrance to the CIA was identified. After several questions, the attendant said, "Oh, you're looking for the CIA." And gave us directions. He said that all the locals knew that even though the sign said Virginia Highway Department, it was really the CIA. The entrance sign has since been properly marked. Our meeting was productive, in that the people we talked to were very receptive to using the Shuttle if we could guarantee the necessary secrecy.

There were a lot of interesting people working at NASA Headquarters when I was there. One of the most interesting to me was Richard "Dick" McCurdy who was Associate Administrator for Organization and Management. He had been President of Shell Oil Company and came to work at NASA for $1 a year. The first time I saw him, I thought, "Who is this hayseed?" He was always dressed in rumpled clothes and had dirty fingernails. He looked like he had just fallen off a turnip truck! I soon saw that, when in meetings, people often seemed unable to come to an agreed decision. Then McCurdy would say, "Here's what I think we should do." All the other participants would just look at each other like "Why didn't I think of that?" and then agree that McCurdy had the right answer. When he was scheduled to meet with Fletcher and Low, he was usually early and would stop by my office to chat. He always seemed to be concerned about how I was doing, how my family was, etc. He relayed to me that he was having problems with the property owner of the apartment where he was staying. A few days later I asked

The Kid From Golden

him how the apartment situation was going and he said that he had solved the problem by buying it. I assumed that he had bought his apartment, but later learned that he had bought the whole building! Another time he brought pictures of his granddaughters wedding. They were taken at what looked like a castle. When I asked where the wedding was held, he said, "At my house in Connecticut." A really nice man and obviously a very rich one. No wonder he could work there for only $1 a year!

Another "character" was Bill Lilly, the Comptroller. He always wore what I called "barber shirts", long shirts with many pockets and never tucked into his pants. No tie ever. He was very gruff and spoke his mind freely, but was highly respected within NASA and around Washington. He tightly controlled the NASA budget and asked all the right questions about budget requests. He clearly understood labor, material and overhead requirements for any projects. On most Friday afternoons, he invited me, Gerry Griffin and Gerry Mossinghoff to his office while we waited for the traffic to clear. I was always amazed at his insight, not just on budgetary matters, but on most all issues facing NASA.

On a trip to Houston, Dr. Fletcher, Mr. McCurdy, Pete Clements and I went to eat at Jimmie Walker's in Kemah (it's now a Landry's). When the waiter brought the check, Dr. Fletcher got out his calculator and started figuring out how much we each owed. McCurdy read him the prices of what we all had to eat. "Now Jerry didn't have a salad, mine was $3.99 and yours was $2.99, Pete had the dessert." I sat there in disbelief! Here were two millionaires actually calculating what each of us owed. Maybe that's how they became millionaires!

Soon after I arrived at Headquarters, Gerry Griffin hired a new Deputy, Judy Cole who had been a speechwriter in the Nixon White House. She hosted a Christmas party in her townhome, to which Linda and I were invited. There I met a guy who also was a Nixon speech writer, Pat Buchanan. I had never heard of him but he went on to seek the Republican presidential nomination twice in the 1990s, and again in 2000 as the Reform Party candidate.

— — —

About six months after moving into Tom and Doris Carter's home in the Lakevale subdivision in Vienna, Tom called saying that the furniture business wasn't what he expected it to be and he would like to come back to the Washington area. This meant we had to find another home as quickly as possible. Linda had already been looking, assuming we would only rent for the first year. With the help of Helga Meyer, our next-door neighbor and a real estate agent, we soon found an acceptable house just a few blocks away on Babcock Road that would allow Mike and Kristi to stay in the same schools. The change from Clear Lake was enough and we didn't want them to have to change once more. However, Kristi's teacher was so bad that changing schools might have been a good idea.

The house that we bought was a nice split-level with all bedrooms upstairs. On the downside, it had a carport rather than an enclosed garage. For some reason that I will never understand, most of the houses there only had carports. Doesn't make sense to me with all the snow they get. The major change we made was to put Holly Hobby wallpaper in Kristi's room. I thought I was an expert at hanging wallpaper, but this was a major project trying to match all the figures.

— — —

After Tom moved back to Vienna, he and I started making plans to attend the Indianapolis 500 race. It was something both of us had wanted to do for a long time and Tom had a small single-engine airplane (Cessna 140A I think) so we bought tickets to the race and started making plans to go. The race was originally scheduled for Monday, May 28, which was the official day for observation of Memorial Day. It was rained out so we didn't go until Wednesday the 30$^{th}$. We flew into an airport about 25 miles away and got a taxicab to the racetrack. It was misting rain by the time we got to the track and the race didn't start until mid-afternoon. We had very good seats, about six or seven rows up at the beginning of the straightway coming out of turn four. The only problem was that the cars were going by so fast we couldn't tell who was leading! Fortunately, a guy in the row behind us had a portable radio so that's how we kept up with the race. It started raining again so the race was called after 133 laps (200 normally), and Gordon Johncock was declared the winner. We caught a cab back to where the airplane was and headed back toward home. Tom hangered his plane at an airport in southern Maryland but when we got there the weather was so bad that the airport was closed. We headed for National Airport in DC, but it closed before we got there, so Tom then headed for Dulles. It was open but they wouldn't give us permission to land. I looked at the fuel gauge and it was on empty. Tom told the tower that he was running out of fuel and was declaring an emergency, so they vectored him to a taxiway. About 20 feet off the ground, the engine started sputtering. We were indeed out of gas but Tom made the landing just fine. It was many years later before I would ever get into a private plane again!

– – –

When the launch vehicle for Skylab 4 rolled out to the pad, Dr. Fletcher and I rode on the Mobile Launch Platform (crawler) for about 45 minutes. From the VAB to launch complex 39, it takes about 5 hours for the total trip at less than 1 mile per hour. It was quite an experience, but became boring very quickly.

We returned to Washington for a few weeks, and then went to Houston during the Skylab 4 mission. Accompanying us to JSC was

Dr. Kohoutek, the Chezch Republic astronomer who discovered a comet which was then named for him. The Skylab flight crew were going to make some special observations of "his" comet during the mission. As we approached Houston, Dr. Kohoutek said something to his interpreter, who relayed the English version to me and Dr. Fletcher. "Want to see Astrodome." Dr. Fletcher explained to him that there would not be time in our schedule to visit the Astrodome but he would have the pilot fly over it so that he could see it. We did that and I'm convinced it was the most exciting part of Dr. Kohoutek's trip.

– – –

Harold B. Lee, the President of the Mormon Church, passed away right after Christmas, 1973. Dr. Fletcher, being one of the twelve Apostles of the Church, flew to Salt Lake City for the funeral. Accompanying us on NASA 1 was several of the other Apostles, including J. W. Marriott, CEO of Marriott Hotels, and the President of Safeway Stores, whose name I can't remember. While there, Dr. Fletcher gave me a tour of all the facilities, including some places where non-Mormons (or even female Mormons at that time) were not supposed to go. This included the chamber where they baptize members standing in for their departed relatives. I was impressed but very nervous being in all those places where I know I wasn't supposed to be. After the very elaborate funeral, the Quorum of the Twelve Apostles met to select the next president. Before we left for the return trip to Washington Spencer Kimball was announced as the 12th President of the Church of Latter Day Saints. On the trip back home, Dr. Fletcher told me that there was initially a split in the vote because some wanted to name Ezra Taft Benson, former Secretary of Agriculture under President Eisenhower. As a compromise, they elected Kimball the new President and Benson as President of the Quorum. Several years later, Benson did become President of the Church, succeeding Kimball upon his death.

While in Salt Lake City, I visited some gift shops and noticed that seagull items where everywhere! The book Jonathan Livingston Seagull was very popular then and one of Linda's favorites, so I purchased a seagull charm for her. I learned later why seagulls were so popular there. In the mid-1800s when the Mormons first arrived, they planted crops. Soon all the crops were destroyed by crickets. They covered the fields and consumed all the plants. The Mormons prayed to God that their crops be saved from the crickets and soon the sky was covered with seagulls who ate all the crickets, saving their crops. They considered this a miracle, and revered the seagull thereafter.

– – –

Back at NASA Headquarters, the big issue was, now that the Shuttle Program has been approved, how many flights can we fly each year and what budget will that require? President Nixon had authorized $5.5 Billion for hardware development in fiscal year 1973, which Congress had narrowly approved, but NASA had asked for $7.45 Billion. Then on top of the development cost, there was the question of operational cost…once it was built, how much would it cost to fly it? To address the operations cost, a contract was issued to ECON, Inc., a world-recognized economic analyses company to help us come up with the answers. The principle economist on the contract was Dr. Klauss Heiss and I was assigned as his liaison with the Administrator's office. His idea was that in the current political environment, the Shuttle would only be viable if it was shown that it would pay for itself. Other government agencies (NOAA, DoD, etc.) and commercial companies would pay NASA to have their satellites launched. It soon became obvious that the only way to keep the price per flight low enough to be attractive to such customers was to fly as many flights per year as possible. There was a "fixed" cost of the entire NASA manned spaceflight workforce, which stayed essentially the same regardless of how many flights were made. This covered facilities and a basic workforce. Above that was an "additive" cost for each flight to pay for fuels, expendable hardware, and some additional workforce. Then the total operations cost was the sum of the fixed and additive components, and the cost per flight was that total divided by the number of flights. When Dr. Heiss would brief the Administrator's staff on the projected cost per flight, the answer always seemed to be that we had to fly more frequently. The required number of flights per year soon got up to 50. We even looked at 75/year. I don't think anybody at NASA believed we could fly that many flights, but if that's what it took to sell the program, that's what the plan became.

After a meeting with President Nixon, Dr. Fletcher assembled his staff and said, "Okay, the president has approved a budget request for development of the Shuttle and this is how much money he will request in the next budget." It was consistently less than $5 Billion/ year. Dale Myers, who was Associate Administrator for Manned Spaceflight and the person who would be in charge of building the Shuttle and then flying it, said that was nice, but he couldn't do it for that. When told by Dr. Fletcher that he would have to do it for that price, Dale said "Well, I guess you will need to get someone to replace me, because I can't do it for that." He resigned shortly thereafter.

Replacing Dale as Associate Administrator was John Yardley, from McDonnell. John had been the McDonnell Program Manager for the Mercury and Gemini programs. At the conclusion of his interview with Drs. Low and Fletcher, he agreed to take the job. Dr. Low sheepishly told him that he would have to fill out an application for Federal employment, a Form 171, and handed him a copy. A few days later, he came by my office and gave me his filled-out application. The Form 171 required that you list each job you had ever held and a reason for leaving. After listing his last job as Vice President of McDonnell Aircraft, he wrote as his reason for leaving, "Dammed if I know!"

— — —

In 1974, as part of the Federal Graphics Improvement Program of the National Endowment for the Arts, NASA hired Richard Danne and Bruce Blackburn to design a more modern logo. They recommended a modernist NASA logotype, a red, stylized rendering of the letters N-A-S-A. It soon became known as the "NASA worm."

**The "NASA worm"**
**Courtesy NASA**

George Low was strongly in favor of the new logo, while Dr. Fletcher took a "whatever" attitude. Most of the Center Directors were opposed to it, but it was officially adopted in 1975. Some Centers were deliberately slow in changing over to the "worm." By 1992 the opposition had risen so strongly that the worm was retired and the old NASA "meatball" came back into use.

**The "NASA meatball"**
**Courtesy NASA**

Also in 1974, NASA was part of a Federal program to celebrate the United States Bicentennial, coming up in 1976. Each center proposed different ideas and Dr. Fletcher asked me to review all of them and make a recommendation to him. The ideas included putting a permanent rainbow over the Potomac River using laser beams, painting all NASA planes red, white and blue, and painting a huge American flag on the Vertical Assemble Building (VAB) at KSC. Since we had a very limited budget, I recommended the flag on the VAB, along with the logo of the Bicentennial. Dr. Fletcher concurred, so the project began. As I recall, it cost in the neighborhood of $50,000, with the paint being donated by Sears.

**Bicentennial markings on the VAB**
**Courtesy NASA**

I tell people that while working in the Administrator's office, I supervised the construction of the National Air and Space Museum, and I did...out my office window. The museum was being built just across Independence Avenue from the NASA headquarters building. It was amazing to watch the American Indians assembling the structural beams, walking so high without any kind of tether or net. Before it opened in 1976, the first Director, Apollo 11 astronaut Mike Collins gave Gerry Griffin and me an exclusive tour.

– – –

When OPEC (Organization of Petroleum Exporting Countries) placed an embargo on oil shipped to the U. S. in late 1973, gasoline prices started creeping up and soon became in such short supply that long lines formed at gasoline stations and at most stations you could only purchase 5 gallons. Gerry Griffin and I car-pooled to work while Sandy and Linda would take turns waiting in line to buy gas.

By the spring of 1974, it was a full blown "crisis." President Nixon asked each Federal agency to come up with things they could do to produce energy and reduce our dependency on foreign oil. After much discussion between the NASA Administrator's office and the NASA Center Directors, it was concluded that there were probably some good things we could do, but it required further study. Gerry Griffin suggested that Jack Schmitt be brought to Headquarters on temporary assignment to study the matter and recommend an approach. After discussions between Jack, Dr. Fletcher and Dr. Low, he agreed to accept the task. He temporarily moved into the spare bedroom in our house while he looked for a place to stay. He was a great cook, specializing in Mexican food, and a great Margarita maker. Most mornings he would leave a list of groceries for Linda to get during the day, and then when we got home from work he would start cooking. Some of the best food I had ever eaten but soon Linda got tired of doing all the shopping and the clean-up.

I was assigned to follow Jack around and to keep Shapley, Low and Fletcher up to speed on what he was doing. As he did for all tasks, Jack approached this one with great seriousness and vigor. He traveled to all the NASA Centers and saw first-hand what they were doing or were capable of doing which was energy related. Within a few weeks, he started putting together a presentation to give to the top staff. One of his conclusions was that an Office of Energy Programs should be formed to direct the agency-wide efforts and to interface with the other agencies that were doing similar things, the White House and Congress. He asked me to put together the organization part while he worked on the technical content. I knew that if he recommended such an office that Dr. Fletcher was going to ask Jack to be the head. Once we had the presentation completed, a time was scheduled for the briefing. As we walked down the hall to the briefing room, I told Jack that Dr. Fletcher would probably ask him the stay in Washington and be the new Assistant Administrator for Energy Programs. He said "No, I don't want to do that. I want to go back to Houston and continue being an astronaut." After a few more steps, he asked me a similar question: "Would you want to do something like that?" I said "No, I agree with you. I want to go back to Houston."

Jack gave the first part of the presentation dealing with which Centers had what capabilities and how they could be brought to bear in trying to help solve the National energy problem. He concluded that NASA could do a lot in that arena and that a new office should be formed to manage agency-wide efforts. He then turned the floor over to me and I started showing an organization structure which would need to be put into place. By the second or third chart, Dr. Fletcher turned to Jack and told him that he wanted him to head the new office. To my great surprise, Jack said "Okay, if that's what you would like for me to do." I continued with my presentation but was thinking in the back of my mind: "Schmitt, you have no backbone! You just told me less than 30 minutes ago that you wouldn't take the job, and now you're agreeing to do it." After a few more charts Jack said "Excuse me, Dr. Fletcher. I may have spoken in haste about taking this job." I'm standing there thinking that finally he had grown a spine and was going to refuse the job, but he said "I will only take the job if Jerry can be my Deputy." Whereupon Dr. Fletcher said to me "Well, would you be willing to do that, Jerry?" I immediately said "Yes." Turns out neither of us had the guts to tell him no.

So, in early 1974, Jack and I set out to put together the Office of Energy Programs. Jack, realizing he was going to be in Washington for some length of time, started looking for a permanent place to stay. He bought a townhouse just east of the Capitol and soon moved out of our spare bedroom. George Low would not agree that I could be the Deputy Assistant Administrator, so I got the title of Special Assistant for Programs. As I began to undertake the organization and staffing of the office, Jack worked vigorously with the NASA elements, other Federal agencies, the White House and Congress to lay out a program and a budget. We both spent a lot of time on Capitol Hill talking to Congressmen and Senators. Sen. Barry Goldwater was a very nice man and a strong supporter. It was on one of our visits to Capitol Hill that I observed that the office space had grown astronomically. When I was there in the 1950s as a Page/Doorman, there were two House office buildings, called the Old and the New, and only one Senate building, simply called the Senate Office Building. Now there were three House buildings; Cannon, Longworth and Rayburn, with a fourth one, Ford, in the planning stage and two Senate buildings; Russell and Dirksen, with a third one, Hart, under construction. We had the same number of Representatives (435) and the same number of Senators (100), so what was going on? After a little research, the answer was clear: the staffs had grown tenfold! When I was there a typical Congressman or Senator had a staff of three people, now the average was over 30 each! Even with all the new office space, each office was now much more crowded than I had ever seen.

One of the first people we hired was my friend Tom Carter. Of course, I knew Tom well and thought he would fit in well with what we were hoping to accomplish. Jack had not worked with Tom before, so he asked Gerry Griffin about him. Gerry's immediate response was "He's a savvy guy. Hire him!" The next person I hired was Steve Copps, with whom I had worked on Apollo, and was still at MIT. Jack also knew him, so he enthusiastically approved.

Our first yearly budget was $4 million, so we started calling Jack "The 4 Million Dollar Man," a take-off on the popular TV show *The*

*6 Million Dollar Man.* As we put the programs together, we organized the office around technology applications, most of which were already available, and research into more futuristic technologies we thought we could develop. In December 1974, I was named Director of the Energy Technology Applications Division, and continued to serve as Special Assistant to Jack.

Most of the NASA centers were eager to get a part of the budget for their pet projects. Some Center Directors, notably Bruce Lundin of Lewis (now Glenn) and Bill Lucas of Marshall, walked the halls of our office almost begging for projects and the dollars that went with them. Ironically, the one Center Director that seemed reluctant to take on terrestrial energy projects was Chris Kraft of the Johnson Space Center. The center had expertise and experience in turning human waste into usable products in space, but Chris did not want to get involved in terrestrial applications. When we tried to give him the Modular Integrated Utility System project, his answer was "This is the Johnson Space Center, not the Johnson Energy Center. The project eventually went to the Langley Research Center, which was glad to take it.

Some of the budgeted money was also available for distribution outside of NASA to Universities, private companies and individuals. One day my secretary said that she was just on the phone with Robert Redford and had scheduled an appointment with me the next week. I was never sure if she was kidding until at the appointed hour, in walks Redford and his wife. They wanted $100,000 for a project to put solar collectors on their ranch in Sundance, Utah. She did most of the talking. After careful review along with the other proposals which we received, they did not get the money.

All of the projects which we undertook proved technically feasible, but probably not economical at that time. Photovoltaic energy was very promising, as well as solar panels. Wind energy definitely had a future. We funded a windmill demonstration project at the Lewis Research Center in Cleveland, Ohio. They contracted with General Electric and built a 60-foot tall windmill. The ceremony on ribbon-cutting day was attended by local, state and national politicians as well as executives from GE. When Jack gave the signal to start the windmill, the blades started slowly moving and it soon became obvious that something was wrong. There was a loud "clunk" in one of the blades each time it reached the top of its arc. In embarrassment, we shut it down and apologized to all the attendees. Within a few hours, it was discovered that the quality inspector for GE had left his flashlight inside one of the blades while doing the final inspection. There was no denying it because his name was on the flashlight!

We also looked extensively at satellite solar power. My friend Frank Van Rensselaer came up from MSFC to help us out in this arena. Unfortunately, like most of the other things we looked at, it was just not economical at the time. The Dryden Research Center kept asking for a little bit of money to test some wind shrouds for trucks pulling long, high trailers. They proposed to build one and test it on the dry lake bed. I finally gave them $50,000, hoping they would shut up and go away. Ironically, that turned out to be the first practical application of all the things we researched! You see thousands of them on the highways now.

Washington was astir with ideas of how to deal with the 'energy crisis.' There were many meetings of the principals from the various government agencies who thought they could contribute to the solution. Jack and/or I attended most of these meetings, usually in the Old Executive Office Building next to the White House. Alvin Weinberg, former Director of the Oak Ridge National Laboratory, had been named by President Carter (after President Nixon had fired Weinberg from Oak Ridge) as Director of the new U.S. Office of Energy Research and Development, so he presided over most of such meetings. John Sawhill, Administrator of the Federal Energy

Administration, had been appointed by Nixon and apparently saw the political hand writing on the wall and resigned in October of '74. Jack and Dr. Fletcher had done a lot of work with him and we were sorry to see him leave. At one of these meetings, Weinberg opened with the statement "What we actually do to solve this problem is not as important as the perception that we are doing something!" I couldn't believe my ears! When Jack and I got in a taxi to return to NASA Headquarters he asked me if I had heard what Weinberg had said. It bothered him as much or more than me. We rode in silence for a while, then Jack said "I think it's time for me to get out of this town."

Shortly thereafter, Jack announced that he was indeed leaving. He would resign from NASA and go back to his home state of New Mexico and run for the U.S. Senate. There was never any question about his principles and beliefs, but there was the question of how best to get elected in a primarily Democratic state. Jack, Gerry Griffin, Gerry Mossinghoff (NASA Deputy General Counsel) and I stayed up all night at Griffin's house considering his platform and trying to decide how best to get elected. Should he run as a Democrat or a Republican? By daybreak, when Gerry's wife Sandy got up to fix us breakfast, it was clear that he was Republican and that was how he should run. Sandy said, "I could have told you that without staying up all night!"

Jack had asked if I wanted to go to New Mexico with him and help with his campaign for the Senate. I was really tempted to do that because I firmly believed in Jack and wanted to help him in any way that I could. I had to tell him that I wasn't sure how much I could help, because I would be an outsider in New Mexico, and that I really couldn't afford to quit my job. He won without me.

Since Jack was leaving and I had been at NASA Headquarters for two years, I was anxious to leave also. George Low had always had a rule that you could not go back to your home Center after serving a tour in Headquarters. He felt that the Center management would not respect what you had learned at Headquarters and would probably just offer you the same, or a similar job to what you had before. So he arranged for me to have several interviews at the various NASA Centers. I went to Marshall, Lewis, Ames, Kennedy and Langley for interviews and had several very nice offers. The only problem was that I didn't want to go to any of those places. I wanted to go back to Houston. Chris Kraft, Johnson Space Center Director at that time, finally convinced Low that he did appreciate the expansion of my knowledge while at Headquarters, wanted me back and would make me his special assistant as Chief of the Technical Planning Office, with responsibilities for JSC technical planning and technology utilization (spinoffs). Dr. Low finally agreed, so I happily prepared to head back to Houston.

– – –

While living in the DC area, we saw the movie *Towering Inferno*, starring Paul Newman and Steve McQueen. I was a horrifying movie about a high-rise office building catching fire and trapping many of the occupants that kept everyone on the edge of their seat. At the same time, a subway system was being constructed in the Washington metropolitan area and many streets were disrupted for months while the tunnels were being built. Mike came up with the idea for a movie about the subway system collapsing and trapping thousands of people. A cliffhanger much like *Towering Inferno*. We did not realize at the time that one day Mike would actually be in the movie-making business. He never made his *Subway* movie.

– – –

On Friday December 13, 1974, I was on a flight from D.C. to Houston which went through Atlanta. As usual, I was tired and just anxious to get to my destination. From D.C. to Atlanta I had a window seat and the adjacent aisle seat was vacant so I was thinking I could really stretch out and maybe take a nap. However, just before take-off, a gentleman boarded and sat in the aisle seat. He said hello and I muttered a hello back at him. When traveling, especially when I am tired, I usually avoid striking up a conversation with strangers seated next to me. When the meal was served, we both started eating. After a few bites, the stranger said "This chicken is pretty good. How's yours?" I just said that it was not bad for airline food. After dinner, I closed my eyes and tried to nap. When we landed in Atlanta and were taxiing to the gate, the flight attendant asked over the speakers for everyone to please keep their seats once we arrived at the gate so that Governor Carter could deplane first because he had an important engagement to make. I had been sitting by Jimmy Carter who just the night before had announced at the National Press Club that he would run for president! What a missed opportunity to carry on a conversation. Since then I have tried to be friendlier with strangers on airplanes.

– – –

One night in 1975, I was up late as usual, thinking about what I had to do the next day. Not being able to find anything of interest on TV, I searched the channel guide and saw something called Austin City Limits. Hoping that it might be something about Austin, Texas, I switched to that channel. It was a music show from Austin and I saw Willie Nelson for the first time. I couldn't believe how much I liked a hippie looking guy singing country music. I became an instant Willie fan. It turned out that it was the first of a new PBS show featuring live music from Texas. I still watch it to this day.

– – –

On our way back to Texas, we planned to spend the night in Birmingham Alabama with Aunt Beece. Since the Jack Daniel's distillery in Lynchburg Tennessee was kind of on the way, I wanted to stop there and go on a tour. That turned out to be a real experience.

There was a house near the entrance which we were told was called the Motlow house, because that was where Lem Motlow, the nephew of Jack Daniel, and later owner of the distillery, had lived. His wife was still living in the house. We were the only ones there, so we had our own private tour. The guide, an elderly man in overalls, started out by showing us the spring where they get the water. He went on and on about how it was the best water in the world and the only source ever used for the whisky. Next, he showed us some stacks of wood ready to be burned to make the charcoal through which the whisky is filtered. That was even more detailed than the water! The stacks had to be three feet tall, consisting of sugar maple wood, 3 inches in diameter, cut from trees growing at an elevation between 2000 and 3000 feet on the north face of a nearby mountain. Then we went into the seven story building where the whisky is stored in barrels. The guide explained that once distilled and barreled, the barrels go to the 7th floor. Then each year they are moved down one floor, and not bottled until they have been on the bottom floor for a year. That ensures that every barrel is aged at the same elevation. I was totally amazed at the details to which they went to finally get a bottle of whiskey. On they way back to our car, a truck loaded with corn came into the distillery. I was almost afraid to ask, expecting another long speech, but I did ask the guide what kind of corn they used. His answer was, "Heck, it don't matter. Any kind of corn will do." So much for everything being so precise!

– – –

We stopped in Golden to see Mother and Daddy before driving on to Houston. Daddy was then a member of the Tennessee-Tombigbee (Tenn-Tom) Waterway Board. The waterway, which would create a shortcut from the Tennessee River to the Gulf of Mexico, had been of great interest to people in that part of Mississippi for many years. Congressman John Rankin had been a big proponent but could never get enough support to fund it. Congressman Abernethy continued that support and got funding approved just before he retired in 1972. Construction started in late 1972 and by 1975 was well underway. The biggest local project was a lock and dam at Bay Springs, about 15 miles from Golden. Daddy told me that if I wanted to, he could get me the job of Port Manager at Pickwick Dam, the beginning point of the Tenn-Tom. He said it would be a GS-13 job. He didn't seem to care that I was already a GS-15, and therefore would have to take a pay cut. I understood that he always had wanted me to live closer to home, and I appreciated that, but I had to decline the offer. I don't think he ever understood why I turned down such a "good deal."

– – –

My new job back in Houston turned out to be great. I attended most meetings involving Dr. Kraft and got a new insight as to what all was going on at JSC. I controlled the Center's Research and Technology money and thus became very popular with all the organizations competing for small research dollars. One day Dr. Max Faget walked into my office and shut the door behind him. I immediately assumed he was upset about me not giving his Engineering Directorate enough Research & Technology Operating Plan (RTOP) dollars. He was on an entirely different mission. He said that his secretary had told him that in a recent survey of all Center organizations, my office had come out on top in terms of efficiency and that his was last, so his question to me was how I did it and how could he improve. Here was the most famous engineer within NASA, if not the United States, asking me for advice!

One of the organizations receiving RTOP money was the Flight Equipment Processing group in the Flight Crew Operations Directorate. I was able to get them some money to experiment with better tasting food for the upcoming Space Shuttle flights. They would give me packets of each new product they came up with and I would take them home and have Mike and Kristi try them. This usually involved following the directions for opening the package and preparation. Many of their suggested changes were incorporated into the final packaging and instructions. They were not too impressed with the taste of most of them! They were correct; it was not gourmet food, but it was much better than what had been used on previous space flights.

Another aspect of my job was Technology Utilization. I searched for projects around the Center which might have applications in the private or public world other than for what they were originally intended. For example, we found a lot of applications for our space suit technology in the firefighting world and in the medical world for our spaceflight monitoring. We hosted a "spin off" conference which was very well received.

Because of my previous work at NASA Headquarters on Space Shuttle cost per flight, I was asked to lead an agency wide Shuttle User Charge Working Group. Our task was to determine how much we should charge users/customers that flew small experiments or large payloads on the Shuttle. We started out talking to major airlines and freight haulers about how they came up with their rates. Some were based on volume and some on weight. It soon became obvious that not only should we consider volume and weight, but also what services (power, nitrogen, coolant, command, telemetry, etc.) the payloads would require. Glynn Lunney and his group in the Shuttle Payload Integration and Development Office, had been spending a lot of time with potential customers and had developed a pretty good feel for what services would be needed and how they potentially could be provided. They proposed a Standard Mixed Cargo Harness (SMCH, pronounced Smitch), which would provide the needed services in various sections of the Shuttle cargo bay. The User Charge Working Group soon concluded that Glynn and his group were way ahead of us on the subject, so, with the Administrator's approval, disbanded and turned to problem over to them. We did develop the basic cost of flying a Shuttle mission, based on what we called "additive cost." That was the cost of flying one more shuttle flight above the base cost, largely based on equipment and fuel. The base cost, which included the facilities required and the "standing army" of personnel it took to service the vehicle and prepare it for launch, was considered to be a National asset and should not be passed on to the users.

— — —

Each week everyone in the Director's Office received "Status Reports" from all the Center organizations. This was usually a stack over a foot high. I actually read them all for the first couple of weeks, but found them to be very boring and devoid of any real information that I could use. One day in a staff meeting I asked Dr. Kraft and Sig Sjoberg, his Deputy, if they actually read the reports and got any useful information from them. They admitted that they did not, so I suggested that the requirement to submit such reports be terminated. George Abbey, who was the Associate Director at that time, argued that they were very useful to him and that the requirement should not be dropped, so they continued to come in each week. After that, each week I would write complete gibberish in my report. After several weeks, I took my reports to the next staff meeting and asked Abbey if he had read them. He said he had. When I showed the nonsensical reports to Kraft and Sjoberg, they immediately issued a memo saying the weekly reports would no longer be required. George never liked me after that day!

— — —

When we moved back to Houston, we purchased a nice two-story English Tudor home in Clear Lake Forest. After settling in, we also purchased a boat, a 1975 18 ½-foot Wellcraft which we named Sundance, because it was yellow and looked like the sun dancing across the water. Of course we tried it out on Clear Lake but got the most use of it on Lake Travis near Austin. The trips to there and back were not a lot of fun for me because of my inexperience in pulling a boat trailer, but the time there was always fun. We usually went with the Sheets' and stayed at Norm Prince's cabin on the north shore (Sandy Creek Cove). Bob and Colette Sheets taught me to ski there. Mike and Kristi had already mastered the art on Clear Lake and were getting very good. Mike's best friend Allan Restrepo went with us several times and they always had a great time. I installed an 8-track player in the boat so we always skied to music. When Mike and Allan were in the water ready to take off they would scream "Ore-Ida". I can still hear Waylon Jennings singing "Rambling Man" as they skied. I have to admit that among all of Mike's male friends, Allan was always my favorite. He had impeccable manners, was industrious, and a lot of fun to be around. I always thought that he would be successful because he was constantly keeping up with all the trends and thinking of how he could make money. That prediction proved to be correct. On one trip there, Mike and Allan had worn the same clothes for 3-4 days and were getting pretty raunchy. One morning Linda told them that they had to change clothes before going out for the day. They went back into the bedroom and came out dressed in each other's clothes, the same ones they had worn for days, but they had "changed" clothes!

Mike and I set a record (for us anyway) by skiing tandem, each on two skis, for 22 miles. I got a little tired but thought that I had made it pretty well until we dropped off at the boat dock and I discovered that I couldn't stand up! My legs were just totally numb!

On one of our trips there in June 1979, around my birthday, I realized that I needed reading glasses and that my hair was beginning to gray. What? Only 40 years old and I'm already turning to pieces?

Getting back to Highway 1431 pulling the boat was not one of my favorite things. There were several steep hills and one in particular that was very difficult. I would go as fast as I could approaching that hill and keep the accelerator floored but we would still barely make it to the top. One of the problems was that we always collected several big rocks to take home with us for a deck/patio we were building behind our garage in Clear Lake Forest. Several hundred pounds of rocks in the boat didn't make it any easier!

**Sundance**

— — —

After being in the technical planning job for almost a year, late one afternoon Dr. Kraft walked into my office and asked, "What do you know about the RMS?" Honestly, I told him I knew that it was the Remote Manipulator System, a mechanical arm that would fly on the Space Shuttle Orbiter and be used to deploy and retrieve payloads, but not much more. He said that Astronaut Gerry Carr had just been in his office complaining about it. In simulations they were not able to get the Orbiter close enough to a payload to retrieve it because of impingement of the Orbiter attitude control system thrusters, and that the arm itself acted like a wet noodle…not strong enough to hold anything. Chris said that he had already talked to Aaron Cohen, the Orbiter Project Manager, and that early the next morning I was to report to Aaron and take over the RMS project. His departing words were "Go fix it!"

At 7:30 the following morning I met with Aaron and he told me to spend a couple of days figuring out what needed to be done and then report back to him. I had known Aaron for several years but had never worked with him or for him. I was immediately impressed with his management style, very much like Kraft and Lunney.

I soon learned that the project was in serious trouble and that it wasn't going to be easy to fix. Without any details, I reported that to Aaron and told him I would need to put together an office and staff it with up to 15 people. He just said "Okay, let me run that by Chris." A few hours later he told me that Chris said I could have as many people as I needed. Just fix it!

The National Research Council of Canada (NRCC) was building the RMS and would give one copy free to the U.S. They had specifications that had been proposed by them and only slightly reviewed and modified by NASA. Bill Middleton, who was the NASA RMS manager, felt that there was little he could do to change it because we had already agreed to the requirements and that there was no money in the NASA budget to change anything. It was immediately clear to me that Middleton had to go, because of that attitude. Even if it was free, it clearly was not going to do the intended job. No money was in the budget for Rockwell International, the Orbiter contractor, to integrate the RMS. Canada was going to give us the thing, but Rockwell was under no obligation to install it on the Orbiter or to do any studies of how/if it would work!

It took me about a week to get back to Aaron with a specific proposal. First of all, I recommender that we send Middleton back to the Engineering Directorate (ED) and replace him with Clay

McCullough, who was an ED avionics expert and had been helping Middleton in the RMS avionics area. In my first discussion with Clay, it was clear to me that having been working on RMS avionics, he fully understood the systems integration necessity and would be the right man for the Manager job. He also seemed to be sensitive to the Canadian/U.S. roles. An office needed to be formed to address not only the RMS, but the total job of deploying and retrieving payloads. It would be called the Payload Deployment and Retrieval Systems Office (PDRSO) and would address the entire problem, not just the RMS. How would the payloads be attached to the Orbiter? How would the latches be released? How would the Orbiter approach orbiting payloads to be retrieved without blowing them away? What was the best way to operate the RMS from the Orbiter? What cameras and grapple fixtures were needed? It was a growing list of questions which I felt had to be addressed. Aaron, and Chris, approved my approach and gave me carte blanche to recruit the people I would need.

As I started looking around the Center for people I would need, I soon realized that the ones who best understood the integration job were from my old organization...Flight Operations. We/they had been taught that you have to look at the total picture, not just your little area of responsibility. First, I enlisted Ed Lineberry and Jerry Bell from Mission Planning to work the problem of rendezvous/approach/ retrieval of payloads. In Gemini, Apollo, Skylab, and ASTP, we had used a terminal approach technique originally proposed by Buzz Aldrin, which really was a brute force/collision course approach. This had been reviewed several times in Bill Tindall's Mission Techniques panel and although almost everyone disliked it (except Buzz), we kept using it because it worked and would be expensive to change. However, it clearly would not work for Shuttle. Ed and Jerry soon came up with what they called the R-Bar approach (approaching the target vehicle along the radius vector) and an entirely new station-keeping technique which they called "proximity operations." They had solved the approach problem!

Since it had been the Astronaut Office that first complained about the system, I asked for 2-3 people to be assigned from there. Within a few days, I was told I would have Bill Lenoir, Sally Ride, Judy Resnik, Ron McNair and Norm Thagard, all on a part-time basis. Over the next three years, these and others who replaced them on a rotating basis, proved to be invaluable. They would be the ones who were going to fly and operate the system, so they obviously wanted to make it work, but at the same time were sensitive to the budget and international problems.

One of the first full time employees that I hired was Milt Windler, a former Flight Director. That turned out to be a wise decision. Milt approached the job vigorously and was a huge help in getting the problems solved. He also was highly respected by the Canadians. To help us solve many of the problems, I was able to get Al Louviere assigned to the office. He aided greatly in improving the mockups in the Manipulator Development Facility (MDF), evaluating the various crew station controls for the RMS, evaluating different proposals for the grapple fixture, and analyzing the structural integrity of the arm.

**RMS on "flat floor" at SPAR Aerospace, Toronto**

— — —

On one of my early trips to Canada, I made arrangements to come back through New York and purchase a 1975 Bricklin. I had seen one while in DC and thought they were the coolest car ever. Our friend Gil Guster had a 1974 Bricklin and that made me want one even more. I had talked to the New York dealer several times and asked every question that Gil and I could think of. It turned out to be a basket case. Even though it was "new", it was incomplete in that it was missing several parts including window roll-up mechanisms. That was not unusual for Bricklins. They were often shipped from the factory with missing parts because they were not available at the time. I decided to pass on it, so I flew back home without it.

In late 1976 I found a used one in Houston and bought it. A young lady who owned a flower shop had given up on the hydraulic door system only a few months after buying it. After getting hydraulic fluid all over the carpet a couple of times, she was eager to sell it.

One unforgettable memory of the Bricklin is when I was on travel in Cape Canaveral in 1977 and got a call that said the car caught fire in our garage! I had installed a pneumatic system to operate the gull-wing doors, replacing the original hydraulic system. The system included an engine vacuum air pump, which filled a tank in the back bumper. The tank valve leaked a little, so the engine had to be run to operate the pump and refill the tank. I had asked Mike to start the car and just let it idle for about 10 minutes to fill up the tank. He did that exactly as I had told him but when the door closed, it locked. He couldn't get into the car to turn it off, so the muffler system began to overheat and set the floor carpet on fire. Linda called the fire department and they pulled it out of the garage and put out the fire. When I got back home a few days later, I found that the damage was not nearly as bad as I had imagined. New carpet (with some insulation to reflect the muffler heat) fixed it right up. Poor Mike, for months if not years, thought it was his fault and I was mad at him, but he did exactly what I had asked him to do and I certainly did not blame him. The car needed new carpet anyway.

Later, Mike had even more bad luck with the Bricklin. I let him borrow it for his high school senior prom. It didn't make it all the way! The neutral/safety switch on the transmission failed and I had to rescue him. He was never too fond of the Bricklin after that.

**Mike in the Bricklin for Senior Prom-1980**

When Kristi was going to Seabrook Elementary, I would frequently drive her to school in the Bricklin. She insisted that I let her out two blocks away from the front door because she thought the boys were much more interested in the Bricklin than they were in her.

I kept the Bricklin for many years. When Vickie and I moved to Virginia in 1990, I dropped it off with Terry Tanner at his new place near Bedford, Virginia for a major overhaul. He replaced several of the body panels, which had started cracking, sand blasted and coated the frame and engine compartment, redid a lot of wiring, installed a new and better air pump for the doors, and installed new carpet. By the time we moved to Marble Falls in 1999, it was beginning to need more work than I was comfortable doing. Because there were not any mechanics who knew what it was (a car they had never heard of, with a Ford engine, a General Motors transmission and a Chrysler rear axle) it was almost impossible to get any reliable help. I had to change the oil myself because it had an oil filter that I had to special order. So soon afterward, I donated it to Hyde Park Baptist School for their annual fund-raising auction. Lauren and Preston were both students there at the time. A few years later, it ended up at an antique car museum in Buda, just south of Austin. I have visited it a couple of times and the museum owner says I can come drive it anytime. They drive every car (over 100) at least once a month.

**My Bricklin in Museum in Buda, Texas in 2008**

— — —

During Mike's senior year in high school, he began trying to figure out where he wanted to go to college. Like many kids in that situation, he was not certain as to what he wanted his major to be. I told him not to worry about that. If some of his friends knew what their major would be, good for them. I have always felt that too much pressure is put on high school seniors to decide what they want to do for the rest of their lives. My advice was to not even consider how much money he might make with a certain degree. I'm convinced that it is much more important to have a job that you really enjoy. If you like what you're doing, you will be good at it and the salary will be adequate. Being happy in your job is much more important than how much money you are making. I encouraged him to list all the things he enjoyed doing. He came up with photography, acting, art and doing projects that involved displays. So, his question then was, "What kind of job can I get doing that?" I told him he should start out in Liberal Arts and take all the business courses that he could. I still firmly believe that regardless of the job you are in, the more you know about finance, accounting and business practices, the better off you will be.

So we embarked on tours of college campuses that he thought he might like. We visited Rice, University of Texas, Texas A&M, and Trinity in San Antonio. He liked Rice but thought it was too science and engineering oriented. He didn't like the large crowded campus at UT, and Texas A&M was a total turn-off for him. The day we visited, most of the students were in uniform and we were told about all the rules for freshmen, i.e. don't walk on the grass. There were very few females there because they were only accepted 6-7 years earlier. After a short time there, he wanted to leave. He said, "This place gives me the creeps! I don't want to go to a military college."

Trinity University in San Antonio was entirely different. He liked the small beautiful campus, all the people we met, and he liked San Antonio. We were allowed to sit in on some classes. The first one was "The History of Rock and Roll." I had a hard time not raising my hand to answer some of the questions. When we left the classroom, I told him that if he didn't enroll there, I would! Contrary to the other schools we had visited, they didn't put any pressure on him to declare a major and thought it would be a good idea for him to start out in Liberal Arts. We stayed on campus for several hours and then headed for the car. When I asked Mike what he thought, he said he thought Trinity was where he wanted to go. He was sold and I was happy with his choice.

- - -

In the middle of my RMS efforts, in the fall of 1977, I was asked to go to Russia with Glynn Lunney and several NASA Headquarters folks to discuss the possibility of a joint US/USSR Shuttle and Salyut mission. Glynn had been the NASA Manager for the Apollo Soyuz Test Project (ASTP) and now President Carter wanted to explore the possibility of another joint space program with the Russians. ASTP had proven that the two countries could rendezvous and dock in orbit, and the Shuttle/Salyut mission would be dedicated to micro-gravity science. The cold war was still going on and in essence, we were declared enemies, but after the success of the ASTP, there was hope that more cooperation in space would lead to closer relations and even maybe an end to the "cold war." To emphasize that it would be a "science" mission, Noel Hinners, the Associate Administrator of Space Sciences at NASA would be the head of our delegation.

One of the first things we had to do was go to Washington for three days of briefings by the State Department. The presenter talked about how we should behave while there. Don't wander off by yourself, don't buy anything from street venders, don't try to sell Rubles (the Russian currency in which we would be paid) or take more than 10 (about $14) out of the country, don't try to sell Levi's or Playboy magazines, etc. At the end of the first day, the instructor told us that by law, he had to inform us that just by the nature of our trip, the Russians would start a file on us. Then he said, "That applies to all of you except Mr. Lunney and Mr. Bostick. The Russians already have files on you." It really caught me off guard. I could understand why they would have a file on Glynn because of his involvement in ASTP, but why would they have one on me? I thought about that all night, so the next morning I went in early and asked the guy why the Russians had a file on me. He said it was because of the high level security clearances which I had. My next question was "How do you know that they have a file on me?' He just looked at me, grinned and said "Oh, we have our ways."

This would be my first trip outside the North American continent. My only previous trips outside the U.S. had been a few trips to border towns in Mexico and Canada. I had always said that I had no desire to travel abroad, but I have to admit I was excited about this trip. For some reason which I can't remember, Glynn and I took different routes. We would meet in Vienna, Austria, and travel the final leg together to Moscow. I flew from Houston to New York City and then to Frankfurt, Germany. I arrived in Frankfurt early in the morning. One of the first things I noticed was a policeman with a machine gun! I had a little trouble trying to get a taxi driver to understand English. I finally showed him my reservation slip for Hotel Intercontinental and U.S. dollars so that he would know that I couldn't pay him in Deutsche Marks. All of the taxis were Mercedes and they drove very fast. The ride to the hotel was beautiful! The trees were turning and it reminded me of Northern Virginia. Everything seemed very clean. At the hotel I was able to exchange money and pay the taxi driver in DM.

The plan was that I would stay one day in Frankfurt to adjust my diurnal cycle. I took a short nap and then hit the streets. Everything looked very neat and clean, just as I had observed on the cab ride into town, but there were a few buildings that I assumed were bombed during World War II and had not been rebuilt or even cleaned up. It was a Saturday, so most of the stores were closed. I noticed, as I had done in the airport, that there were a lot of "Sex Shops." They all had large, full color billboards outside. All of the biergartens were open, and there was standing room only. The beer was strong, but very good. All the people seemed to be happy. I just wished I could speak their language.

I had read in the airline magazine about restaurants in Frankfurt. One that they recommended was Henniger-Turm, which was a revolving restaurant on top of the tallest building in Europe, so I decided to try it. The view of Frankfurt was fantastic! I had Pippchen auf Sauerkraut, which is salted pork cutlet and sauerkraut. I thought it was outstanding. Just felt lonely there by myself.

The next morning I arose early and headed for the airport. Another Mercedes taxi and I noticed that he was going 140 km/hr, almost 90 miles/hour! I checked in at the Austrian Airlines counter and my bags were checked through to Moscow. I had breakfast in a small airport restaurant. I couldn't believe that a cup of coffee was the outrageously high price of $1.75! (Now I pay 2-3 times that at Starbucks.) I had oeufs and swine lard (eggs and bacon). At the boarding gate, they wanted me to point my camera at my face and expose one picture. Since all of their directions were in German, it took me a while to understand what they wanted. Before we got on the plane, all of the luggage was out on the apron beside the plane. You had to identify your bags before they would load them on the plane. The plane was a DC-9, which we boarded through the tail door, a first (and last) for me.

When I arrived at the Vienna airport, there was Glynn waiting; tired, unshaven and sleepy. It was good to see him. The police in the Vienna airport were carrying machine guns, just like in Frankfurt. We soon boarded our flight to Moscow. They served mineral water with the meal and it tasted awful, like carbonated water. Of course that's what it was, but it was my first taste of "water with gas."

We arrived in Moscow about 4 p.m. their time, or 7 a.m. Houston time. I soon figured out that I should forget about trying to keep up with all the different times. The Moscow airport was very drab and old looking. At passport control, there were two lines and Glynn and I got in separate lines. There was a guy in a little booth who looked at my passport, then at me and then at something else on his desk…I couldn't see what. He repeated this routine three times, then reached up and pulled the cord on an overhead light, turning it on. He stamped my passport and handed it back to me with no expression or comment. I waited for Glynn who soon came through his line. He said, "You won't believe what the passport guy did." He had gone through the very same routine. We assumed that they were signaling someone of our arrival. Four people from the Soviet Academy of Sciences soon met us. We retrieved our luggage and headed for customs. One of the Academy people said something to the customs guy, who then waved us through without the inspection we had expected.

Once outside the airport, the Academy people very obviously led us to a certain car, which I assumed was a taxi although it had no markings. On the ride into town, Glynn said a few things to the driver who just shrugged his shoulders, indicating that he didn't understand English. Then Glynn tapped me on the leg, turned his head around quickly and said "Holy Mackerel, look at the boobs on that broad!" The driver, who obviously understood English very well, turned to look and almost ran off the road. It was overcast and raining, so I couldn't see much, but noticed that there were no billboards, no gas stations, and hardly any signs on any of the buildings. The ones with signs were all uniformly white neon. The only color I could see at all was St. Basil's Cathedral as we approached our hotel. It was lit by floodlights and very colorful and beautiful. It looked like a very elaborate cake. According to Glynn, it was commissioned by Tsar Ivan the Terrible in the 16th Century. Legend has it that once it was completed, Ivan had the architect blinded so that he could not re-create it anywhere else.

**St. Basil's Cathedral on Red Square in Moscow**

Soon we arrived at our hotel, the Rossiya (sometimes they spelled it without the y), adjacent to Red Square and St. Basil's. At the time, it was the largest hotel in the world, with 3,000 rooms. The driver got out and disappeared into the hotel. We never saw him again. Glynn and I unloaded our luggage and started into the hotel but the doorman wouldn't let us in. We showed him our passports, but it was obvious that he wanted to see something else. Soon someone from the Academy who Glynn knew came over and we finally were allowed in. The Academy person took our passports and gave them to the desk clerk, who in return gave us a slip of paper with our room numbers and 72 Rubles (about $100) for spending money while in Russia. Glynn's room was on the 4th floor and mine on the 8th. The hotel is huge! It's in the shape of a quadrangle, divided into four sections, with each section having its own "Floor Clerk" or "Key Lady" as Glynn called them. When you give her the slip of paper with your room number, she gives you your room key. When you leave the floor, you give her your room key and she gives you back the slip of paper. When you leave the hotel, you must have the slip of paper to get back in. That's what the doorman was asking for when we first arrived. Each even numbered floor of the hotel has a buffet in each of the four sections where they sold meat, cheese, boiled eggs, beer and wine.

While the Rossiya was the largest hotel in the world at the time, I think the rooms were the world's smallest: about 10' x 10', with no closets. There were two small clothes in the bathroom which were like fragments of an old tablecloth, starched and ironed. I assumed that one was for washing and the other for drying. There was a curtain rod over the tub, but no curtain. The toilet paper was like waxed paper! There was a TV in the room with a remote control, but only one channel, which was Russian propaganda. The bed was very small. Carpet throughout the hotel; rooms, hallways, lobby and restaurant was all the same low grade indoor-outdoor.

The rest of our delegation arrived later and we met in the hotel main restaurant for a snack. In addition to Glynn and me, there were 13 others, including Noel Hinners, his Deputy, Ichtiaque Rasool, Len Jaffee, the NASA Deputy Associate Administrator for Applications, three "delegation advisors" from the NASA International Affairs Office, Gerry Wasserburg, a scientist from Cal Tech, two interpreters, and two "State Department" guys who we thought were really from the Central Intelligence Agency (CIA). I tasted caviar for the first time, which I thought was very salty but quickly learned to like. There was a rock band on stage in the restaurant playing Beatles' songs in English. Some people were dancing. The interpreter assigned to Glynn and I, Nick Timacheff, said they were tourists. The other interpreter, Steven Seymour, then proceeded to tell us how he hated the Russians. I thought that it was strange that the State Department would assign somebody like that to us.

The next morning before leaving my room, I decided to see if I could determine if the Russians were going to spy on me. Since there was no closet or dresser, everything had to stay in my luggage. I carefully placed several items in exact positions and then carefully shoved it under my bed. When I returned that night, it was obvious that someone had gone through it. The same happened each day I was there.

We all climbed on a waiting bus and rode to the Space Research Institute, the lead organization of their Academy of Sciences, which is in charge of Soviet long-range planning of space research programs. It was my first view of Moscow in daylight. My first thought was how gray everything was; no color anywhere! Once outside the immediate area of the Kremlin, there was nothing but apartments. Almost every apartment building had a shop of some sort on the first floor; produce, meat, children's clothing, etc. There were many signs along our route, all in red, promoting the 60th anniversary of the Revolution, pictures of Lenin, and several that said "Glory to the Communist Party!" At least there was some color, but to me, they were creepy.

Most of the cars and trucks on the street were very old, dirty and dilapidated. All of the trucks looked like military vehicles. Equipment at construction sites also appeared to be very, very old. The buildings all looked poorly constructed. We passed by the Academy of Sciences which looked like an old cathedral.

Upon arrival at the Space Research Institute building, it obviously was newer than most: probably 1960s. Other buildings on the site were still under construction. Now I could see up close how poorly constructed their buildings were. The tiles on the outside walls were crooked, the concrete was crudely finished, metal door frames sloppily welded, very poor quality glass in windows, etc. A Russian interpreter met us and took us inside. There was a Sputnik spacecraft hanging from the ceiling on the first floor. I assumed it was a replica, but the interpreter told us that it was the actual back-up for the one launched in 1957. He took us to the second floor where all of our Soviet counterparts were waiting. There was a big table in the middle of the room with all the Soviets on one side and empty chairs for us on the other side. At other tables in the room, there were 35-40 Soviets, two of which were women. The center table had Soviet and U.S. flags and several bottles of mineral water. Academician Petrov, Chairman of Interkosmos, and the head of their delegation, welcomed us, introduced his associates and proposed an agenda for the day and the rest of the week. Noel responded for us and introduced our delegation. There were several exchanges concerning what we each hoped to accomplish and then Petrov suggested we take a coffee break. We all then walked to another building where we had coffee and pastries, neither of which was very good. I noticed that the two women in our initial meeting cleaned the dishes we had used.

After the break, we divided into two working groups; Science & Applications (S&A) and Operations. In the Operations Group, there was Glynn, our interpreter Steve, and I. On the Soviet side were 14 people. Glynn led our side and a General Semenov led their side. At the beginning, Semenov proposed that we do nothing until the S&A group had come up with some proposals. We pointed out that there were certain spacecraft characteristics which should be made available from both sides in order for the S&A group to discuss a relevant science mission, and that we were prepared to discuss Shuttle characteristics. Semenov said that they would try to answer any questions we had about Salyut, but they didn't have any material to give us. After discussing this back and forth for a few minutes, we were informed that it was time for lunch...2:30 p.m.!

For "lunch", we went to a cafeteria banquet room in yet another building. I had never seen such a feast! At each seat they had bottles of vodka, wine, mineral water (with and without "gas"), and something like cola. In the middle of the table, they had cold cuts, cheese, smoked salmon, caviar, steak, roast beef, a salad consisting of roast beef, chopped potatoes, carrots and English peas, ice cream and all kinds of pastries.

We started the lunch with toasts. Glynn had warned me about this. He said we should drink a jigger of vodka after each toast; no sipping allowed, just throw it down. When it was our turn, each of us would be expected to say a few words. They did the toasts by chain of command, alternating between Soviets and Americans. I was number six, and therefore had already consumed five jiggers of vodka, so I don't even remember what I said. Probably something really stupid.

We finished the lunch at 4:30 p.m. and reconvened the working groups. Semenov agreed to draw up a list of parameters for each spacecraft for the minutes and then to provide us details by the end of the year. We agreed that the next day, one of their guys named Gorshkov and I would draw up the list, and then present it to the entire delegation. Glynn and Semenov will sit in on the S&A group to see what they're coming up with.

We adjourned at 6:30 and left for a reception for us and the entire Soviet delegation to be held at the apartment of Allen Greenberg, the Science Counselor for the American Embassy.

The Greenberg's apartment was on the top (14th) floor of an apartment building not too far from the Institute. A military guard was stationed in the small lobby. The elevator would only hold four people at a time, if they deeply inhaled. It took forever to get everyone upstairs. There were about 40-45 Soviets plus their wives, a dozen or so U.S. Embassy folks plus their spouses, and the 15 of us. Even though this was an "upscale" apartment, the construction was even worse than the Institute. Their apartment was four rooms, which ordinarily would be four separate apartments. Even Academicians only get a one or two room apartment. All of the Russians appeared upset that this American was taking up so much space.

More cold cuts and caviar. I'm beginning to love caviar! They had trays of meatballs and cheese along with bowls filled with toothpicks. I saw several Russians, including Academician Petrov, picking up the toothpicks and putting them into their pockets. Steve, our interpreter, said that toothpicks were very rare and considered a real luxury.

We rode the bus back to the Rossiya and all met to caucus in one of the corner buffets on a floor where none of us were staying, hoping to have privacy. Our "State Department" folks told us that we should assume that all of our rooms were bugged. In general, we concluded that things were going pretty well, but it sure was hard to get any information out of the Soviets. Glynn, who had a lot more experience in dealing with them than anyone else, said that should be expected. They like to hold all information close to their vest.

Each night when we got our room key from the "Key Lady", she would also give each of us a pint of vodka and a small tin of caviar. Not really caring for vodka, I just usually left mine in my room, thinking I would bring the caviar back to the U.S. and give the vodka to some of our Russian counterparts. Apparently, the housecleaner or the KGB (Soviet equivalent of our CIA) agents who searched my room took it.

The next morning our session started with Semenov making more proposals about specific mission profiles and bilateral responsibilities. We explained once again that the Ops group needed to start out with spacecraft characteristics, and then we could work with the S&A group to start developing missions. So, as agreed the day before,

Gorshkov (I asked through the interpreter what his first name was, but he said, "Just call me Gorshkov." He, and the other Soviets pronounced my name "Djerry.") and I broke away to start working on spacecraft characteristics and capabilities. He brought four others with him, so it was just me against five of them. Gorshkov turned out to be a real hard nose! He initially would not agree with anything I suggested. We finally agreed on a list and then proceed to fill it out. I was able to convey to Glynn at lunch how uncooperative Gorshkov was being.

I noticed that each day when we left the Institute, a guy locked each inside door, put a string across the opening and then sealed it with wax. Strange!

That night, after our second day of meetings, we were invited to a special concert for the members of the Soviet Academy of Sciences in honor of the 60th anniversary of the Great Soviet Revolution. The concert was held in the central hall of the Rossiya and was a fine variety show; orchestra, ballet, folk dancers, pianists, comedians, singers and even rock groups.

After the concert, Glynn and I met in his room to drink a little vodka, eat a little caviar, and debrief. Glynn started pointing to the ceiling and began by saying that some things weren't going all that well, but that he had noticed that Gorshkov was very cooperative, and that if I was having any problems, I should just go to him and he would agree to almost anything we proposed. I finally figured out what he was up to, so I agreed with him. I said, "Yes, I have found Gorshkov to be a push-over. He will agree to almost anything."

We got started late for our third day of meetings because the bus didn't show up, so our Russian "handler" finally ordered three taxis to take us to the Institute. The one in which I was riding ran out of gas. Luckily, one of the other taxis had a can of gas. When our meeting finally started, Gorshkov was not there, so I gave a status report on our progress (or lack thereof). Then, without any comment on our report, Semenov said we should start writing the minutes of our meetings. So, Glynn and I went to a separate table and started writing. This turned out to be a very interesting, and sometimes frustrating, process. We would write something, give it to the Russian translator, who would translate it into Russian and then give it to our counterparts for their review. They would mark it up and give it to our translator who would translate it into English and then give it back to Glynn and me. Much was lost and changed in the translations. For example, we would write, "The Space Shuttle will be launched from Cape Kennedy." It would come back as "The Space Shuttle will escape from Cape Kennedy." We made very little progress in producing anything substantial. I still wonder what happened to Gorshkov. He's probably still in a labor camp in Siberia!

That night was free, so I decided to take a walk around the Kremlin. We had been told to not go out alone, but Glynn didn't want to go, so I headed out by myself. It was soon obvious that I was being tailed. Two guys followed me out of the hotel and into Red Square. They were either not very good or they didn't care if I knew I was being followed. I walked around St. Basil's and just marveled at its beauty. I watched the changing of the guard at Lenin's tomb (his body is in full view) and visited the tomb of the Soviet Unknown Soldier. I saw a round pedestal, which had a plaque in front of it, but since I couldn't read Russian, it wasn't of much help. I stopped for a few minutes and imagined all of the military parades in Red Square that I had seen on TV, with either Premier Khrushchev or General Secretary Brezhnev watching from atop the Kremlin wall. One such parade of soldiers, tanks and missiles, celebrating the October Revolution, had occurred just a few weeks earlier. Chills ran up my spine!

I then walked to the opposite side of Red Square to the Gum (pronounced "goom") Department Store. It was truly a "department store." It was like an indoor shopping mall, but instead of individual stores, it had separate departments for men's shoes (all black), one for women's shoes (both black and brown), another for combs, one for handkerchiefs, etc. In the shoe departments, all of the shoes were stacked on a wall with nowhere to try them on. I guess they just select a pair and hope that they fit. To me, it all appeared to be low quality stuff that I couldn't imagine people would wait in line three different times in order to purchase. In the first line, you select what you want to buy and give it to a clerk, who then gives you a ticket with which you get into another line to pay for it. Once you have a receipt, you then get into a third line to take it to the clerk who is holding your merchandise! The customers were pushing and shoving and the clerks were very rude and unhelpful. On the first floor was a lot of produce: fish, meat and vegetables. There the customers were really fighting over stuff that I wouldn't even consider buying!

My bodyguards, as I called them, followed me back to the Rossiya.

On the bus to the Institute the next morning, I happened to sit with Dwight Cramer, one of the "State Department" guys. He asked how my last evening had been, so I told him about my stroll around Red Square, the Kremlin and Gum. He went ballistic! He reminded me that I wasn't supposed to go out alone. I told him that I was perfectly safe because of my "body guards." He still was not too happy.

In our final meeting, both sides reviewed drafts of the meeting records. After several iterations, we finally came to agreement. There were no specific recommendations, just a general conclusion that a joint Shuttle/Salyut mission was feasible. We had tried to put something in the record that such a mission could produce valuable science, but it was obvious that the Soviets did not want to make any commitments.

We then split into our separate groups and exchanged gifts. Glynn and I gave them pictures and decals from the Shuttle Approach and Landing Tests, and several Shuttle decals, which they asked us to autograph. They gave me a Samovar, a very nice Russian teapot. Several of the Soviet members of our working group gave us various lapel pins and medallions, which they said had been flown on ASTP.

The entire group then assembled in the building where we had met the first day. There were banks of portable lights and TV and movie cameras set up. Noel and Petrov made a few remarks for the cameras and then we adjourned for lunch.

After lunch, Glynn, Gerry Wasserburg and I got someone to drive us back to the hotel. The three of us then went to Gum for some shopping. We had all those Rubles they had given us, so we needed to spend them for souvenirs. The place was packed! We figured out that it must be fresh produce day, because there were lines of people over 200 feet long. Fresh fruit is really rare, so those lines were even longer. I had noticed that the coffee cups and plates were the same at the hotel and the Institute. The ones on sale at Gum were exactly like them. The only place I saw anything different was at the Greenberg's apartment. There they were all U.S. made.

Glynn then told us about the Beriozka store (he called it the Dollar Store), not far from the Rossiya, which sold high quality goods for foreign currency. Soviet citizens (except for high-ranking officials) were not allowed to enter these stores as they were legally forbidden to be in possession of hard currency. The selection for things to take back to the U.S. was much better there. I got Kristi a Matryoshka doll set, wooden dolls of decreasing size placed one inside the other, a necklace and a satellite set. For Mike, I found a different satellite set and a Cosmonaut/Astronaut set. For Linda, I got an amber necklace. Amber jewelry is big in Russia and Glynn said there were other places where you could buy better stones for cheaper prices, but we were not going to be there long enough to find them. They had some really neat hand carved wooden plaques that I went crazy over. I bought five of them; one each for Mother & Daddy, Hobson & Elwa, Mary & Joe, Bob & Colette and Gil and Evie Guster. I think the Guster's were the only ones who really appreciated what they were.

That night we all went to a final banquet at the "House of Scientists" which is a club for scientists in downtown Moscow. Before the banquet began, Anatoly Aleksandrov, the President of the Academy of Sciences for the USSR, walked over to a wall where there were pictures of all the Soviet Cosmonauts. He turned the picture of Valentina Tereshkova, the first woman to fly in space, so that it faced the wall. As he did that, he said something in Russian, which of course I didn't understand, so I asked our interpreter Nick what he had said. Nick told me that he said, "PR", meaning Public Relations, indicating that she was only flown for propaganda.

It was a nice banquet, but nothing like the "lunch" we had on the first day at the Space Institute. I sat by Cosmonaut Konstantin Feoktistov. He flew on Voskhod 1 in 1964 as an engineer apparently to prove that the spacecraft could hold three people. It was the first flight by any nation to fly more than one person. He was a spacecraft designer who was on the design team for Sputnik, Vostok, Voskhod, and later Soyuz, Salyut, and Mir. In order to get three people into Voskhod, they took the ejection seat out and the three crewmen flew without pressurized suits. After that mission, they cut back to two crewmen with suits. I asked him about the pedestal I had seen in Red Square. He told me that it was where the Tsars had people beheaded! He also verified what Glynn had told me about Ivan the Terrible having the architect of St. Basil's blinded so that he couldn't design another one like it. To my surprise, he knew that I had attended Mississippi State and asked if I knew Dr. Gus Raspet, the head of the Aerophysics Department at State. Dr. Raspet was a pioneer in aircraft flight efficiency and wing design. Unfortunately, he was killed in an experimental plane crash while I was in school there. I did not really know him, but had met him a couple of times through our next-door neighbor, who worked with him. Feoktistov said that he had read everything Dr. Raspet had published and was a big fan of his. I guess they really did have a file on me because nothing that was sent to them concerning our visit mentioned where I went to college.

After the banquet, the entire U.S. delegation met in Glynn's room, at his suggestion, and discussed what had been accomplished during the trip. He just wanted to make sure that we didn't go back to the States with two or three different impressions of what had happened. Our consensus was that some good science could be conducted on such a joint mission and it was operationally feasible, although the Salyut was at a higher orbital inclination than the Shuttle was being planned to reach, but it really was a political question as to whether it should be undertaken. We were pretty frank in the discussion and concluded that it would take the KGB a long time to transcribe the tape!

We got up early the next morning to leave. After you get packed and vacate the room, the "Key Lady" inspects your room to see that you haven't stolen anything. What you would want to steal, I don't know! She then gives you a slip of paper that says you have paid for your room, you haven't stolen anything, and tells how many bags you have. The doorman won't let you out of the hotel without that slip of paper.

Semenov and Logastaov met us and drove us to the airport. The airport was a real hassle to get through customs, check baggage, go through passport control and security inspections. Once I was through all of that, I felt like I was out of jail.

The flight to London was on Aeroflot, the Russian airline, so I felt like they still had me. On the flight, I reflected about where I had been and what I had seen. The best word for Moscow is "gray". The sky is gray, the buildings are gray and so are the people. Very little color anywhere. Every day we saw old women out on the street sweeping with brooms, which were sticks with bundles of straw tied to them. They were all fat and wore overcoats and boots. I saw very few men in the 50-70 age range. Most of them were killed in World War II. Nobody ever smiles! I got no news while I was there. The TV in my room only had one channel...propaganda, no entertainment and no news. We had Nick buy their newspapers each morning; Pravda and Izvestia, and tell us what they said. All they had was editorials about the Communist Party, copies of speeches given by Party leaders, stories about factories that were producing great products and about the new airport they were building for the Olympics. There was no mention of the outside world except for natural disasters such as fires, earthquakes and storms. There was one article about how the "Capitalistic Americans" were aiding Israel to take away land from the Palestinians. When the Russians park their cars, they take the windshield wipers off to keep someone from stealing them. There are very few gas stations and they have no identifying signs. They are spread out over Moscow, 25-30 miles apart. The ones I saw had very long lines. One of the guys on my working group told me that sometimes he waits in line for two hours to get gas. One of our taxi drivers had a picture of a Datsun 240Z on the dashboard. He said it was his dream car, but probably would never be able to own one. My conclusion? Moscow is a very sad place and I'm not sure I ever want to return. One thing which I wanted to see but didn't have the opportunity, was the subway. Glynn, Arnie Aldrich, Ken Young and others who spent a lot of time there during ASTP, all say it is very beautiful. I'll just take their word for it.

Just a few weeks after our trip, Seymour was chosen by the State Department to be President Carter's personal interpreter when the president visited Poland in December 1977. This time, he made International news for his screw-ups. In his speech, the president said that he wanted to learn about the Polish people's desires for the future. Seymour translated that as "I lust for the Polish people." Carter later mentioned leaving for his journey back to the U.S., which Seymour translated as "I have abandoned America forever." As a further insult to the Pole's, he used a lot of Russian words in his translations; a big no-no in a country with a long history of anti-Russian feelings.

Several weeks later we learned that President Carter had decided to not pursue the mission. We never knew exactly what NASA Administrator Robert Frosch recommended, but felt that based on the consensus of our delegation, it was positive. We suspected that Zbigniew Brzezinski, Carter's National Security Advisor, who was of Polish decent, didn't want to have that much cooperation with the Russians and talked the president out of it.

– – –

When our flight arrived in London, I couldn't get over the feeling of happiness and relief! I was out of Russian and off their airplane! I had never been to London before, but I felt like kissing the ground. There was color, the people were friendly and polite, and they were even smiling! What a difference from Moscow!

Glynn and I caught our flight to Dublin, Ireland a couple of hours later. Glynn had graciously invited me to go with him to visit his brother Bill and family who lived in Kilkenny. Bill met us at the Dublin airport and took us by the hotel where he had been staying and we each had a pint of ale in the hotel pub. I couldn't get over how nice and friendly the people were. I noticed on the drive from the airport that everything looked clean with bright colors. Each door on the townhouses was a different color. What a change from Moscow. The drive down to Kilkenny is through beautiful rolling hillside. They drive on the left side of the road in Ireland, which took a bit of getting used to. I kept trying to get into Bill's car on the driver's side. It's only 75 miles from Dublin, but it takes about 2 hours because the road is very narrow and curvy. The fields are all divided by hedgerows or stone walls. We passed a horse drawn wagon, shaped like a big barrel, filled with a family in very colorful clothes. Bill said they were Gypsies and probably lived in the wagon/barrel. He said there were still a lot of Gypsies in Ireland and they frequently traveled in caravans.

Bill was the manager of the Fieldcrest Mills towel factory in Kilkenny. Fieldcrest, based in North Carolina, was a very popular brand of medium to upper priced towels and sheets in the U.S., and had just expanded to Ireland in an attempt to penetrate the European market. His wife, Becky, and two young teenage sons, Tim and Will, were very nice and appeared to be happy to see folks from the U.S. They had a very nice two-story duplex, but lacking some of the amenities they were used to, like closets and washers and dryers.

Our first night there we went to Tynan's Bridge House Bar, selected by Guinness as the best pub in Ireland. What a fun place! Everybody was just standing and sitting around laughing, drinking, playing darts and having a good time. We did notice that there were several young girls at the bar, just talking among themselves. The men didn't seem to be paying any attention to them, for some reason which we couldn't understand. Bill had obviously been there before. Most of the patrons called him "The Man from Fieldcrest", a take-off on a TV ad at that time featuring "The Man from Glad", advertising Glad plastic cling wrap.

Our first full day there, we toured Kilkenny. Everything was green. We're told it's that way all year. Lots of moss growing everywhere.

Bill says they have to continually scrape it off the driveway and the roof. Kilkenny is an old town with narrow streets and lots of shops. The population is about 12,000, of which Bill says over half are under 25. We visited Kilkenny Castle which was built in 1195 and is only partially restored. It's a magnificent building and grounds with fountains and rose gardens.

We stopped off at another pub, Kytelers Inn, one of the oldest in Ireland and exactly what I expected an Irish pub to look like. The tavern bar downstairs looks like a dungeon. There is a courtyard out back, which according to Bill, is where they once burned a witch. The upstairs bar is especially great, with beautiful wood walls and brown cordovan leather booths. They have entertainment there at night and a disc jockey's box which was originally a church pulpit.

Linda had requested that I bring her some Waterford crystal, which was made just 20 miles down the road from Kilkenny. In the first shop, when I asked for Waterford, the clerk said, "We don't sell that cheap stuff here. Only genuine Kilkenny crystal." Bill took me to another shop where he thought they might have Waterford. Sure enough, they had it, but they insisted that I buy Kilkenny. I bought some Waterford anyway, because I had heard of it before and that's what Linda had asked for.

That night Becky prepared a real Thanksgiving feast, turkey and all the accompaniments. After dinner, Bill took us out behind their house to cut some peat bricks to burn in the fireplace. I couldn't believe that they really did that, but the bricks burned great. We sat around the fire for a while and then went back to Tynan's. We had met some of the same people there the night before, and given them some Shuttle patches and decals. They instantly recognized us and started buying beer for "the astronauts." We tried to explain that we were not astronauts, but finally just gave up. I was amazed again at how happy and friendly the people were.

– – –

We arose early the next morning for the drive to the Dublin airport. I was catching a plane to Amsterdam to spend a few days with Steve and Cathy Copps, friends from the Apollo and Energy Office days.

Steve and his son Stevie met me at the Amsterdam airport. The weather was really bad; cold and rainy. On the drive to Leiden, where the Copps' lived, I could see that what I had read about Holland was true. It's mostly below sea level, so there are canals and dams everywhere. I kept looking for the little Dutch boy with his finger in a dike, but never did see him. A lot of windmills also. I had figured that they only saved a few for tourists, but they are everywhere and all appear to be working. Steve said they were used mainly to pump water from one canal to another. When we arrived at their house in Oegstgeest, we visited with Cathy for a while and then Steve and I drove to Noordwijk (about 5 miles) to see Mel and Dorothy Brooks. Mel and Steve were both employed by NASA on assignment to the European Space Agency (ESA), which had their Space Research and Technology Center in Noordwijk. I had not seen Mel and Dorothy in several years and it was good to see them again. They had just recently moved from the ESA facility in Darmstadt, Germany and had a very large cellar full of German wine. Mel was worried how he would ever get all of it back to the U.S. I told him to just drink it all and the problem would be solved.

The next day Cathy drove me around the area. We saw a lot more windmills and canals and some beautiful old buildings with thatched roofs. Unfortunately, the weather was still rainy and cold. I tried not to think about how much nicer it had been in Ireland. She drove me to Den Haag (The Hague as we know it) and dropped me off. On the way there, she tried to explain to me that The Hague is the Capital of Holland and the seat of the Dutch government, but is not the capital of the <u>Netherlands</u>, which is <u>Amsterdam</u>. I didn't get it. The Hague also is the home of the International Court of Justice, where cases involving more than one nation are tried under United Nations law.

I walked around some of the government buildings and into a few shops along the way. Then I came upon the Netherlands Picture Gallery, which had some fantastic paintings including about 15 Rembrandts! I had never dreamed that I would see a real Rembrandt. I spent over an hour there just pinching myself that I was really looking at such famous paintings.

Upon leaving the Gallery, it was snowing very hard but the ground was too wet for it to stick. I got soaking wet, so decided to catch the train back to Leiden, where Cathy would pick me up. Everybody here rides bicycles. All the streets have a bike lane marked off and there seems to be as many bikes as cars. I'm surprised, because the weather is so bad, but they just ride right along in the rain.

Mel and Dorothy came for dinner that night and brought a mixed case of German wine, asking us to help them drink all of their wine before they go back to the States. Cathy and I helped them, but Steve insisted on drinking his Grolsch Beer, which they have delivered to their doorstep three times a week, just as people used to have home delivery of milk.

The next morning, even though it was raining harder than ever, Cathy and I rode bikes to the market. The market had lots of root vegetables, some I had never heard of, and plenty of flowers, Dutch chocolate and cheese. I went crazy for the cheese!

Cathy explained to me that while it was Thanksgiving season in the States, it was Sinterklaas season in Holland. Sinterklaas, which translates to Saint Nicholas, is the source of our Santa Claus. He arrives in Holland each November 19 on a boat from

Spain with his Svarta Petes, our equivalent of elves. He then rides over the rooftops on his white horse listening to the chimneys to see if children are being good. If they are, he sends the Svarta Petes down the chimney each night with fruit and candy. The children leave a carrot or an apple on the hearth in their wooden shoes (they really do wear them in Holland) for Sinterklaas' white horse. The Svarta Petes are black because of all their trips down sooty chimneys. On December 5, Sinterklaas brings gifts for everyone who has been good. Twenty days later, Christmas is celebrated as strictly a religious holiday.

That afternoon Steve took off from work and he and I piled into his Mini Cooper for a drive through North Holland. That was the first (and last) time I had ever been in a Mini Cooper and I quickly saw why it was called a Mini. My knees were up in my face! We saw more windmills, more canals and more rain. Unfortunately, it was not the season for tulips, so the fields were bare and they were just beginning to plant bulbs. Flowers are plentiful and cheap in Holland. I wanted to buy some tulip bulbs for only four cents each, but Steve said I wouldn't be allowed to take them on the plane.

We went to Edam, where the cheese is made; to Zandvoort, home of the Dutch Grand Prix Formula 1 race course; to the IJseelmere, a large fresh water lake formed when they built a dike cutting off part of the Zeiderzee.; and then to Amsterdam. Amsterdam is really a "different" place. The heart of the city is the "red light district" where the prostitutes display themselves in windows! There are more porno shops even than I saw in Frankfurt. In the middle of all this was a bar which only served Texas beer and the juke box had nothing but Willie Nelson and Waylon Jennings songs. Made me feel at home.

Next, we visited the Anne Frank house. Anne and her family, Germans of Jewish descent, hid there during the Nazi occupation of the Netherlands during World War II. She kept a diary, which was discovered after the war. A very sad place, but a strong reminder of the atrocities carried out by the Nazi Germans.

Steve and I then had dinner at a coffee shop just across the square from Anne Frank's house. At the bottom of the menu was "cannabis." I thought I knew what that was, and Steve confirmed it was marijuana! I had smelled something when we entered, but had no idea what it was. I had wiener schnitzel, and a black beer, both of which were delicious.

Almost everywhere we went, I saw several people in wooden shoes, mostly farmers who trudge around in the mud. And there was plenty of mud from all the rain. Steve said that the Pilgrims stopped off in the Leiden area for about 10 years before sailing on to Plymouth Rock. I don't blame them for leaving!

I got up early the next morning to catch the bus to the Amsterdam airport. Unbelievably, it isn't raining! I looked through the duty free store at the airport to find something to buy with my remaining Gilders. I had hoped to buy some Delftware pottery, but it was incredibly expensive, so I ended up buying a Royal Holland pewter candle snuffer.

— — —

My flight to Paris was on an Air France Caravelle, smaller than a DC-9, but one of the quietest planes I had ever ridden. Cathy and Steve had told me that I probably wouldn't like Paris because the people were all rude and go out of their way to intimidate Americans. I thought about that on the flight and determined that I would just refuse to be intimidated. Steve had called and made reservations for me at the Hotel Neva, just a couple of blocks from the Arc de Triomphe. He gave me fairly detailed instructions on how to get there from the DeGaulle airport.

After landing, I exchanged Dollars for Francs and caught a bus to Maillot Terminal where I catch the Metro to L'Etoile. Finding the right subway train turned out to be harder than I had expected, but I finally did. When the train arrived at L'Etoile (Charles DeGaulle Circle where the Arch is), I went up to the street lever only to discover that I was on the opposite side of the circle from the hotel. When I finally got to the Neva, they said they had no record of my reservation, and had no rooms available. The manager, who spoke enough English that we could communicate, rudely told me there was nothing he could do to help. So, I hit the streets thinking Steve and Cathy were right; Parisians are rude and I may not have a great time here. With two bags strapped around my neck (this was before the days of bags with rollers), I stopped at every hotel I could see, but no rooms were available. My bags were weighing one ton each by now, but at least it wasn't raining like it was in Holland! Finally, I was able to get a room at the Hotel MacMahon, just one block off the circle. It turned out to be a nice room with a view of the Arch, about 500 feet away. The rate was about double that of the Neva, but at this point, I thought it was a real bargain!

As soon as I could unpack, I started walking. I walked all the way down the Champs Elysees to the Louvre and back. The Louvre was closed, so I just took in everything else along the way. It helped to have a guidebook, otherwise I would not have known what I was seeing. There were a lot of cars and a lot of people. Very vibrant place! Also, a lot of sidewalk cafes. I really enjoyed the afternoon.

For dinner that night, I selected Rech Restaurant, which was listed in my guidebook as one of the top 100 in Paris and only about 10 blocks from my hotel. I had salmon terrine, brochette (shish kebab), crème de caramel, and a great glass of montrachet. They had menus in English, so that was not a problem, and the waiter was very nice and helpful.

The next day was Thanksgiving. Made me a little homesick. I rode the Metro to Chatelet and started walking again. I visited la Sainte-Chapelle, a very old church with the most beautiful stained glass I had ever seen. Absolutely incredible! I saw the Temple Prison where Marie Antoinette was kept, Notre Dame and the Louvre. I spent a lot of time at Notre Dame. Climbed the tower which was a real work out. Only an engineer would count the steps—384. Fantastic views of the entire city from up there. I looked for the hunchback, but he was nowhere to be seen.

I ate lunch; pate, haddock, bread, cheese and vin blanc, at the Brasserie de l'Isle St. Louis, with a great view of Notre Dame.

At the Louvre, I joined a tour with an English-speaking guide. I really liked Venus de Milo and Mona Lisa. Mona looked alive and her eyes really do follow you as you walk from side to side! In the gift shop, I saw a large poster of an American astronaut being suited in front of a bunch of nude women. It was very strange and the clerk was of no help in explaining it to me.

It was getting late so I took the Metro back to the hotel. During the ride I thought about all the wonderful things I had seen and wished that Linda, Mike and Kristi were with me to share them. After dark, I walked down to the Eiffel Tower. I had intended to eat at another three star restaurant on the way, but they were not open for dinner until 8:00 p.m. As I approached the tower, it started raining so I rode the elevator up to a restaurant, thinking I would eat while it was raining. It was a café that served only hamburgers and French fries before 8:00 p.m. They sure do eat late in France! I didn't complain however, because the view was so great. I could then understand why Paris is called "The City of Lights." My waiter reminded me a lot of Daddy, which was very strange hearing him with a French accent.

It was still raining a little, so I walked to the nearest Metro station and rode back to the hotel. I was getting pretty good at the subway business. That night I planned my last full day in Paris. First on my list was to go back to the Louvre and buy that poster which I had seen but couldn't understand. I thought that maybe somebody back in Clear Lake could explain it to me.

The next morning, before leaving the hotel, I called National Airlines to confirm my flight the next day. My heart skipped a beat when they told me that it had been cancelled! They started laying out options, which involved delays of a day or two, so the first thing I did was catch the Metro to their office, where I hoped to do better talking to them in person. It turned out they could get me on an Air France direct flight to Houston, with about the same departure time as the cancelled flight but getting to Houston four hours earlier.

With that problem solved, I went back to the Louvre and purchased the poster*, then headed for Montmartre, the highest point in Paris. After I had climbed the many steps from the Metro station up to Sacre Coeur (Church of the Sacred Heart), I saw that there was a tram that I could have taken. Sacre Coeur is a beautiful church and offers a fantastic view of Paris from it's front. In the narthex, I saw several phones on the wall that people were listening to, so I waited for one labeled English. I heard a nice message about the church and it's history. Then the recording ended with something like "If you are a tourist in our city and seek a closeness with God, feel free to light a candle and pray inside." I did both.

* *Upon returning to Clear Lake, I had the poster framed and hung in my office. The framer told me that the background was a famous 19th century painting titled **The Turkish Bath**. Why some French artist named Erro, superimposed an American astronaut donning his spacesuit and giving it the title Programme Spatial (Space Program), I will never figure out. Astronaut Joe Allen denied*

*that he had posed for the drawing, even though there is a distinct*
*similarity.*

The area just to the left of Sacre Coeur (as you face the church), is full of small restaurants and crepe shops. In a large square, there are dozens of artists displaying their paintings. Over the years, many famous artists worked and/or lived here, such as Salvador Dali, Claude Monet, Pablo Picasso and Vincent van Gogh. I could have spent all day there just watching the artists and eating crepes. But I still had a lot to see and not much time, so after walking by the Moulin Rouge, I headed back to downtown Paris.

L'Hôtel des Invalides (Home of the invalids) is a collection of war museums, hospitals and retirement homes for French veterans. For me, the most impressive thing there was Napoleon's tomb. After seeing so much old historic stuff, I decided to check out the Pompidou Center, a brand new, ultra-modern building that I had seen from the top of Notre Dame. From there it looked like a power plant that someone tried to dress up with stainless steel pipes, glass and big tubes of all different colors. I tried to locate it on my tourist map, but it wasn't identified there, so I just marked where I thought it was. When I asked people on the street where it was, they made mad faces and waved me off. Supposedly, all true Frenchmen hate it. When I finally found it, I thought it was really neat and a nice change of pace.

On the first floor (they call it the ground floor and what I call the second floor, they call the first) they had the largest, most cluttered hunk of art I had ever seen. I had no idea what it was, but it was intriguing, with all sorts of moving parts and making weird noises. It was really a strange building and even stranger considering where it was.

On the way to the Pompidou Centre, I stumbled upon another very old and very large church, Saint Eustache. When I first saw it, I thought it was Norte Dame. It had buttresses just like Notre Dame, just as large, but without the twin towers. I discovered that it was under a rather major restoration. Inside it was as big and bold as Notre Dame, but looked very old and badly in need of repair.

Since this was going to be my last night in Paris, I decided that I should assume it would be my last time there, so I got out my Michelin guide and selected a four star restaurant, Traktir Prunier (they since have dropped the Traktir), supposedly one of the best in Paris. They didn't have an English menu and the waiter was absolutely no help, but I struggled through without too many surprises. I had moules (mussels) and croquille de crabe (crab cakes), a half bottle of Pouilly Fuisse, and vanilla glace for desert. As I was leaving, my waiter helped me with my coat and said in perfect English, "Thank you Sir. I hope you enjoyed your meal." I just looked at him and said, "You son of a bitch."

After dinner I walked back to the Champs Elysees and had coffee and a cigar at Le Deauville, a sidewalk café. I just sat and watched all the people walking by. Gray and brown seemed to be the "in" colors. Most of the women wore fashionable leather boots, slacks and some of the nicest coats I had ever seen. There were carts on almost every street corner selling chestnuts. They sure did smell good, but I didn't try any. I looked at the Arch and imagined Hitler and his troops marching through there during World War II. I almost couldn't believe I was there.

I whispered under my breath "Well, here's the kid from Golden on the Champs Elysees. Who would have ever thunk it?"

My last day in Paris, I had to get up early to get to De Gaulle airport for my flight to Houston. I was excited about getting back home. My bags were checked all the way to Clear Lake. It was a long flight, 10 hours 15 minutes, but a lot quicker than having to change planes. I had time to reflect on where I had been and what I had seen. I had no great desire to return to Russia, although I hoped that the Shuttle/Salyut program would be approved and I would be going back. I definitely wanted to go back to Ireland and to Paris and would like to go back to Holland in the springtime when the tulips were blooming and hopefully it wouldn't rain every day. We arrived in Houston at 2:10 p.m., and I then caught the commuter flight to Clear Lake. Linda, Mike and Kristi met me and I sure was glad to see them. I learned that the kids had kept diaries for me. That was a real treat to read about what they had been doing while I was away.

– – –

It took me a few days to get back on Houston time, but the next Monday, I was back at work, catching up on what had happened in the RMS world while I was away. As I had expected, Clay had taken care of everything and the program was moving forward.

We all traveled to Canada a lot. I grew to love Toronto, where SPAR Aerospace, the RMS contractor was headquartered. We also traveled frequently to Ottawa, the home base of NRCC. We had many long and sometimes contentious meetings. One such meeting in Toronto lasted until 2:00 am. Several of the Houston crowd wanted to replace the SPAR proposed snare end-effector with one that looked and operated like a hand. We argued back and forth and finally I said, "Okay, we're going with the snare." All of the Canadians seemed happy and most of the NASA crowd disappointed. Years later in the Atlanta airport, I ran into one of the lead end-effector engineers at SPAR at the time of my decision. We reminisced for a few minutes and then he told me that he thought I made the wrong decision that night. That is so typical of how the Canadians operated. Here was the guy who had argued against us, now telling me that I should have forced them to change to a different end-effector!

If nothing else, the Canadians had a lot of pride and we had to be careful never to insult them. I recall several occasions when I would get a call from the head of NRCC saying that we were right in trying to get them to change or add something, but he wanted me to hear them out. "Let my engineers make their case, and then make whatever decision you think is right." At first, I thought this was a waste of time, but soon learned that it was necessary if you wanted to keep them happy. They didn't mind being overruled if you had given them their day in court.

– – –

On one trip to Canada in 1978, Linda and the kids drove with me. We were in our Cadillac Eldorado, which had front wheel drive. Near Akron, Ohio, the constant velocity unit on the front wheels went out so we had to spend an extra day there to get it fixed. We stayed at a very nice hotel which had an indoor heated pool that the kids loved. We then went to Lavonia, Michigan, to a Bricklin shop owned by Terry Tanner, who had been the Chief Engineer at the Bricklin factory before it closed. That's when I first saw the pneumatic door system that Terry had developed and was to be standard equipment on the 1976 Bricklins, which never made it to production. I purchased a kit to install the system on my car and Terry shipped it to Texas.

After that brief visit, we went to Niagara Falls, which was a first for all of us. What a beautiful place. We rode the boat which goes underneath the falls and still got wet even though they gave us raincoats. I think Mike and Kristi were more impressed with all the attractions in the town of Niagara Falls, such as a wax museum and Ripley's Believe It Or Not. That didn't make me too happy.

**Linda, Kristi and Mike at Niagara Falls**

In Niagara Falls we also went to the Bricklin convention, which was really exciting for me. They had over a hundred cars (only 2854 were made…mine was VIN # 2444) on display and I got to meet Malcolm Bricklin. He told me the story about when he was building a prototype of his Bricklin SV-1, John DeLorean, who at that time was head of the Pontiac Division of General Motors, would stop by at night and give him ideas on how to improve the car and make it easier to manufacture. I guess DeLorean also picked up some ideas from Bricklin, because a few years later he left General Motors and built his own gull-wing car, the DeLorean DMC-12, which gained prominence in the movie *Back to the Future*, but soon suffered the same fate as Bricklin…bankruptcy.

Once we arrived in Canada, I was busy with RMS meetings while Linda and the kids got in a little sightseeing. I went with them to the top of the newly completed CN tower in Toronto, the tallest free-standing structure in the world. After a couple of days in Toronto, we drove to Montreal, where I had more RMS meetings with the NRCC staff. For the return trip home, we drove down through Vermont and saw the most beautiful foliage I had ever seen. We visited the Von Trapp Family Lodge near Stowe, Vermont. It was a beautiful facility and I could just hear "The hills come alive with the sound of music." The manager of the gift shop told us that Maria was there, but she didn't come down until much later.

We then drove toward New York City. We stopped to eat at a Howard Johnson's restaurant near New Rochelle. That night we went to see the play Grease on Broadway. About halfway through the play, Kristi started throwing up on the floor of the theater. Linda left with her to go back to the hotel, while Mike and I saw the rest of the play. By the time we got to the hotel, Mike was also getting sick. During the night, Linda also got sick, and I wasn't feeling so well myself so I called the desk for a doctor to come to the room. He determined that we all had food poisoning from the bacon cheeseburgers we had all eaten at Howard Johnson's. He called them and told them to immediately shut down the kitchen and that he was calling the New York food inspectors to get there as quickly as they could. He wrote a prescription for us that I took to an all-night pharmacy to be filled. On the way there, I got really sick and threw up in a trash can on Times Square! The next day we all stayed in bed and ate nothing but saltine crackers. By the third day, we felt well enough to take a Gray Line tour of the city. That night we say Annie on Broadway. Sarah Jessica Parker, who was Kristi's age, played the part of Annie. We all thought it was wonderful. I don't think any of us have caten a bacon cheeseburger since!

The next day Bob and Colette Sheets called to tell us that our house had been broken into. Their son Chris was housesitting for us while we were away and was the one who discovered that we had been robbed. He did the right thing by then calling the police and waiting until they arrived. Other than our car breaking down, me working one day until 2:00 am the next morning, the entire family getting sick and our house being broken into, it was a great trip!

— — —

We finally were able to get a budget for the PDRSO that allowed us to bring Rockwell International on board to integrate all the payload fittings and the RMS onto the Orbiter. Sy Rubenstein and Bo Bejmuk were very helpful in making necessary changes both to the Orbiter and our equipment. One of the first things we discovered was that some things had to be moved on the Space Shuttle Orbiter longeron in order for the RMS to fit when the payload bay doors were closed. Both the RMS and the longerons were beefed up to handle the launch loads. We also realized that the same payload fittings we were putting on the Orbiter had to go into the Payload Ground Handling Mechanism (PGHM...pronounced Pig-em), a part of the Rotating Service Structure (RSS) which takes the payloads from their canisters at the launch pad and then installs them into the Orbiter. I feared that this would slow things down, but the Cape people were great to work with. They just said "Do what you need for on-orbit and we'll use the same here."

In 1978, Aaron Cohen called me to his office and asked if I could use Kenny Kleinknecht on some of the technical issues we were having with the RMS. Kenny had been Manager of the Mercury Project, Deputy Manager of the Gemini Project and Manager of the Skylab Program. He now was assigned to Aaron as Deputy of the Orbiter Program, and Aaron thought he might be able to help us. I quickly agreed. The next day Kenny came in my office and said he would be happy to do whatever I asked of him and he promised not to interfere. He became my de facto chief engineer and did a wonderful job. The Canadians were blown away by the fact that they were now dealing with such a famous NASA project manager and outstanding engineer.

The entire Orbiter payload deployment and retrieval system, especially the RMS, turned out to work magnificently. I am very proud of what we were able to accomplish in a very short time period and of the job that Clay did after I left.

— — —

One day in the fall of 1979, I was sitting in my office and in walked Glynn Lunney. He told me that he had been asked to go to NASA Headquarters as the Acting Associate Administrator for STS Operations. Since I had spent several years there, he wanted to know all about the area, how much houses cost, where the nice subdivisions were, etc. After a couple of hours, as he was leaving, he said "Oh, by the way, since I'm now going to Headquarters, you will be taking over my job here as head of STS Operations. I've already discussed it with Chris and he agrees that next week you'll be moving into that job." He said that his job in Washington was to get the program started and since he would be in an acting capacity, he would retain his title as Manager of the JSC office and I would have the title of Deputy Manager. I was shocked and not sure what to say. My first reaction was that I couldn't leave my current job, but then immediately thought "If Chris and Glynn want me to do that, then that's what I will do." The next day Chris asked to see me. His only question was "Who should take over your current job?" I was prepared to make a long pitch for Clay McCullough, but Chris just said, "I agree", so the conversation was over.

I was aware of what Glynn, Leonard Nicholson, Larry Williams and the others had been doing in the STS Operations Program Office. I had worked with them on Shuttle user charges and knew that their primary job was to integrate user payloads into the Shuttle system. They had developed a Payload Integration Plan (PIP), which outlined all the services the system could provide (power, gases, fittings, astronaut support, etc.) and the requirements which customers must meet (size, strength, safety, etc.) to fly on the Shuttle. I was shocked however, to see how the customers were reacting to the PIP. One of the first NASA customers was Galileo, a scientific probe designed to go to Jupiter propelled by a Centaur rocket. The Centaur was a potentially dangerous rocket fueled by liquid oxygen and liquid hydrogen. The fuel tanks were very lightweight and were only rigid when they were full of pressurized hydrogen and oxygen. Prior to propellant loading, they had to be pressurized with nitrogen. Andy Stofan, from the Headquarters Space Sciences Office, was our interface. At our first meeting, I asked if they had any questions about the PIP, which we had supplied them in advance. Stofan said that they had looked at it but didn't think they could meet it and we would just have to accept whatever they built and provide all the services they needed. Things went downhill from there. Efforts to make the Centaur and Shuttle compatible and safe continued for several years, but were terminated after the Challenger accident when everyone involved agreed it was just too risky to fly the Centaur on the Shuttle.

My first Department of Defense (DOD) payload was highly classified*, of course. The payload manager was Gen. Wesley Clark. When asked about the PIP, he threw his copy on the floor and said, "You just don't understand. We're not here to meet your requirements, you're here to meet ours. We don't like being forced to fly on the Shuttle, but we will and you must provide all the accommodations and services that we need." Things really went downhill from there. After several more unproductive meetings, Gen. Clark went to see Chris Kraft, the JSC Director, to complain. Chris asked him with whom he was working in our office. Clark told him Jerry Bostick and Leonard Nicholson. Then Chris said, "I see that you are a one-star General. I need to explain to you that Nicholson is a two-star, Bostick is a three-star, and I am a freaking four-star, so you had better get back down there and do what they tell you to do, or you won't be flying on my Space Shuttle!" After that, he did cooperate to an extent, but was still a real pain to work with. Unbelievably, Gen. Clark later became the Supreme Allied Commander of Europe for

NATO (North Atlantic Treaty Organization) and even ran for the Democrat Party Presidential nomination in 2003. He dropped out of the race after about five months. He did become a four-star General before retiring in 2000.

- *I was surprised to learn that I must get some even higher security clearances than what I already had. I filled out all the paperwork, which included a list of every doctor I had seen since birth. When Linda and I were having problems in the early '70s, I had agreed to see a marriage counselor, who was a psychiatrist. He turned out to be an absolute nut case in my opinion, but he was a medical doctor, so I had to include him on my list. Very shortly after turning in my paperwork, I got a visit from the agent checking out my clearance application. He wanted to know all the details of why I was seeing a psychiatrist. I guess I convinced him that I was only seeing the doctor for marriage counseling and that I was not having mental problems. I got the necessary clearances.*

Gen. Clark's DOD payload did eventually fly on the Shuttle, but with a different manager. In contrast, at about the same time we were having so much trouble with those payloads, we worked very well with Jesse Moore of NASA and with other DOD managers, such as Gen. Neil Beer. Both of them were a dream to work with.

– – –

Our neighbor in Clear Lake Forest was Lee Swope, who owned several restaurants in Clear Lake and Pasadena. One afternoon I was working in the front yard and Lee came over to talk. He told me that on their last trip to London they had met a nice couple who now planned to come visit them. He said that he and his wife, Coleen, wanted to show them a good "Texas" time and asked if I had any suggestions beyond the Astrodome and the San Jacinto Monument. I suggested that if the couple cared about country music at all, they should take them to Gilley's. The very popular movie Urban Cowboy had just been released a few weeks before and Gilley's, where a lot of it was filmed, had become very popular. (I thought all the new attention had ruined it. I liked it a lot better before all the tourists showed up.) Lee said, "Really? That's probably a good idea. I know Mickey Gilley, so I will call him and make reservations." I went in the house and laughed to Linda that Lee was going to "make reservations at Gilley's." They don't take reservations! The next day, Lee came over and said that he had spoken with Mickey Gilley and had made reservations for six people, hoping that we would go with them because we had been there before and they had not. Lee had served free meals to Gilley at one of his Pasadena restaurants several times, so they really did know each other. I still wasn't sure about the reservations until we showed up and sure enough, they was a table set up for six people, roses, white table cloth and all, on the dance floor right in front of the stage. Gilley was the featured performer that night and at the first break, he came and sat with us. His piano playing ability came up and he said that he didn't think he was as good as two of his cousins, Jerry Lee Lewis and Jimmy Swaggart. He explained how he and those two cousins grew up together in Louisiana and all played the piano very much the same way. I had never heard of Swaggart. Gilley told me that he was a Pentecostal preacher who sang and played the piano, and that he was on TV every Sunday morning at 6:30. The next Sunday I got up to watch, and sure enough, he probably was a better piano player than Gilley.

— — —

In addition to integrating payloads onto the Shuttle, the STS Operations Office controlled the budget for operation of the Shuttle. This was not one of my favorite activities because all the operators wanted more money than what we had, so all the requestors left our budget meetings unhappy. George Abbey, then Director of Flight Operations, usually came to the meetings with no prepared charts, just some hand written notes, which we accused him of writing as he came down the stairwell to the meeting. He always started out with a plea for money to replace the T-38 training aircraft that the astronauts used. He said they were outdated and cost too much to maintain. He wanted to replace them with F/A- 18 Hornets like the Blue Angels used. He never got the money. In fact, when I was chairing the meetings, I told George just to skip the T-38 part and get on with his presentation of other items. He liked me even less after these meetings. I find it interesting that 30 years later the astronauts are still using the T-38s.

Astronaut John Young, already in training as Commander of the first Shuttle flight, was always asking for money to buy another Shuttle Training Aircraft (STA). The STA was a Grumman Gulfstream-II modified to simulate the Shuttle Orbiter approach and landing. The Orbiter, having no air-breathing engines, lands like a glider with no "go around" capability. Some astronauts have likened it to a "falling brick." If you miss the first landing attempt, you don't get another. To approximate the Orbiter drag profile and descent rate, the instructor pilot deployed the STA's main landing gear and reversed the thrust on the two engines at about 40,000 feet. Then the astronaut would take over and complete the approach. The left-hand side of the cockpit had the same controls as the Orbiter, while the right seat had regular Gulfstream controls. Each Commander and Pilot assigned to Shuttle flights had to complete 1,000 STA training runs before their flight. John was enthusiastic about the STA as a training vehicle and was afraid that one of the only two we had at that time would be damaged, setting the program back.

To convince me on the value of the STA, John invited me to ride with him and instructor pilot Ted Mendenhall for a day of training at the White Sands Shuttle Landing Facility in New Mexico. I was excited about the opportunity to ride in the STA and to also see the Missile Range where I had fired Nike missiles during my Artillery training there in 1962. Ted was a personal friend, so that made it even better.

For the training runs, John was in the left cockpit seat and Ted in the right seat. I rode in a jump seat between, but slightly behind, them. I was listed on the manifest as "Flight Engineer" because "Observer" didn't sound professional. Our first run started at about 43,000 feet altitude, where Ted took his hands off the controls and said, "Okay John, it's yours." I knew, intellectually, how steep the approach was, about 23 degrees, but was totally unprepared to actually experience it. It appeared that we were going straight down! All I could see was desert below! We continued this dive until about 1,700 feet, when John started a flare maneuver to prepare for the simulated landing. At this point, we were pulling about 1.8 gs. John deployed the nose gear at about 150 feet, just in case of an unplanned touchdown. At 20 feet altitude, which approximated what the pilot would see at Orbiter touchdown, Ted turned off the simulation mode and took control, flying back up for another training run. For the remainder of the approaches, he would climb to between 25,000 and 30,000 feet before handing over to John. We did a total of 10 approaches.

**Shuttle Training Aircraft during approach at White Sands**
**Courtesy NASA**

My view from the STA cockpit

Our STA (NASA 947) on runway at White Sands

Those runs convinced me that we needed to scrape up enough money in the budget to buy another one. We eventually bought two more for a total fleet of four.

Incidentally, the Third Shuttle flight, STS-3, landed at the same White Sands facility because the planned landing site at Edwards Air Force Base, California had flooded due to excessive rain and the flight crew had not trained to land at the new KSC Shuttle Landing

Facility. It took us months to get all the sand out of the Orbiter and we avoided ever landing at White Sands again.

— — —

On March 30, 1981, I was in a meeting in the Executive Conference Room on the 9th Floor of Building 1 when we got word that President Reagan had been shot. We stopped the meeting and turned on the TV to find out what was happening. It initially looked very bad and we were all sad. After a few minutes, we canceled the meeting and went back to our offices. For me it brought back memories of November 22, 1963, when President Kennedy was shot. Fortunately, it turned out a lot better this time.

— — —

The first orbital flight of the Shuttle occurred in April 1981, with John Young as the Commander, and Bob Crippen as the Pilot. This was the first time we had ever flown a new spacecraft system with a crew onboard for the maiden flight. Once clear of the launch tower, I was shocked to see how quickly the entire configuration rolled to the intended azimuth. It actually rolled no faster than previous launch vehicles, but the unsymmetrical configuration made it look very different. The two-day flight went very well, but with a few anomalies. Once on orbit, the crew noted several thermal tiles were missing from the Orbital Maneuvering System pod and some tiles on the nose looked damaged. High-resolution photographs taken from a classified Air Force tracking site in Hawaii also showed a few tiles missing from the bottom of the Orbiter. These photographs were so detailed that you could read the serial numbers on each of the tiles. It was concluded that despite the damaged and missing tiles, the Orbiter should make it through reentry with no problem.

After that first flight, Bob Thompson, who had been the Space Shuttle Program Manager for over a decade, left NASA and Glynn Lunney took over as Program Manager. One of the first things Glynn did as Program Manager was to question why the external tank was painted white. On STS-1 Crippen had observed paint flecks coming off the tank and sticking to the Orbiter windows. Turns out that there was no technical reason for painting the tanks, so he ordered that they not be painted in the future, saving over 600 pounds. It was a "no brainer." It is rare that changes can be made to save both money and weight. The tank for STS-2 had already been painted, so beginning with the third flight, all external tanks were left the natural orange color of the insulation.

The STS Operations Office stayed in place for about another year with me as the Acting Manager. Just prior to STS-3 the two offices were consolidated and I became the Shuttle Program Deputy Manager for Operations. After only being there for a few days, Glynn asked that I do a radio interview for him. He said that he had agreed to do it, but now had to be at the Cape, so would I do it for him? Of course, I said "No problem." It turned out to be a problem however. The interview was live from 11:00 p.m. to 12:30 a.m. Houston time, with someone named Larry King from Atlanta. I had never heard of him but of course, he went on to be a very famous TV host on Cable News Network. A staff person called me the day before and said they wanted me to talk about why the Space Shuttle was such a good deal for America. They would call me on my home phone number. So, I set up shop on our breakfast room table and waited for them to call. When we got on the air, King introduced me and then also introduced Vladimir Pozner, a space commentator on Soviet radio and television. King started out by saying something like "Mr. Bostick will tell us later why the Space Shuttle is such a wonderful machine, but first, Mr. Pozner, what do you think of the Shuttle?" Pozner then ranted for about five minutes about how the Shuttle was a "war machine" designed primarily to deliver bombs to drop on the

Soviet Union. So for the next hour and a half, we debated the purpose of the Shuttle. I think I held my own, but it came as a total shock that Pozner was going to be on with me and that he would argue that the Shuttle's only purpose was to be a "space bomber." We were planning to fly Department of Defense payloads, but none of them came close to being "bombs."

The night of the STS-2 landing, Chris invited a bunch of us to go with him to his favorite local place to eat, Ella's in Alta Loma. We took the JSC bus and planned to be back at Ellington to officially greet the flight crew, Joe Engle and Dick Truly when they landed there on the Gulfstream. They had a tailwind from Edwards to Ellington and we were a few minutes behind our schedule, so they landed at Ellington, taxied to the far end of the runway, turned their lights off and waited for their "official" welcome group. The public and news people were wondering what was going on. Finally, we arrived, about 10 minutes later, and got on the reviewing stand to welcome the crew home. How embarrassing!

We continued to implement the DOD security requirements. We spent about $35 Million on facilities at JSC with the only visible elements being the large flowerpots in front of the control center entrance (to keep vehicles from being driven through the doors) and the security gates inside the lobby at the first floor entrance. Most of the money went into electronic security, which was all hidden in the walls of the building. The DOD insisted that we develop the capability to electronically transfer flight software from the Software Production Facility (SPF) in the office wing of Building 30, where it was developed, to the Real Time Computer Complex in the control center wing. They gave us money to filter the line for their flights so that the flight software could not be tapped into. After several months of trying to find a filter that would meet their requirements, I called General Neil Beer to tell him that we could not meet their requirements. I told him that the best filter we could find still fell short of what they were asking for. His reply was that he wasn't surprised, because they also could not find one that would meet their requirements and we should just install the best one we could find. I made a final plea to just allow us to walk the flight software tapes from the SPF to the RTCC, which we did for non-DOD flights, but he said no, we had to implement the electronic transfer.

Other "invisible" requirements which we implemented were to replace the glass in the windows of my, Glynn's and Dr. Kraft's offices. To show that this was necessary, with my permission, the DOD had set up an eavesdropping system in a hotel across the road from JSC and recorded conversations just by aiming a listening device at the windows of my office. We also built a secure "vault" in which we could discuss Top Secret information and store documents. Initially, the DOD said that Dr. Kraft could not have access to the vault, but he explained to them that it was his Center and he would not allow the construction of any room to which he would not be allowed. His name was added to the access list.

One of the big disagreements with the DOD was over who would operate their payloads in orbit. They insisted that it must be one of their people and we insisted that a NASA astronaut could be trained to operate the payload a lot easier, and less costly, than training a military person to fly on the Shuttle. In reality, there usually was not much to do with the payloads to activate them. The launching from the Shuttle was much more involved and there was no way we would ever let a non-NASA specialist do that. It seemed crazy to us to put a military person through training just to have him/her turn the payload on. Once it was deployed from the Shuttle and we had separated to a safe distance, all other necessary functions could be performed by the military from their ground control centers.

The same argument applied to civilian payloads, but in some cases flying a non-NASA Payload Specialist made sense. This applied to the Spacelab, which was co-sponsored by the European Space Agency (ESA), and stayed inside the payload bay where unique international scientific experiments and observations were made. We flew the first two Payload Specialists on STS-9, the first Spacelab flight, and it worked out well. For commercial payloads, especially those that would stay attached to the Shuttle, a non-NASA Payload Specialists also made sense. Our first experience with this was the Continuous Flow Electrophoresis System (CFES), which was developed by McDonnell Douglas Corporation. One of the patent holders on the system was one of their young engineers, Charlie Walker. He obviously knew more about the system than we could ever teach an astronaut, so we had no argument with Charlie flying along to operate it. McDonnell Douglas and NASA could not agree initially on the cost for flying Charlie, so the CFES flew on STS-4 without him. That flight demonstrated how difficult it was to operate the experiment by relaying instructions from the ground (Charlie wasn't allowed to speak directly to the flight crew), so McDonnell Douglas and NASA finally agreed to fly him on STS-41-D, the 12th Shuttle flight. So he became the first non-government person to fly in space. That worked so well that Charlie flew twice more with the experiment on STS-51-D and STS-61-B.

We eventually lost the argument about military Payload Specialists, and Gary Payton flew on STS-51-C, the 15th Shuttle flight in January 1985. The payload, still highly classified, was deployed on an Inertial Upper Stage (IUS), which sent it to a geosynchronous orbit.

This dispute about flying non-NASA astronauts also involved civilians who, in my opinion, had no real purpose in flying. The first such civilian who pushed hard to fly was Senator Jake Garn, who was Chairman of the Senate NASA appropriations subcommittee. NASA management apparently was afraid to tell him no, so he was assigned to fly. On his flight, STS-51-D in April 1985, he became so sick during the flight that a new scale for space sickness was developed, the "Garn Scale", where "one Garn" is the highest possible level of sickness. Next was Congressman Bill Nelson, who held a similar position in the House of Representatives, who flew on STS-61-C about a year later. I thought that both were mistakes and that we probably had made Shuttle flight look too easy. I knew that it was risky and no place for "observers." However, flying them worked to some extent because both Garn and Nelson became even stronger advocates for the Shuttle program and did everything they could to keep the money flowing.

Trying to gain more public support for the Shuttle program, NASA decided to sponsor a Teacher in Space Program. The first one chosen was Christa McAuliffe, a social studies teacher in New Hampshire. She was assigned to STS-51-L, which exploded during the launch phase on January 28, 1986. That was only 10 days after Congressman Bill Nelson's flight landed. I'll have more to say about the "Challenger Accident" later.

My argument against flying any such civilians switched to "If we're going to fly civilians, why not fly someone like John Denver who can probably describe the experience better than anyone?" Gerry Griffin, a friend of Denver, actually contacted him to determine his interest, which was "Hell yes, I want to fly!" Gerry and I pursued getting him assigned until it soon became obvious that NASA management wasn't interested.

— — —

In October, 1981 I went on an AIAA sponsored speaking tour of Europe to promote the Space Shuttle. I was allowed to take Linda with me. We went to Munich, London and Paris. In Munich, we stayed at the Hilton International hotel on the English Garden. It was a great hotel with an even greater view. We visited the 1972 Olympic site where the sporting events were overshadowed by what became known as the Munich massacre. Eight Palestinians took eleven Israeli athletes and coaches hostage and eventually killed all of them plus one West German police officer. Five of the Palestinians were subsequently killed and the other three captured. The only positive thing which I saw there was the swimming pool where United States swimmer Mark Spitz won seven gold medals. Not only was that a record number of gold medals in a single Olympics, but he set new world records in each of the seven events.

On the advice of Gil and Ev Guster, we went to Dallmayr's delicatessen and got a ton of stuff for a picnic. The Gusters were right, it was the most fabulous delicatessen I have ever seen. Also on their advice, we saw the Glockenspiel on the Marienplatz (main plaza). It is a fantastic clock that puts on a great show at noon each day. We enjoyed the beer and sausage at the Hofbräuhaus. The servers walked around with five mugs of beer in each hand. The entire city was immaculately clean and the subway system was wonderful. Overall, we liked Munich a lot.

Before going on to London, Linda and I rode a train to Salzburg, Austria where one of my favorite movies, *The Sound of Music*, was filmed. We quickly learned that it was definitely not the favorite of the citizens there, because they thought it distorted Austrian history and culture. I wanted to walk around singing "The hills are alive with the sound of music", but refrained for fear of being run out of town. We visited many of the sites where the film was made; the Salzburg Festival Hall; the Nunnery where Maria von Trapp lived; and the Hohensalzburg Castle, which required riding a cable car, but didn't go to the place outside of town that was shown in the movie as the von Trapp home. The locals said it was a movie set and the von Trapps never lived there.

We visited the Cathedral of Salzburg, which was absolutely beautiful. A United States bomb hit the dome during World War II causing severe damage, but it had all been reconstructed. I silently said, "I'm sorry, but we knew Hitler's troops were hiding here." Salzburg was a beautiful town with flowers everywhere. We also visited Mozart's birthplace (they actually sell Mozart chocolate bars there) and a fine restaurant for lunch on a mountaintop overlooking the entire city, Restaurant Getreidegasse. We entered a large cave at the base of the mountain where we caught an elevator up to the restaurant. The view of Salzburg from there was fantastic in all directions and the food was very good. Years later, I was watching a show on the History Channel about Adolf Hitler, and there he was standing on the porch of the same restaurant! It turns out that the cave we walked through was one of the places where Hitler hid his tanks and artillery during World War II, and he visited there frequently. What was once one of his many hideouts was now a fine restaurant.

Then it was on to London for my second speech. It was nice to be among English speaking people again and I enjoyed much of what we saw; Tower of London, Westminster Abby, Buckingham Palace, Big Ben, etc., but it was cold and rainy and not my favorite place. We attended church at Westminster Abbey on Sunday. One of my favorite sites was a statue of Winston Churchill smoking a large cigar. We walked down Downing Street to number 10, the home of the British Prime Minister. There was a single guard at the door. Now, you can't even walk down Downing Street. The food in London was so-so. We ate at Samuel Pepys and Simpson's In-The-Strand. Both were good, but not as good as I wished. My favorite food in London was fish and chips with Muscadet wine. I'm pretty easy to please. We saw two great plays there; *Evita* and *Barnum*.

Our final stop was Paris. I had not been there since 1977 and was anxious for Linda to enjoy it as much as I had. We stayed at the same hotel in which I stayed on my first trip, The Hotel MacMahon. I made the mistake of assuming that she would enjoy walking around the city as much as I did. I tried to replicate all the experiences from my previous visit. At least she got to see the Louvre before they built the pyramid entrance in the main court. I think it is one of the ugliest things I've ever seen and is totally out of place. By the second day, she was ready to leave, saying, "I don't get it." I hopefully learned to not oversell things and places which I like, but with Paris, that's hard for me to do.

By the way, my presentations in all three cities went well. Of course, I was "preaching to the choir" because most of the attendees were somehow connected to the European aerospace industry and already were big Space Shuttle fans.

— — —

For the launch of the fourth Space Shuttle flight (STS-4) in June 1982, I got tickets for Mother, Daddy and sister Mary to sit in the VIP viewing stand at the Cape. I think they were really impressed. I was able to see them for a few minutes the night before the launch at their hotel and again the next morning after the launch. As a souvenir, I got a picture of the launch signed by the crew, Hank Hartsfield and T. K. Mattingly with a note from T. K.; "Hope you enjoyed the launch as much as we did."

— — —

In the summer of 1982, I took Kristi to a Spinners concert in the Hofheinz Pavilion at the University of Houston. They were an R&B/Soul group with a big hit, *Rubberband Man*. I probably liked them more than Kristi. Hofheinz Pavilion is a basketball arena and is structured so that when you enter at street level, the court and surrounding seats are below you. I had been there several times to see either the Houston Cougars or the Rockets play basketball. I immediately noticed that there was a haze over the entire seating area and wondered if the place was on fire. Kristi said, "No Dad, it's marijuana smoke." I was never sure how she knew what marijuana smelled like, but I didn't press the issue. We enjoyed the concert anyway and I thought it was a great father/daughter outing.

— — —

While serving as Deputy Manager for Operations of the Space Shuttle program, the Air Force was still trying to figure out how they could control their own flights. The Shuttle launch pad at Vandenberg Air Force Base was under construction and they were planning for their first launch in 1986. In late 1982, the Space Command was formed and some within the Air Force wanted to build their own Shuttle mission control center at Peterson Air Force Base in Colorado Springs. General James Hartinger, Commander in Chief of the North American Aerospace Defense Command (NORAD), was named to also serve as the Commander of Space Command. Of course, we at NASA did not want them to have their own control center. We felt we were the only ones with the experience and expertise to safely control the flights.

I paid Hartinger a visit shortly thereafter to discuss what they planned to do, what the Shuttle control facility would need capability wise, and to hopefully talk them out of their own control center. They put me up in the Officer's Quarters at Peterson and treated me like royalty. They even had a big sign up at the main gate welcoming me. Jim gave me a great tour of the NORAD complex in Cheyenne Mountain. As a Flight Dynamics Officer, I had done a lot of coordinating with NORAD over the past years, but had never been to their highly classified facility. It was something to behold! From the outside, it just looks like a tunnel drilled into the mountain, but inside there are at least a dozen buildings, all separated from the surrounding granite and from each other by springs and flexible connections. It is about 5 acres in area and was designed to withstand a 30-megaton nuclear blast. The blast doors inside were the most massive doors I had ever seen, weighing about 25 tons each. In addition to the main NORAD control room, where they track aircraft and space vehicles, they have a cafeteria, a gymnasium, sleeping quarters, food and water storage, a barbershop, and medical facilities staffed with doctors, dentists and nurses. I was impressed and comforted to see the capability they had to protect the US and Canada from attack. However, I was not convinced that the expertise they had at NORAD would translate to a similar expertise in controlling Shuttle flights.

We came to no great decisions about their Shuttle facility at Peterson, but I left thinking that Jim Hartinger was a great guy with whom we could easily work. I also felt that after hearing the details of what it would cost and the talent they would have to develop, his enthusiasm for their own facility was waning. It helped greatly that AF Col. Larry Griffin, twin brother of Gerry, was assigned by Hartinger as the liaison between Space Command and NASA.

Preparations were still underway at Vandenberg when the Challenger accident grounded the entire Shuttle fleet. Shortly thereafter, the decision was made to cancel all west coast launches and the AF dropped the idea of having a control center in Colorado Springs.

— — —

Between the first and second Shuttle flights in 1981, Jim Beggs became the NASA Administrator with former Ames Research Center Director, Hans Mark as the Deputy Administrator. We knew little about Beggs, who came from Westinghouse Electric, but were very familiar with Mark, who was not considered a strong supporter of human space flight. It was obvious upon their coming into office that they did not agree on much of anything with our Center Director, Chris Kraft. Chris had been talking about maybe retiring for a couple of years and finally announced it in April 1982. It was generally accepted at the center that when he did retire, Glynn

Lunney would become his replacement. Beggs and Mark were dead set on not filling the job with anyone supported by Chris, so we all wondered, with some dread, who would be named. A few months later, to our pleasant surprise, Gerry Griffin was announced as the new Center Director. Most of the employees felt very much the same as we had when Jack Schmitt replaced Joe Engle on Apollo 17. We all liked Joe and felt very sorry for him but were happy that Jack was going to get to fly. Glynn was most everyone's first choice to replace Chris, but if Beggs and Mark wouldn't allow that to happen, Gerry was an excellent choice. I was particularly frustrated because Glynn and Gerry were two of my closest friends and while I was extremely happy for Gerry, I felt sad for Glynn.

One of Gerry's priorities upon becoming Director was to reorganize so that not so many people would be reporting directly to him. In April 1983, he consolidated several Directorates into three super-directorates. In the flight operations world, he made Cliff Charlesworth Director of Space Operations, with three Directors reporting to him; one for Mission Operations, one for Flight Crew Operations and one for Mission Support. Gene Kranz was named Director, Mission Operations, George Abbey, Director, Flight Crew Operations, and I was named Director, Mission Support. I would be responsible for development, implementation, configuration management, operation, and maintenance of the Mission Control Center, flight software, ground and flight crew training systems, vehicle and procedures development, simulation systems, and mission planning activities. I would also be responsible for development and coordination of space flight tracking and data network instrumentation requirements, providing JSC institutional computational support, and for acquisition of all automatic data processing equipment.

This was a huge promotion for me, not in dollars, but in prestige. I would have five Divisions reporting to me; Spacecraft Software, Mission Planning and Analysis, Ground Data Systems, Flight

Simulation, and Institutional Data Systems. I had about 4500 civil service and contractor personnel answering to me and an average annual budget of $350 million. To top it off, I would have the northeast corner office on the top floor of Building 1 at JSC, originally occupied by Chris Kraft. Who would ever have believed that the kid from Golden would occupy that office? There was still a dent in one of the ceiling tiles made by a champagne cork popped by Chris and George Low after the Apollo 11 landing. It was the first drink of alcohol that Low had since becoming the Apollo Program Manager. The facilities people remodeled the office for me but I told them not to replace that tile. It was a daily reminder of how far we had come.

It also was a Senior Executive Service (SES) position, which for most people was a real big deal. There were only 435 SES positions within NASA, which was about 2% of the total Civil Service workforce, so I guess it was kind of a big deal.

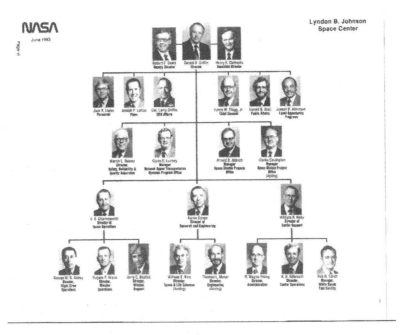

**JSC Organization under Director Gerry Griffin**
**Courtesy NASA**

Lyn Dunseith, who had been the Director of Data Systems and Analysis (essentially what I was taking over) and would now be Deputy to Cliff, came to give me a short hand-over briefing on my first day. Literally, on his way out the door, he said, "Oh, by the way, if I was staying in this job, I probably would abolish the Institutional Data Systems Division. It was formed originally to provide computing services for the entire center, but now everybody wants to do their own thing. Maybe we should just treat computers like pencils and paper and let everybody buy their own." This came as a big shock to me, so I told him I would consider that.

— — —

One of the first things that I had to do was get ready for a visit from Vice President George H. W. Bush. He was from Houston and a strong NASA supporter, so we wanted to give him a good tour. STS-6 was to be in orbit during his visit. The walkway to the SMS was covered with cables so we asked Singer/Link, the SMS contractor, to install them beneath the wooden walkway, where they were supposed to be. The night before Bush was scheduled to arrive, nothing had been done, so Bob Ernull and I spent a couple of hours correcting the problem. It was bad enough to ask the astronauts to walk carefully and not step on cables, but I wasn't about to ask the Vice President. Later the Singer-Link union filed a complaint against us, but dropped it when it became clear they had dropped the ball and had no valid complaint.

The Secret Service had requested that the VP be escorted into MCC from the side loading dock rather than the main entrance, so Gerry Griffin and I were there to meet Bush and Administrator Beggs. As we walked down the corridor toward the MOCR, Bush turned to me and said, "Just like all the places I visit." I said, "Excuse me?" to which he replied, "Fresh paint!" Indeed, we had repainted the day before.

**VP Bush, Administrator Beggs and JSC Director Griffin in MCC**
**Courtesy NASA**

— — —

On STS-6 as Mission Specialist was astronaut Don Peterson, from Winona, Mississippi. Don was appointed to West Point by Congressman Tom Abernethy, so we came up with a plan for Don to fly a Mississippi flag on the flight which we would later present to him. After the flight we had the flag framed with each of our pictures and a message of thanks for all that he had done for us. Years later I asked his son Tommy what the Congressman thought of what we had presented to him. He said it was his dad's prized possession. He hung it over the fireplace in their Jackson home and he would point it out to all visitors saying, "These are my boys." Tommy said that he always muttered to himself, "I thought I was your boy."

— — —

Management wise, one of the first things I did as Director was to ask my five division chiefs for a "will." They all wanted to know if I planned on killing them, but I explained that we all needed to have someone in mind to take over in case we got run over by a truck. If they didn't, then we needed to start developing someone. This began to pay off when I selected Bob Ernull, the previous Chief of the Flight Simulation Division, to be my Deputy. Bob had prepared Phil Barnes to take over the division and the transition went very smoothly.

I had never enjoyed "appraisal" time for the people who reported directly to me. They were usually contentious and resulted in some bad feelings. To solve this problem, I asked each of the division chiefs to write down what they thought their jobs were and what their goals for the upcoming year should be. How many software drops, how many upgrades to systems, etc. When they came back with their job descriptions and goals, it was enlightening to see how much difference there was between what they and I thought their job was. Once we agreed on the goals, they became the basis for their performance appraisal. The Personnel office was not initially too excited about this approach. There were standard government approved job descriptions and appraisal forms, which they insisted that I use. I finally convinced them to let me try it. We had mid-year reviews, which sometimes led to slight alterations of the goals, but overall, the plan worked great. There could not be much argument over mutually agreed performance standards.

Another change I made was to develop a standard format for presentations. Some of the divisions (MPAD was by far the worst) would come in with view graphs (transparencies projected onto a screen) that looked very much like this page. The font size was 12, which made it almost unreadable if you were a few feet away. Also, there usually was no conclusion. They just put up a page of unreadable information which conveyed some message, but no conclusion. The new format specified a landscape layout with a minimum font size of 36, and a heading on the top of each page stating the desired conclusion, such as FLIGHT SOFTWARE DEVELOPMENT IS ON SCHEDULE FOR STS-6. That was something I had learned from Glynn Lunney—"Always tell the audience what you would like for them to conclude. Don't just throw up a bunch of data and let the audience draw their own conclusion."

John Aaron, Chief of the Flight Software Division, had been developing a Flight Load Preparation System (FLPS...pronounced Flips), to track the various flight software loads they had to develop and to automate the delivery of these loads to the various users: MCC, SMS, MPAD and the flight vehicle. With the help of IBM, we adopted this system in the directorate office for our weekly staff meetings. Since it was a computerized projection system, it solved many of the presentation problems we had in the past. More importantly, it brought to light the inter-dependencies of the five separate divisions. They soon learned that their successes were dependent on the success of the directorate as a whole.

We also developed a new Directorate logo, which would go on each document we produced as well as on each presentation page.

**MISSION SUPPORT DIRECTORATE LOGO**

We also did away with weekly Activity Reports from each of the divisions to the directorate office. They typically ran on and on for 4-5 pages and included such items as: Joe Blow attended a meeting at MSFC. My reaction was, "Great. What was accomplished at the meeting?" I wanted to only be informed of important items, so we changed the name to weekly Progress/Problem Reports and limited them to one page. I wanted to know what progress was being made to meet our goals, and if the Division Chiefs were having trouble meeting those goals (and thought that I could help) they should let me know. I didn't like last minute surprises. Everyone seemed to like the new approach and it certainly improved the communication of important information.

– – –

I began vigorously perusing the question Lyn had raised about how the center should manage our computer resources. I told Gerry Griffin about Lyn's recommendation, but told him I needed a few months to look into it. He agreed. The first thing I did was ask our major contractors, IBM, Univac, and Ford Aerospace, the question: "How should an organization the size of JSC manage its computing resources? Should we continue to have centralized control or just let everyone go do their own thing?" They all said that was a good question and they would be back in a couple of weeks with an answer. One by one, they came back and said they didn't have a good answer because their own companies had varying experiences. IBM, for example, let each of their major centers around the world do their own thing, but it turned out to be very expensive and resulted in major incompatibility around the globe. The Boeing Company marketing representative at JSC heard about my question and said I should visit their facility in Seattle to see what they were doing. They had formed the Boeing Computer Services Company, which funded and controlled computer resources throughout the Boeing Company. With doubts, Bob Ernull and I agreed to pay them a visit.

They completely understood my question and concluded, based on their own experience, that we should maintain centralized control. When we reported this back to Gerry Griffin, he completely agreed.

After the first year of enforcing this policy, Bob suggested a brilliant change to the system. We had tried to adequately budget for all the computer requirements around the center, but we always ended up with a stack of money one foot high and requirements from the end users two feet high. Each organization would come to us with their requirements and leave unhappy because we didn't have the money necessary to fund what they wanted. Bob suggested that the center policy should be that each organization would ask for and defend their own computing budgets, then once they were approved, the money would come to us for implementation. We took that idea to Griffin and he too saw the brilliance of the concept. Once that was in place, there were no more arguments. If an organization did not have an approved budget for what they wanted, then they didn't get it.

We had realized that once NASA Headquarters saw what we were doing, they would get the idea to apply it agency wide. Gerry appointed his Deputy, Bob Goetz, to work with us and try to establish JSC as the lead NASA center for computational support. One of the first things we did was get approval, along with dollars, to build a new building to house all the computers we thought would be heading our way, Building 46. Just about the time the building was completed, MSFC pulled an end run on us and convinced Headquarters that they should be the lead center and that they could do the job less expensively. As usual, MSFC would do anything as long as they were named the lead center.

In the early part of our search for an answer to the computer management question, Ernull and I traveled to Univac, just outside the Minneapolis/St. Paul, Minnesota area. That trip was only notable because Bob's luggage was lost. Univac picked us up in a limo and

Bob asked the driver if he would stop at a Target or Walmart so that he could buy some toiletries and underwear. The driver pulled right up to the door of a Target store and stayed parked there while Bob went inside. The windows in the limo were dark so that people couldn't see inside, but you could clearly see outside. After a few minutes, a crowd gathered around wondering who the "celebrity" was. When Bob came out they were all disappointed because no one knew who he was. It turned out to be a wasted trip because Univac didn't have any answers to our question. They just wanted to sell computers, caring nothing about how they would be managed.

I'm sure partly due to their embarrassment in not being able to answer my computer management question, IBM invited me and Ernull, with our spouses, to go to a conference in San Francisco where they said the subject would be discussed. So, Bob, his wife Judy, Linda and I went on a nice little vacation. The conference barely mentioned our computer management question, but did give us insight into what new products IBM was planning. We rode the cable cars, ate wonderful Chinese and seafood and had drinks at the Top of the Mark, a bar atop the Mark Hopkins hotel. After San Francisco we went to the Napa Valley, a first for all of us. We toured at least a dozen wineries and had an absolutely wonderful meal at Auberge du Soleil. We were there at sunset and looked down on the valley, a fantastic view. When they delivered the food, the presentation was so good that I didn't want to disturb it! It tasted even better than it looked. The restaurant became one of my favorites and I have returned there several times and have recommended it to lots of people. Recently, however, I learned that it is owned by Nancy Pelosi's husband, so I refuse to go back.

— — —

On July 3, 1983, Dan and Grace Germany hosted a luau in their back yard in Nassau Bay. Bob Crippen supplied the pigs (he raised them at his mother's farm in Tomball), Ellison Onizuka supplied the lava rocks and palm leaves. He said he got them from Hawaii, but I couldn't figure out how he did that. I found out later that he, Gerry and Kirk Griffin and Dan Germany had "borrowed" the rocks from the border of the duck pond behind Building 1 at JSC. They were initially brought from Hawaii and used on a back lot at JSC for lunar landscape training during Apollo. We all pitched in to dig the pit. We got the first hole about a foot deep and ran into a natural gas line, so we had to move over several feet and start again. It was an involved process and we all had plenty of time to consume beer. Once the pigs were roasted, it had to be the best meat I had ever eaten.

**LUAU AT GERMANY'S HOUSE**
**Me, Judy Resnik, Gerry Griffin & Ron McNair**

**Bob Crippen and the pigs**

— — —

Just prior to the launch of STS-8, Hurricane Alicia formed in the Gulf of Mexico and made landfall at Galveston on August 18, 1983, as a category 3 hurricane with winds about 115 miles per hour. We had had hurricane warnings in the past, but this one was for real. Kristi was baby sitting in Clear Lake City, so we were obviously worried about her. Mike was safely in San Antonio at Trinity. I stayed up all night watching trees fall all around our house. Thankfully, none made a direct hit. Electricity and phones went out soon after the high winds reached us. When the eye of the storm came over, everyone gathered in the street for a few minutes but soon went back inside to wait for the backside to hit. It seemed ever stronger than what we had experienced already. Roof shingles and fences were flying everywhere. The cul-de-sac in front of our house was filled with debris and fallen trees. Again, we were very lucky that none of the trees fell on our house.

Daylight brought an ugly sight. It was the most devastation I had ever seen. Some people started trying to clean up immediately, but my priority was to get Kristi home safely. Amazingly, the phones came back up, so we made arrangements for her to meet me at the Hilton Hotel, where the parking lot was dry. NASA Road 1 was still flooded between the hotel and Clear Lake Park, so I waded in waist deep water to get to the hotel, then brought her back in my arms. Twice while we were wading back, I saw snakes swimming not too far away. To divert Kristi's attention I pointed out boats and other debris that had floated up on the road. I was scared to death of the snakes, but I don't think Kristi ever saw them.

**NASA Road 1 after water subsided. Hilton Hotel in background.**

We made it home fine. Streets in Clear Lake Forest were still blocked with fallen trees and we couldn't drive anywhere for about three days. A man about a block away from us had gotten his sailboat out of the marina and parked it in his front yard. Unfortunately, a tree fell on it, almost cutting it in half. We had stocked up with canned goods in anticipation of the electricity going out, but didn't expect it to be out for a week! We got tired of Vienna sausage and pork and beans fairly quickly! What we had not anticipated, and couldn't have done anything about even if we had, was the lack of ice. I had never realized how dependent we are on ice. After 3-4 days, word begin to spread in the neighborhood that there would be a truckload of free ice the next day at the Safeway on the corner of Kirby Road and NASA Road 1. Hundreds of people showed up. I saw grown men actually fighting over a bag of ice. Everyone else had obviously missed it as much as we had. I was able to get two bags (without having to fight anyone).

By now, I had accessed the damage to our property. The roof and our cedar fence had to be replaced, but that was about it. I contacted our insurance agent and he said just get everything fixed and send him the bill. He didn't have time to come out and inspect. Our neighbors, the Swopes, did not fare as well. Most of the siding on their house blew away.

As soon as the roads were clear, I drove to the storage place where our boat, Sundance, was stored. The facility was almost completely destroyed, but miraculously, Sundance was not damaged very much. I had to clean it up and replace the carpet, but other than that, it survived.

After this experience, we paid more attention to hurricane warnings.

**Sundance after Hurricane Alicia**

— — —

When Kristi began her search for a college to attend, she, like Mike, was uncertain as to what she wanted her major to be. I gave her the same advice; if you aren't sure, that's fine. Just start out in Liberal Arts and take all the business courses that you can. We visited UT, Baylor and Texas A&M. Much to my surprise, her reaction to A&M was the opposite of Mike's. She loved it! After she was accepted, we attended an orientation day. I waited outside the auditorium while she attended a briefing. To kill time, I started looking through all the brochures that they had given us. I started with the one about food service. It was a very nice, four-color brochure describing all the food plans available. It read, "Entering freshmen at Texas A&M must choose one of two food plans, A, B or C." I read it again and again to make sure I was reading correctly. I said to myself, "I'm not sure I want my daughter to go here! They can't even count!" It turned out to be a great choice for her and I loved attending bonfires and football games.

— — —

Unfortunately, I was totally absorbed in my new job. Linda was, of course, not as thrilled as I was. Soon after taking it on, we agreed to an amicable divorce. Dick Morrison served as attorney for both of us and there were no disputes on splitting up property. I stayed in the house, which immediately went up for sale, and she and Kristi moved into an apartment. I kept Pfeiffer, our Miniature Schnauzer, so I went home every day for lunch and to let him out. While eating lunch (usually a grilled cheese sandwich), I played music very loud. All of our neighbors worked, so I could crank up the songs that reflected my feelings at the time: *I Am I Said* by Neil Diamond; *Understand Your Man* by Johnny Cash; *Going Where The Lonely Go* by Merle Haggard. It was cheaper than seeing a psychiatrist!

— — —

Our new Deputy Administrator, Hans Mark, visited JSC frequently. He was known for flying "red eye", or all-night flights. He would usually arrive in the early morning hours and sleep on the couch in my office. I gave him the key to my private bathroom so that he could shave and freshen up. He continually harped on me and others in management, that we had to get "operational." His definition of operational was to become more like the airline industry. He thought we were spending too much time (and money) on turnaround and flight preparation. Regardless of what we told him about how the Space Shuttle was much more risky than the airlines, he never gave up. He left NASA in the fall of 1984 to become the Chancellor of The University of Texas System. I believe he finally understood after the Challenger accident, but would never admit that he was wrong. I see him occasionally now and he is always very nice and friendly to me but deep down, I'm afraid he is still not a great fan of human space flight.

— — —

Another thing, which Lyn told me at our handover, was that the head of the JSC employees union, Bob Bryant, was in the Ground Data Systems Division and that he was a troublemaker. He had complained about just about everything and had accused the Directorate office of operating in secret. Not long after I took over, I invited him to come to our weekly staff meetings. He hesitated but finally started showing up. When he was there, I would ask him, just like everybody else, if he had any questions or anything to report. He always said no. After a couple of months, he told me he thought it was a waste of his time to attend, so I never saw him again. Jack Lister, Head of the Personnel Office, told me that was the smartest thing I had ever done.

— — —

All of the MSD contracts were evaluated every six months. We could give the contractor grades of Outstanding, Satisfactory, Marginal or Unsatisfactory, and their bonus was determined by those grades. Singer-Link, which had the contract to operate the Shuttle Mission Simulator, had a tremendous backlog of work that needed to be completed. The trainer/instructors and astronauts had accumulated a large number of discrepancies and Singer-Link didn't seem to be too interested in fixing the problems. When the division came to me with their evaluation, they recommended a Marginal grade. I disagreed and changed it to Unsatisfactory. Before any contractor can be given such a low grade, it must be approved by the Center Director, so I took the case to Gerry Griffin. He agreed with the Unsatisfactory grade, but asked that I deliver it to the contractor in person. The center had never issued such a low grade and he wanted to make sure it was handled properly.

Therefore, I flew up to Binghamton, New York to deliver the bad news to the Singer-Link president, George Barna. At the beginning of the meeting I told him that I was there to deliver an Unsatisfactory grade and that the only reason it wasn't "Shitty", was because NASA didn't officially have such a rating. That got his attention and the next week he came to Clear Lake to personally oversee the work. One of the first things he did was fire the local manager. He stayed for several weeks until all the problems had been resolved. The next rating period we gave them a Satisfactory grade.

While in Clear Lake, George invited me to fly their helicopter simulator that they were building in their facility on Saturn Lane. I had flown the Shuttle Mission Simulator and found it rather easy to fly. I even landed it, but blew out all the tires in the process. The helicopter simulator was something else! I found it to be an unnatural act, like patting your head and rubbing your stomach at the same time. I never got the hang of operating the cyclic stick, the collective lever and the pedals at the same time. On my third or fourth attempt, I got it up to about 30 feet before crashing. I learned two things from that experience: helicopters were not meant to fly, and I had even more respect for Gerry Griffin for learning to fly them.

– – –

The JSC Public Affairs Office received a request for a speaker at the Computer Aided Manufacturing-International (CAM-I) Spring Seminar in Montreux Switzerland, May 8-10, 1984. They forwarded the request to me. Who wouldn't want to go to Switzerland! I called the CAM-I person who had made the request, Rhonda Gerganess, their Manager of Conference Services. She explained that CAM-I was a not-for-profit international organization devoted to cooperative research and development activities in computer aided design and manufacturing. Their funding for such R&D projects came from industry, government and educational organizations. Their headquarters were in Arlington Texas and had offices in England, Japan and Australia. I explained to her that I was not directly involved in such projects, but that we used computers in everything we did. She said that what they would like to hear from me was how we integrated all our computers. I told her I would think about it and call her back. After thinking about it for a few days, I called her back and said I could talk about the design, implementation and integration of the Space Shuttle flight support and flight computer systems, with emphasis of how we managed them. Her reply was, "wonderful", so I committed to speak at the seminar and began preparation of a 45-minute speech.

I flew from Houston to JFK airport in New York and changed planes for the flight to Geneva. I was seated upstairs on a Swiss Air 747, which was a first for me. However, the plane was old and dirty. Not what I had expected from Swiss Air. We arrived in Geneva at 9:30 a.m. on a Saturday and thankfully, my luggage was there. None of the luggage for passengers from Dallas arrived, so there was a lot of unhappiness at the baggage claim area. We rode a chartered bus to Montreux through very lush, green country. CAM-I had a small reception for us at the hotel, the Montreux Palace. I noticed a small blond girl at the reception who obviously was with CAM-I. She was wearing a very wrinkled pant suit and had on no make-up. I felt sorry for her and the other people who flew from Dallas whose luggage didn't make it.

After the reception, I went for a walk along Lake Geneva into the town of Montreux. I went into several watch shops, looking for a graduation gift for Mike. I saw nothing like what I thought he would like, but the prices seemed to be very good. I passed a Bally shoe store and went in to see what they had. I had previously owned one pair of Ballys, which I bought at Neiman Marcus in Houston and thought they were the most comfortable things I had ever worn. The only problem was that they were very expensive. I ended up buying two pairs, one black and one brown, for about $65 a pair, which was less than half what they cost in the States.

The next day, Sunday, I went on a three-country bus tour which CAM-I had arranged. As we rode through the Swiss countryside on the way to Italy, the tour guide pointed out a beautiful waterfall not far from the road. One of the others on the bus asked the name of the falls. The guide thought for a minute and then said, "Uh, I think in the U.S. it would be called 'Cow pee-pee on flat rock.'" At the Swiss-Italy border, the driver had to wake the guard in order to pass. A slow day I guess. We drove through the St. Bernard pass into Aosta Italy. I looked for live St. Bernards, but didn't see any. Aosta is a very old Roman town with ruins everywhere. We saw ruins of an amphitheater, which was supposedly older and larger than the Coliseum in Rome and an arch, still in pretty good shape, which was built in 23 BC and allegedly, the inspiration for the Arc de Triomphe in Paris. At a gift shop, I bought a stuffed St. Bernard for Kristi.

**Roman ruins in Aosta Italy**

We drove on to Courmayeur, a ski resort town at the foot of Mont Blanc, where we had lunch. I had spaghetti, veal, and some very good red wine. Then we drove through the seven-mile Mont Blanc tunnel into Chamonix France, the site of the first winter Olympics. It was not as cloudy in Chamonix as it had been in Courmayeur, so we could clearly see the top of Mont Blanc.

Monday was arrival day for most seminar attendees with no scheduled events, so I decided to ride the train to Lucerne, where several people had told me I would find a better selection of watches at good prices. I had to change trains in Lausanne and Bern, but made the trip with no problems. Lucerne is a beautiful city filled with historic sites and lots of tourists. Plenty of watch shops. I found Gubelin, which several people had recommended. They specialized in Omegas, which is what Mike wanted. I selected an understated one with a leather band. It was a very good deal at about $200. I was getting pretty good at converting from Swiss Francs to U.S. dollars.

I walked along the lake and stumbled upon the Swiss Museum of Transportation. It was a pleasant surprise with lots of old airplanes, cars, trains and quite a bit of US space hardware, including the Gemini 10 flown spacecraft. When I got back to Texas, I told John Young about it and he said, "Yea, nobody in the US wants it, so the Smithsonian lent it to Switzerland."

It was time to go back to Montreux, so I raced back to the bahnhoff (train station) to catch the train. Once again, I was impressed with how lush and clean the countryside was. They raise all kinds of animals there; cows, sheep and deer. I had never before seen deer raised in captivity. I arrived at the hotel just in time to clean up for the reception. I was invited by one of the CAM-I folks to go to dinner with them, so about 10 of us walked 3-4 blocks to the Casino. At the dinner I sat by the young lady I had seen on the day of arrival with no makeup and the very wrinkled pant suit. Her luggage had obviously arrived and she now looked very nice. Her name was Vickie Proffitt and she was one of the CAM-I Directors from Arlington. We had a nice conversation and learned that each of us was divorced. (My divorce was scheduled to be finalized that very day, but I learned when I got back to Texas that it was delayed one week.) We both shared our intent to never marry again. We danced several times and she didn't complain about my short-comings on the dance floor. It was getting late, so Vickie and I decided to walk together back to the hotel. We went into the hotel bar and had a nightcap. Overall, I found her to be very forthright, somewhat cynical, but very enjoyable to be with. There was a good piano player in the bar, but he didn't know Willie Nelson, so we decided it was time to call it a day. Actually it was 1 o'clock in the morning, so we parted ways.

We saw each other the next day at the seminar, but didn't spend any time together. The following day, Wednesday, I asked her if she would like to walk up the street and have lunch rather than eating the buffet at the hotel. Much to my surprise, she eagerly accepted my invitation (because she hated buffets) and we had a very nice lunch at which I asked too many personal questions. She shut me up by telling me that before CAM-I she was a streetwalker in Fort Worth.

The next morning, I gave my presentation. I saw Vickie in the hallway afterward and asked her how she thought it went. Her reply was, "You gave a great presentation, but unfortunately, it had nothing to do with what we're interested in." So much for hours and hours of preparation, but once again, I admired her honesty. Since I was finished with the seminar, I asked her if she would like to take a train ride to Lausanne that afternoon. I had changed trains there on my way to and from Lucerne and thought it would be a pretty town to explore. She said she would love to go, so after changing into more comfortable clothes, we headed for the bahnhoff.

**Vickie waiting for train to Lausanne**

In Lausanne we found a beautiful park, bought a bottle of wine, some cheese and bread and had a nice picnic. During our conversation, the subject of dogs came up. I said that I loved dogs except for miniature poodles. Tom and Doris Carter had one, which I thought was useless. Then Vickie told me that's what kind she owned! Way to go, Jerry! However, all in all, we both had a good time and enjoyed each other's company. We had dinner together back in Montreux that night and agreed that when we got back to Texas, we should keep in contact. I would be flying back home the next morning, but she was continuing with the CAM-I group to tour Italy.

The next morning as I was checking out of the hotel I ran into her again as she was buying a cooler to take her Diet Cokes on the bus. Once again, we said good-bye and agreed to keep in touch.

A couple of days later, back in Clear Lake, Mike came from Trinity for a short visit. As I was giving him his watch and telling him about my trip, the phone rang. It was Vickie, saying that she just wanted to make sure I made it home okay and to say that she missed me. Mike heard me say, "I miss you too." After I hung up the phone, he was very inquisitive as to whom I was talking.

— — —

The house sold very quickly, even though we were asking a high price, expecting to negotiate down. Within a few weeks, it sold at the asking price. That meant I had to find an apartment and move all my junk. I rented one on NASA Road 1 in Seabrook. At NASA we had this group of guys known as "The Ace Moving Company" who helped friends move. It usually consisted of George Abbey, Jay Honeycutt, Dan Germany, Bob Crippen and an assortment of others who had a pickup truck and might be available. I set the move up for Saturday, November 17th, 1984. Astronaut Rick Hauck had volunteered to help, but I didn't expect to see him because his second Shuttle flight, STS-51A, was scheduled to land at KSC the day before. Lo and behold, on Saturday morning Hauck showed up with his pickup, along with Dave Walker, the Pilot on 51A, and helped me move. Amazingly, not too many things were damaged and it sure was a cheap way to move.

– – –

While living in the apartment, I would go home every day to take Pfeiffer for a walk and feed him. Not once, while living in the apartment did he have an accident inside. One Saturday I took him with me to check on the boat, docked on Clear Lake. I went ahead of him on the walkway down to the boat. I heard a large splash, looked back and saw him going down in the water. I immediately dove in, wallet, watch and all, found him on the bottom and raised him to the walkway. He was not breathing. I took him to the car and headed for the emergency veterinarian. Once there, they pronounced him dead. I asked for an autopsy, but was questioned as to why. "He's dead. What will an autopsy tell you?" I told them I just wanted to know why he died. Did he fall in the lake and drown because I wasn't watching closely enough? The autopsy found no water in his lungs, so he did not drown. The official cause of death was determined to be by heart attack. He just had a heart attack and fell into the water. That made me feel less responsible, but still very sad.

— — —

In the spring of 1984, Astronauts Dave Walker, Dan Brandenstein, John Creighton, Rick Hauck, Judy Resnik, Sylvia Stottlemeyer and I took Neil Hutchinson's sailboat, Panache, for a sail on Galveston Bay. Neil was on assignment in NASA Headquarters and had left his boat in Dave's care. Everything went fine until we saw a thunderstorm approaching off to our left. Dave, who had just returned from meteorology school, said it was okay and not to worry about it. Suddenly, as the storm crossed in front of us, it turned and headed straight for us. We panicked! It was coming fast. Before we could lower the sails, the mainsail ripped! We were taking on a lot of water and I thought for sure we were going to sink, but the storm passed quickly and we made it back to shore. We all chipped in to replace the mainsail and I'm not sure if Dave ever told Neil. For years we kidded Dave about being a meteorologist.

— — —

Also in the spring of 1984, Kristi was selected as Rendezvous Princess for the Lunar Rendezvous Festival held each year in the Clear Lake area. I proudly escorted her to the ball.

**Princess Kristi and her proud escort**

— — —

Astronaut Judy Resnik and I became very good friends while working on the RMS project. I found her to be extremely intelligent (she had a Ph. D. in electrical engineering) and she had a wonderful sense of humor, never passing up the opportunity to play a joke on someone. When she heard that Linda and I were getting a divorce, she came to my office just to "see if you're okay." She told me that she too had gone through a divorce (which was a surprise to me) and assured me that I would survive. She was already in training for her first Shuttle flight. Frequently, when the flight crew was in the simulator late at night, she would call and ask me to bring her a cheeseburger and fries from Whataburger. She was usually with Steve Hawley and Charlie Walker, so they started complaining that I didn't bring them anything to eat. Soon, it seemed if I was feeding the entire crew a least a couple of times a month.

During the next two years, Judy and I became even closer. Our relationship was completely Platonic. Her true love was Tom Selleck, star of the TV show *Magnum, P.I.* When she hung pictures in her Seabrook apartment, his poster had to have a prominent spot. We just enjoyed a lot of the same things like music, cars and art. She had a great appreciation for most kinds of music and was a good pianist. A favorite singer of both of us at the time was Earl Thomas Conley. She drove a Pontiac Fiero, a small mid-engine sports car and she loved driving the Bricklin. We both were in the market for houses, so we spent many weekends looking at property for sale on Galveston Bay. We also went to several art shows in Clear Lake, Houston and Galveston. We never bought anything, but usually the wine was free. She liked homemade ice cream and we experimented with different recipes. We came up with a great recipe for chocolate and took a batch to a swim party that Dick and Sheri Morrison hosted in their back yard. Gary Dorman said it was the best he had ever eaten.

On the first launch attempt for her flight, the main Shuttle engines came on and then immediately shut down before the hold down arms were released. She said that Hank Hartsfield, the Commander, had always made a big thing about never saying "What." He insisted that his crew be very specific if they had a question. It was okay to say, "What was that clanging noise I heard on the mid-deck?", but never acceptable to just say "What was that?" Judy said that when the main engines lit and then shut down, there was an almost deafening noise in the crew compartment. The first crewmember to say anything was Hartsfield, who screamed, "What the _ _ _ _ was that?"

One of the things people remember about that flight, STS-41D, was Judy holding up a sign that said "Hi Dad". Everybody thought that was really cute for a female to say "Hi Dad" rather than "Hi Mom". Little did they know that Judy and her mother had not spoken in several years and she was very close to her dad.

– – –

Vickie and I talked on the phone several times and she agreed to fly to Austin where Dick and Sheri Morrison and I would pick her up for a weekend on Lake Travis. Dick had a brand new 36-foot fishing boat which he was anxious to try out. We stayed at Lake Travis Lodges where the boat ramp was exactly the same width as the wheels on his boat trailer. It took us forever to get it launched. Finally, with the boat in the water and some fried chicken that Sheri and Vickie had bought, we headed out to open water. We stopped at a nice spot and started eating the chicken. Dick was very particular with his new boat and picked up every crumb of chicken that anyone dropped. It soon got dark and we decided to head back to shore. Dick said he didn't know where we were, so I said, "I know this lake like the back of my hand. I'll drive us back." I gave the boat full throttle, went about 100 yards and ran up on a sand bar. The entire length of the boat was on dry land! I did know that lake pretty well, but I didn't realize it was down about 10 feet exposing all those sand bars which you couldn't see at night. Like fools, we got out and tried to rock the boat and get it back into the water. It was hopeless. Finally, a boat about the same size came by and stopped to help. We broke every rope in both boats trying to pull it into the water, but to no avail. We gave up and let the guy take us back to Lake Travis Lodges. There we found a man with a huge barge with a crane and made arrangements for him to get Dick's boat the next morning. Dick and I went with him to observe the operation. He put straps fore and aft under the boat and lifted it into the water. Great deal, but it costs us $300!

I figured that would be the last time Vickie would ever want to have anything to do with me, but she just thought it was funny and we continued to talk almost every day on the phone. We started making plans for her to visit me in Clear Lake. I considered a number of fancy restaurants, thinking I should impress her on her first visit. Then I realized that if she didn't like the places I normally frequented,

I should find out quickly. I took her to Joe Lee's in Kemah, a local hangout on the water that served great seafood. Earl Campbell and Kenny Stabler usually showed up there on Sunday afternoons after Houston Oiler football games. She loved it! I certainly had made the right decision about restaurants.

On this visit, Vickie met Gary and Myrna Dorman for the first time. They had us and the Morrisons over for dinner. We began discussing the possibility of us all taking a vacation together. Dick said he had a bail bondsman friend who had a beach house on Grand Cayman Island that we could probably use free just about anytime we wanted. We soon began planning the trip for August 1984. Gary, trying to save money, took along a fully baked ham. Nobody questioned it until we got to the airport on the island. The customs guy there would not allow Gary to keep it, so that didn't turn out to be a money saver. We caught a van to the beach house. It was pretty run down and you had to walk about 50 yards through thick brush to get to the "beach", which was only about 3 feet wide. We spent the night there but started looking for a better place early the next morning. We ended up at Lacovia, where we rented a three bedroom condo right on the beach. It had a large living/dining room and a modern kitchen. Everybody was happy except Gary. He thought it was too expensive.

**Our condo at Lacovia, Grand Cayman Island**

**The beach in front of our condo**

**Relaxing on the beach**

The beach was fantastic, the cleanest I have ever seen. The water was so clear that you could wade out in it up to your armpits and clearly see your feet.

Vickie and I went parasailing, which was the first time for both of us. We launched from a platform out in the water and returned to splashdown in the water nearby. The view was fantastic! I vowed to do that again whenever I had the opportunity. We also rented a car and drove around the island. It took a little time to get use to driving on the left side of the road. We went to Hell, which is on the eastern end of the island. Vickie found postcards there and we sent several to people saying "Wish you were here."

On our last night there, we all went to the Grand Old House restaurant in Georgetown, famous for its seafood, for dinner. It was wonderful! After everyone had ordered dessert (except Gary, who said he couldn't afford it), Vickie excused herself to go to the restroom.

After we finished dessert, Dick asked the waiter to bring our checks. The waiter said, "It's all been paid for by this young lady", pointing to Vickie. After hearing that, Gary said, "Hell, I wish you had told me you were going to pay for it. I would have ordered a dessert!"

In the meantime, I had visited Vickie in Arlington a couple of times and met her parents, Bob and Sue Burnet and her daughter Marnie, age 15. Bob was actually her stepfather, but Vickie and Marnie called him Dad. I immediately loved them all. They welcomed me with open arms. Bob was a State District Judge and former member of the Texas legislature. They owned a weekend cabin (house trailer) on Lake Possum Kingdom and we spent some time there. It was a great place to fish and water ski. Bob usually cooked a brisket and sausage on his big bar-b-q pit. He had a "secret" recipe for bar-b-q sauce which was wonderful. Sue (Bob and I called her Susan) liked my margaritas, which I made from a recipe given to me years earlier by Judy Ernull. After two or three, I stopped putting tequila in them and nobody seemed to notice.

Their neighbors at the lake house were Carolyn and Monte Land and their daughter Amanda. They were both high school teachers, with Monte also being the football coach. Amanda was about 12 years old and as cute as a bug. They had a jukebox on their covered porch that had great records from the 50s, 60s and 70s. Just a couple of houses down were an older couple, Francis and Henry Pitzer. They both loved fishing and usually went out early in the morning. Henry would come in the back yard and yell, "Victoria, it's time to go catch a mess of fish." The three families usually shared dinner each night and then played Rummy Cube. I had never played before but soon learned to love it. Frances was a very serious player and usually won. Bob always had a problem distinguishing the colors of the tiles.

On my first visit there, they were just finishing a new floating boat dock with a huge walkway. Bob had designed the entire project himself. I was impressed and loved doing what I could to help them finish it.

There was a concrete boat ramp just beside their house, which was for use by all in the neighborhood. It was great entertainment to sit on the back porch and watch people trying to back their boat and trailer down the narrow ramp, usually with a man doing the driving and his wife/girlfriend giving directions. We often wondered how many breakups/divorces were caused by that boat ramp.

– – –

The longer I lived in the apartment, the more I craved a house. I had no garage, no place for all my tools, and I actually missed yard work. I had a one-year lease on the apartment, so that became my deadline. There was a house on Long Grove in Clear Lake Forest which had been on the market for over a year and was in really bad shape. It was owned by Dow Chemical, who had transferred one of their employees and taken over the house. They had a local real estate agent, but had done nothing to make it sell, other than put a For Sale sign in the yard. It needed new floors, paint inside and out, kitchen and bath room makeovers, and landscaping just to name a few things. I made a ridiculously low offer, which they rejected. I started gradually going up and they gradually came down on the price. After about 4 months of this back and forth, I finally bought it for about 60% of their initial asking price. Now I had plenty to do before my apartment lease was up. I did most of the remodeling work myself. All of the horrible wallpaper came down first. I ripped out all of the carpet and rented a scraper to remove the linoleum in the kitchen and breakfast area. That turned out to be a horrible job! It took me a week of working long hours every night. Once it was up, I started laying tile. That was a fun job. Engineers like to figure things out. Next came the bathroom. I started there with a sledgehammer! Out came the lavatory, the commode and all the cabinets. I had hired a plumber to install the lavatory and commode, but he never showed up so I did that myself (against the law in Texas). The only thing I needed help with was installing the new mirror. It covered the entire wall and weighed about a ton, so I got Gary Dorman to help me with that.

- - -

In the fall of 1984, Ford Aerospace, one of my biggest contractors, with responsibility for maintenance of MCC, opened a new office building just outside the JSC gate on Saturn Lane. For the grand opening ceremonies, they held a big banquet in the atria on the first floor. I sat beside Philip Caldwell, the CEO of Ford who started out by saying he was a car guy and not an expert on space. They had several new Ford Taurus' on display on the sidewalk outside. It was to come out officially in January 1985 as a 1986 model. After talking about the Taurus for a while, he asked what kind of car I drove. When I told him about my Bricklin, which had a Ford engine, he got really excited. He knew a lot about the car and had personally dealt with Malcolm Bricklin on the switch to Ford engines for the 1975 model. Then he started telling me about the new Ford Mustang. He obviously was more excited about it than the Taurus. He was interested in learning that I had once owned a 1965 Mustang convertible. I thought if strange that he wanted to know the color of the Mustang and the Bricklin. They were both white. A couple of weeks later, I got a call from Chuck Miller, the local Ford dealer telling me that "my" white Mustang SVO V-8 convertible was ready for pickup. He explained that Philip Caldwell had shipped it with instructions that it was mine to drive for six months and then give him a report on what I liked and didn't like about it. I told Chuck that there was no way I could do that because Ford Aerospace was one of my big contractors and it was illegal for me to accept any favors, especially the use of a new car. Chuck said if that was the case, I would have to call Caldwell and explain it to him, because he certainly was not going to tell him that he couldn't follow his instructions. So, I called Caldwell and amazingly got through to him on the first try. After listening to why I couldn't accept his generous offer, he said that was the dumbest thing he had ever heard, but since it was the US government, he wasn't surprised at their "crazy rules." I surely wish I could have accepted the offer. It was a great looking car.

— — —

Later in 1984, IBM's chief marketer, Laird Landis, invited me to attend another conference, this one in Germany. He was still trying to recover from their not being able to help me with the JSC computer management question. Laird, his wife Jill and I flew to D/FW and then non-stop to Frankfurt Germany, an over 10-hour flight. We then drove to the Hotel Krone in Tubingen, near Stuttgart. That was our home base for the next four days. The conference was held in a different location each day, in various old castles in the surrounding area. IBM knows how to put on elaborate conferences, with wonderful food, but I didn't get much out of this one that I didn't already know. At the end of the conference, we drove further south in Germany, crossed into France and spent the night in Colmer. From there I drove the Mercedes rental car to Frankfort on the Autobahn with Laird and Jill asleep in the back seat, averaging over 90 mph. The Autobahn was wonderful. Doing 95-100 mph, there were faster cars passing me. I enjoyed the trip, but felt as if I should be back working in the office.

— — —

That Christmas, Mother and Daddy came to see me. Mike and Kristi came for a delicious home-cooked meal.

**Christmas 1984**

Because they knew I missed Pfeiffer, Mike and Kristi gave me a puppy for Christmas that year. Kristi's friend Ricky Almato's dog had a large litter of pups so they selected one for me. He was only about 7 weeks old and very tiny. They brought it into the house in a Christmas stocking. He was mostly white and when they told me he was born on Halloween day, I named him Spook.

**My new best friend Spook**

— — —

During my two-year tenure as Mission Support Director, I received several job offers from within NASA. I had outright offers from Jesse Moore, the Associate Administrator for Space Flight to go to Washington as his Deputy, and from Congressman Don Fuqua, Chairman, House Subcommittee on Space Science to be the Subcommittee Executive Director. I also was asked if I would like to be considered as Deputy Director at two different NASA Centers. These were not out-right offers, just opportunities to be considered. I was deeply honored by all these offers, but I declined them all. I didn't want to go back to Washington in any capacity, and I considered my job at JSC better than what any other Center could offer. I felt pretty comfortable in my decisions, but wanted to talk to someone about the situation. I asked Kristi what she thought. After patiently listening to the offers I had and my reasons for turning them down, she looked at me and said, "Dad, you sound like an old fart who's already retired in place."

Her response gave me cause to reconsider. I quickly came to the decision that if I was going to leave my current job, I would leave NASA. Several companies had hinted, "If you ever decide to leave NASA, come talk to me." I decided that I should see what they had to offer. For the first time in my career, money became an important consideration.

When JSC decided to award the Space Transportation System Operations Contract (STSOC) for just about all of the Shuttle operations, my decision was made easier. Most of what we did in Mission Support would go to the new contractor. About the only thing left would be Data Systems Division. I had already lost my Deputy, Bob Ernull, to Rockwell, who was going to bid on the contract. Other companies who had announced their plans to bid were Grumman, Lockheed and Ford Aerospace. Both my good friend Bob Sheets, who was with Grumman, and Rocco Petrone, who was with Rockwell, had "jokingly" asked why I didn't come work on the contract proposal with them. I had purposely avoided making any personal inputs to the Request For Proposal (RFP) because I wanted to avoid any appearance of conflict of interest in case I did go to work for one of the bidders. Finally, I told Bob that I would consider an offer from Grumman. They were teamed with American Airlines and Singer-Link and had formed a new company, Grumman Space Operations Company within Fred Haise's Technical Services Division, because they could offer more attractive rates there.

Before officially talking to anyone, I told Gerry Griffin what I was thinking about doing. He completely understood and even encouraged me. He said that if I did go into private industry I would find it very interesting but also very different.

Soon after I told Bob Sheets that I would consider an offer, I got a call from Fred Haise saying that he would love to have me at Grumman and that he had set up an interview with Tom Kelly who would be heading up the STSOC proposal. When I met with Tom, who I had known from the Lunar Module days, he said he couldn't talk about salary but would like me to be his Vice President for Operations. Dave Lang, formerly the JSC Procurement Director, had already accepted a job as Vice President for Business.

Shortly thereafter, Bob and I traveled to New York to talk with George Skurla, who had recently been named as President of Grumman Aerospace. I had known him back in the '60s when he was Director of Lunar Module Operations at KSC. George and I had lunch together and then went to his office for cigars and wine. I think Bob had let him know what made me happy. He said that he, Fred and Tom all wanted me and that all we needed to do was work out a contract. I then met with Danny Knowles, Grumman Vice President, Personnel and Administration. We talked about salary, benefits, stock options, restricted stock, bonuses, pensions, etc. One of my big concerns was that I was three years short of being able to retire from NASA. He said that they would guarantee that when I retired from Grumman, my retirement would be equal to or exceed what it would have been had I stayed at NASA. Another question which I had, was what would happen if Grumman didn't win the STSOC contract? He said the plan would be for me to go to the Kennedy Space Center as Fred Haise's Deputy on the shuttle processing contract. Fred had mentioned that to me earlier. I asked him to put all of that in writing and I would surely consider it.

A few days after I returned to JSC, I received a phone call from Skurla's office saying that I should expect a call from him the following day. The next day I was in Gerry Griffin's office discussing another matter when the call from Skurla came. I had told my secretary to forward it to Gerry's office if he happened to call while I was there. Since Gerry already knew what I was thinking about doing, I didn't care if he heard the whole conversation, and I didn't want to make George wait. He outlined all the things that Knowles and I had discussed and made me a verbal offer. He said an official letter and contract would be in the mail the next day if I was in general agreement. I told him it seemed like a good offer and I would strongly consider it once I received the official letter.

Soon after receiving the official offer, I accepted and agreed with NASA and Grumman that my separation date would be March 1, 1985. It was a life changing decision but I was comfortable with it and excited about the new opportunities I would have.

— — —

Many people at NASA have since told me that I was the best manager they ever had. I greatly appreciate the compliment, but it was my goal to be a good leader, not a good manager. I tried to be a good leader in the vein of Bob Gilruth, Chris Kraft, Glynn Lunney and Gerry Griffin, all of whom I consider great leaders. My definition of a leader is one who entrusts his people with responsibility and lets them know that they are trusted. Great leaders inspire their co-workers rather than manage them. They teach people by example rather than directing them to do things a certain way. It has been said that a leader gets out in front of his co-workers and says, "Follow me!" A manager follows his co-workers and kicks them in the butt.

– – –

# Chapter 6

# GRUMMAN AEROSPACE CORPORATION

I immediately headed for Bethpage to get all the paperwork completed to become a Grumman employee and start working on the proposal. One of the things they gave me was an employee's handbook. It clearly stated, "Nepotism is encouraged." In other words, if one or both of your parents worked at Grumman, you are almost guaranteed a job. It was a big family. The proposal center was an entirely new environment for me. Very few of us had a small office, but most of the workers were in a large open area. There were no windows. I keep hearing what I thought was a noisy air conditioning system, but learned that it was coming from speakers in the ceiling playing "white noise." Someone had figured out that workers in that large a space with no windows needed to hear something that would be soothing.

Bob Sheets, Gary Stone and even George Skurla had warned me that as an "outsider", it might take a little while to fit into the Grumman "family". I was only the third company officer, after Fred Haise and Dave Lang, to be hired from the outside. Just a few days after being there, I saw first-hand what a family it was. One of the guys working on the proposal found out that his wife and mother, who were vacationing in Mexico, had become sick and needed to get back home quickly. When Skurla found out about the situation, he ordered that his private Gulfstream jet be flown to Mexico, along with the company doctor, to bring them back. No expense, no questions asked. Everyone seemed surprised that I thought this was a very generous undertaking. It was just the Grumman way of doing business.

They had booked me into a nearby Howard Johnson hotel, but after two nights of strange noises in the adjoining room (I think they were filming a porno movie), I requested a change. They then booked me into the closer and much nicer Long Island Marriott, located on what was once Roosevelt Field where Charles Lindbergh departed on his historic flight across the Atlantic.

Proposal writing was a new experience for me even though I had been involved in writing several requests for proposal. It involved long ten to twelve hour days, which didn't bother me that much because that's what I was used to at NASA. Tom Kelly, Dave Lang and I usually ate lunch in the Executive Dining Room. Some days we would go to the Grumman owned Linden Tree restaurant nearby. It was a very nice restaurant open to the public, but with a separate room for Grumman executives. When Bob Sheets and/or Gary Stone were in town, they knew all the good Italian restaurants, so we would go to one of those. I learned to love linguini with white clam sauce. The kind of food I missed most was Tex-Mex. Any kind of Mexican food was unheard of on Long Island. Finally, someone told me about one that was several miles away. On Easter Sunday, I drove there to try it. It was terrible! I had enchiladas with a red sauce that turned out to be Italian Prego sauce. So much for Tex-Mex!

Vickie came up for a weekend visit, so that was a wonderful change of pace. We went to see the Four Tops and the Temptations performing together in Manhattan. It was a great show! I took her to a couple of my favorite Italian restaurants where we both enjoyed good Long Island seafood.

We wrote drafts of the proposal on sheets of paper that had "PROPOSAL" at the top and bottom. Thinking I was being clever,

I wrote a proposal for marriage on one of the sheets and mailed it to Vickie. A couple of days after mailing it, I talked to her and asked if she got my last letter. Her reply was, "Yes, that was cute." I didn't press the matter, but we did start talking about the possibility of marriage.

— — —

NASA had planned a going-away party for me later in March at the Gilruth Center. I thought it was a great event. Pete Clements was the emcee and kept us all in tears laughing at his jokes. More people attended than I had expected. Several Grumman folks were there, many of my Clear Lake non-NASA friends and just about everyone I knew at NASA. Mike and Kristi were both there, which made it especially nice.

**Kristi & Mike at my NASA going-away party**

Among the gifts I received was an authentic astronaut jacket, only the second one given to a non-astronaut. The first one was presented to Joe Algranti, Chief of Aircraft Operations at JSC, and pilot of the JSC Gulfstream for most of our trips, upon his retirement. John Young, who was Chief of the Astronaut Office at the time could not be there, so the jacket was presented to me by Lyn Dunseith. As he helped me put it on, he said, "Where in the world do you wear something like this?"

**Lyn Dunseith presenting me with astronaut jacket**

— — —

When it came time to present our proposal to NASA, Tom Kelly, Dave Lang, Sam Sanborn and I flew to Clear Lake on the Grumman Gulfstream, along with George Skurla. It was traditional that after the technical and business presentations, the company president or CEO would talk for a couple of minutes about how the company would support the effort. It was our goal to be a close second on the technical side (how could Rockwell not be first, since they were the builder of most of the Shuttle?), and first (lowest cost) on the business side. It was a little awkward for me to be presenting to people who I knew well and had worked with for so many years. Charlie

Harlan was the head of the source selection committee. My "old friends" asked a lot of tough questions, but I felt we did pretty well.

Then it was back to Long Island to start our recruiting process, assuming we would be the winner. Most of the staff would have to be hired outside the company since very few Grummanites wanted to go to Texas. We also had to put the finishing touches on plans for the facilities we would need in Clear Lake. We had already begun construction on a new three-story building across from the Nassau Bay hospital, and had plans to build a similar building just across the street, plus tentative lease agreements on other existing buildings.

After a couple of weeks, we moved into temporary quarters on Upper Bay Road in Clear Lake and started the interview process for new employees. That summer we hired Kristi as a secretary.

**Kristi, my favorite Grummanite, summer 1985**

In September, NASA issued their source selection. Sadly for us, Rockwell was awarded the contract. The selection was primarily a technical one and on that basis, it was hard to argue against their decision. NASA did not consider the Grumman cost proposal to be that much better than the others.

— — —

I convinced Vickie to drive to Mississippi with me for Thanksgiving '85. She said she would love to go, but wanted to fly because she hated riding in a car for a long period. Reluctantly, she finally agreed and we departed on the 12-hour drive. To hopefully make it a little easier on her, I fixed a dozen bags/packages for her and told her she could open one each hour. They were all silly little things like chocolate bars and crossword puzzles, but they did help pass the time.

On the way, we stopped in Tupelo at Elvis Presley's birthplace. She enjoyed sitting in the swing on his front porch.

**Vickie in Elvis' front porch swing**

Then it was on to Golden to meet my parents. They welcomed her with open arms, as did all my aunts and cousins. She was a big hit.

Daddy really enjoyed showing her Tishomingo State Park and she seemed to enjoy it also. Her favorite part of the park was the swinging bridge.

**Vickie & Daddy on swinging bridge**

— — —

Back home in Clear Lake, the big question for me was what do I do next? The plan for me to go to KSC as Fred Haise's Deputy had not worked out because Wiley Williams, who had been head of the NASA KSC test and operations office, retired and was then available for the Grumman job. Both Fred and George Skurla told me about the situation before it was announced, and assured me that I would be "taken care of" if we didn't win the STSOC contract.

The Nassau Bay office building we had planned to use was almost complete, so a portion of the third floor was built out to only accommodate a few of us until Grumman figured out what to do with us.

Jack Buxton, head of Grumman Houston, a small manufacturing facility across from Ellington Field, had been trying to get more business moved from Bethpage for many years. Skurla liked the idea of moving some projects and programs away from Long Island because they could be done less expensively elsewhere. He and I had several long discussions late at night about the possibilities. One of the problems was that a lot Grumman employees had never been west of the Hudson River, so they weren't anxious to move, especially to Texas.

George hired a search consulting company and formed a Grumman committee to start looking at the possibilities for moving some projects, both aircraft and space, away from Long Island. We traveled to Denver, Atlanta, and Houston to see what was available. This involved quite a few helicopter rides, which I enjoyed. In Denver, they landed us on the 50-yard line of Mile High Stadium, which was a thrill. Of course, I was pulling for Houston.

By the end of 1985, Alex Alexandrovich, President of the Grumman Space Systems Division, asked me to be his Vice President for Civil Space. He reorganized the division into two groups, military and civil. I would be responsible for all civil programs including Space Station, Orbital Maneuvering Vehicle, Space Shuttle Wings, Thermal Systems, Robotic Systems, and numerous other civil space-related advanced technology projects. The contracts in place at that time amounted to approximately $100 million. A key condition of my acceptance of the job was that I could stay in Clear Lake and only go to Bethpage "occasionally." Alex was also in favor of moving projects to the Houston area.

At my introduction to the Grumman Civil Space employees, I was not exactly greeted warmly. I even had one question asking what made me qualified for the job. I definitely was considered an outsider. However, most of the employees came around within a few weeks and I was accepted as their leader, but still an outsider. Dick Kline, who had been with Grumman for a quarter century, was certainly not happy. He left Space Systems shortly to work with Fred Haise who was bidding on the NASA Space Station Engineering and Integration contract, which was being bid out of Fred's Technical Services Division, just as we did on the STSOC program. The competitor was TRW. Grumman won that contract. More about the TRW reaction later.

Early in 1986, George Skurla retired from Grumman. I knew I was losing a good friend, but he deserved it. He was a big open-wheel car racing fan. In his office, the only picture he had on the walls was one of A. J. Foyt standing by his number 14 Indy car. He and his son had completed the Bob Bondurant Indy and Formula 1 racing school, and were certified to drive in races. I thought a good retirement gift would be an autographed picture of A. J. Foyt, so I called his office in Houston and explained what I wanted. The secretary said, "Let me put you through to Mr. Foyt." After explaining again who I was, who Skurla was and what I wanted, he said that he was sure he could do something and asked that I come pick it up the next day. When I got there, he showed me an official A. J. Foyt racing jacket that he had signed. I couldn't believe it. When I presented it to George at his retirement party, all of the long term Grummanites were mad at me because it was obvious that George liked the jacket better than anything else he received.

— — —

On January 28, 1986, I was in the conference room at the Grumman Nassau Bay facility talking to some local real estate people about putting together some Clear Lake area brochures that I could give to the Space Systems people in Bethpage. I had turned the TV on because I wanted to see the Space Shuttle Challenger launch. We all sat quietly for the last few minutes of the countdown and the lift-off. At 73 seconds into the launch phase, I couldn't believe what my eyes were seeing. Something was obviously bad wrong! Elements of the launch vehicle and spacecraft appeared to be shooting off in several directions, accompanied by huge trails of smoke. I begged for the TV commentators to shut up until they had some word from Mission Control. Finally, it came, "Obviously a major malfunction. We have no downlink." Then, "We have a report from the Flight Dynamics Officer that the vehicle has exploded."

My immediate thoughts were of the flight crew. I knew them all very well, with the exception of Greg Jarvis, the Hughes Aircraft Payload Specialist, and Christa McAuliffe, who was to be the first teacher in space. Mike Smith, Dick Scobee, Ron McNair, Ellison Onizuka and Judy Resnik were all close friends. Jane Smith was helping Vickie choose a wedding dress. When it became obvious that it was highly unlikely that none of them survived, I canceled the meeting, went to my office, locked the door and cried.

The next day, I was invited to sit in the VIP section for the ceremony scheduled for the following day at JSC. President Reagan would deliver the eulogy. After thinking about it for a few hours, I called back and declined. I was afraid that it would be like some of the splashdown parties; a whole bunch of people who didn't even know the flight crew just seeking publicity. I felt that I could better honor them alone. I did watch the ceremony on TV and I thought it was the best speech President Reagan ever delivered. I was dismayed to see Judy's mother, who she hadn't spoken to in years, in attendance. Years later, I wished that I had attended the public ceremony.

I had to fight the urge to go to NASA and "help." I wanted badly to be there with my comrades and help find out what caused the explosion and make sure it never happened again. Glynn Lunney had left NASA in late fall, '85, and Gerry Griffin left in early January '86. One of my thoughts was "Would this have happened if we had been there? Surely we would not have launched in those freezing conditions." But, I had to realize that I was not a NASA employee anymore and that the best thing I could do was to stay away and not bother the people who were trying to figure out exactly what happened and why.

Vickie and I were invited to the Challenger tribute held in the Old Post Office Building in Washington D. C. We sat at a table near the front, next to the table where Oprah Winfrey sat. It was a moving affair, with Lee Greenwood singing *God Bless the USA* while walking around all the tables up front, including ours. It was the first time I witnessed him singing that song, only a couple of feet in front of me. The next year, it happened again when June Scobee invited me to the dedication of the first Challenger Center in Houston. I was seated at a console in the center of the first row, and there was Greenwood again singing what now is one of my favorite songs, only a few feet away.

— — —

Gerry Griffin had left NASA only a couple of weeks before the Challenger accident to become President of the Houston Chamber of Commerce, so that was a tremendous help in my efforts to get some programs moved to the Houston area. Unlike the Denver and Atlanta economic development people we talked to, Houston was interested in getting us to move to anywhere in the Houston area, with no prejudices about exactly which part of town. Gerry linked me with Paul Gaines, Director of the Houston Airport System, which included Ellington Field. Paul and I hit it off wonderfully.

For our first meeting he suggested that we meet in the Executive Club at Hobby Airport, have a few drinks and only talk about our backgrounds. No discussion of current plans allowed. At first, I thought that was strange, but it worked great. We found that we had similar roots, beliefs and goals. We both concluded that the other was trustworthy.

In the meantime, Grumman Space Systems Division was bidding on a Space Station Freedom development contract. The proposed site for doing all the work was "in the Houston area."

Gaines and I then started meeting frequently on the subject of Grumman leasing several acres at Ellington on which to build our Space Station facilities if we won the contract. He wanted to get some commitment whether we won or lost the contract, so I began working on the Bethpage management for such a commitment. I proposed that we commit to one office building and if we did not win the Space Station contract, we could use it for other civil space work. Alexandrovich agreed with that idea. Skurla also liked the concept and told me that he would assign Jake Bussolini, the Grumman Vice President of Business Operations, to lead the effort to lease the Ellington land and determine if the company should commit to something even if we lost. Jake jumped in with both feet and tried to take over all of the negotiations with Paul Gaines and the city of Houston. After a couple of meetings with Gaines, Paul called me and said he understood that Jake had to be involved from a corporate standpoint, but that he would like to reach a deal with me on what we really wanted and then that's what he would insist upon with Jake. That method of operation worked very well, and soon we had Jake convinced that "he" had negotiated a great deal with the city, and he would take it to the Grumman Board of Directors for their approval. Gaines also let me know that he didn't want to talk to Jack Buxton any more. He said, "I don't know who he is and how he fits in, but I am going to be unavailable when he calls." That suited me fine, because I never figured out how he fit in either.

While Bussolini was doing a good job convincing the Board of Directors on the Ellington project, I was more concerned with selling the idea to the employees we would be asking to move. Without them, the facility would be useless. In this area, I had great help from Bob Sheets and Gary Stone. They did a lot of good work convincing some of the key people that Clear Lake would be a great place to live and work.

Jake also had his own Bethpage facilities "experts" who wanted to start designing everything from sewer systems to carpet colors. Ed Carl, who was the facilities director at Grumman Houston and had worked on our office building in Nassau Bay, was my go-to guy for such things. Ed said we should start by talking to the contractors for that building, Bailey-Matthews Construction. When we outlined for them what we were thinking about for office space, they suggested that we look at the Boeing Clear Lake facility which they had recently completed. Their idea was that if it came close to what we needed, they could use the same plans and save a lot of design work. After looking at the Boeing building, we concluded that it would serve our purposes just fine. Some exterior treatment changes would need to be made, but the basic structural design could be duplicated. When Ed and I presented this idea to Jake, he almost went ballistic. "Why are you doing all of this without talking to my facilities people? Why are you talking to a potential contractor?" Fortunately, after getting all of the "right" Bethpage people involved, they came to the same conclusion that Ed and I had reached several weeks earlier.

Before Jake got involved, I was already working with several local, state and national politicians. On the local level, I spent some time with Houston Mayor Kathy Whitmire and a lot of time with city councilman Frank Mancuso. Ellington Field was in Mancuso's district and he was very eager not only to get us there, but also to make other improvements at Ellington that would draw other businesses. He wanted to construct a new entrance from Beltway 8, to the north, and to fix up the golf course. I made clear to him and Mayor Whitmire that I certainly had no objection to those improvements, but they were not critical to the Grumman deal. On the state level, through my friend Dick Morrison, I talked to Gov. Mark White, who volunteered to go to Bethpage and talk to the board about doing business in the state. That turned out to not be necessary.

Mayor Whitmire, along with Lee Hogan, President of the Houston Economic Development Council, did travel to Bethpage to make a pitch to the board. The Grumman headquarters building had been recently redesigned and expanded. The old and new parts were connected with a large glass atrium. When we stopped in the parking lot, Lee said, "Boy, that's an interesting design. I wonder who the architect was?" Mayor Whitmire responded, "What makes you think there was one?"

– – –

A big celebration of the Texas Sesquicentennial was held at the San Jacinto monument on April 21, 1986 to commemorate 150 years since the battle at San Jacinto when Texas defeated General Santa Anna and won her independence from Mexico. Governor Mark White was the host, and through our mutual good friend, Dick Morrison, we were invited. Willie Nelson was the featured entertainment. Dick, Sheri, Vickie and I, along with Mark and Linda Gale White, had front row seats. The Governor promised that he would introduce us to Willie after the performance, but it never happened. I'll never forget Willie singing *Living In The Promiseland*. I was a tear-jerker!

At the time, I had no idea that my "cousin" had played an important role in the capture of Santa Anna. Years later, Michael Corenblith, the production designer on the movie *Apollo 13*, was also the production designer on the movie *The Alamo*. When we visited him on the set near Hamilton Pool, not far from Marble Falls, he asked me about my "cousin" Sion (pronounced Zion) Bostick. I didn't know what he was talking about. He said that his name was on the wall inside the San Jacinto monument because he was one of the guys who captured Santa Anna. It turns out that on April 22, 1836, the day after the battle, Bostick and two others were ordered to scout around in search of escaping Mexican soldiers. They spotted and captured a Mexican soldier hiding in tall grass, dressed in a woman's dress. When they returned to camp, they discovered that their prisoner was Mexican President and General Santa Anna, because the Mexican soldiers already captured all stood and saluted him saying, "El Presidente." I have never been able to reconstruct how we might be related, but he did live in Alabama before coming to Texas and we are bound to be distant cousins. Since then, I have visited his grave and a Texas Historical Society monument honoring him, in the San Saba Cemetery, about 65 miles northwest of Marble Falls.

Just a couple of months later, the statue Goddess, which had been removed from the dome to the Texas State Capitol for repair and refurbishment, was ready for reinstallation. It was totally recast in aluminum, in large part from aluminum cans collected by schoolchildren for the project. Once the statue was finished in June, the Texas National Guard made several attempts with a helicopter (three as I recall) to position her back on top of the dome. Each ended in failure, attributed to high winds. The Mississippi National Guard had volunteered to place it back after the first failure, but Gov. White refused the offer. Finally, he relented and told them they could try. On June 14, 1986 (a day of infamy for Texas), they were successful on the first attempt, even in higher wind conditions than before. I kidded Dick Morrison about Mississippi coming to the rescue. He gave me the Governor's private phone number in the Governor's Mansion, so I called him late one night. To my surprise, he answered immediately. I told him who I was and said that he was welcome for Mississippi coming to his rescue. He hung up while mumbling several curse words.

--- --- ---

Vickie and I had set our wedding date for Saturday, July 12, 1986. Rev. William Miller ("Brother Buddy"), pastor of the Clear Lake United Methodist Church, led the ceremony. We wanted it to be at Clear Lake Park in what was once the Webster Presbyterian Church, and became "The Little Church on NASA Road 1." Mike agreed to be my Best Man and Marnie was the Bridesmaid. Amanda Land was the flower girl. The ceremony went just fine. We had our reception at the Windemere Mansion, a part of the Bal Harbour Yacht Club, where Mike proposed a very nice toast. We spent the night at the Tremont in Galveston, ate dinner at the Wentletrap and were back in the house on Long Grove Sunday, where Vickie wrote thank you cards to everyone. The next day we left for our honeymoon in Barbados.

In Barbados, we stayed at Sam Lord's Castle, a very nice resort. The beach was adequate, but not as nice as Grand Cayman. We rented a Moke, sort of a mini Jeep, built by British Motor Corporation, very much like their Morris Mini, but completely open. We really enjoyed touring the island in it. We traveled single lane dirt roads through the sugar cane fields and came upon a Bacardi rum factory. We could smell it for a long way off. We went for a tour but left early because the smell was getting to us. I saw bananas growing for the first time and realized that they grow upward, not like you see them sometimes on stalks in grocery stores. We also passed by a Belmont Funeral Home, which Dean Deaton swears he does not own.

**Vickie in our Moke**

There was a woman on the beach in front of our hotel who did hair braiding. Vickie told me one night that she just might get hers braided. I told her that would be fine with me if that's what she wanted to do. The next day, she did it. It took several hours.

**Vickie with braided hair**

In the Sam Lord's bar they had a towel with the inscription "Sir Robert Burnett's White Satin Dry Gin." We offered to buy it when we first saw it, but the bartender said it wasn't for sale. Each time we were there, we offered again to buy it, explaining that Robert Burnett was Vickie's dad's name. Finally, he agreed to sell it to us. Upon our return home, we had it framed and gave it to Bob. It now proudly hangs in our game room.

– – –

Moving Vickie and Marnie from Arlington proved to be quite a task. I borrowed a Grumman bread truck (we had several old ones at our Clear Lake facility) and headed for Arlington. I got almost to Ennis when one of the tires blew out. I limped into town on the frontage road and luckily found a tire shop, where they put on a new tire.

We spent the next day packing the truck and Vickie's car to the brim, and then drove in convoy to Clear Lake the following day. Vickie proved to be a whiz at unpacking and placing furniture, so we had everything in order within a few days.

Marnie took some summer courses at University of Houston downtown and got an evening and weekend job at the Oasis, a local restaurant and bar on the lake. She also worked at the Cargo furniture store in Baybrook Mall. That fall she went to North Texas State University in Denton. She later transferred to South West State University (Now Texas State University) in San Marcos and graduated with a degree in Applied Sociology. While at school there, she experienced her first severe stomach pain and was admitted to the hospital. Unfortunately, the pains have persisted and she has had at least 20 hospital visits since.

In the meantime, Marnie asked if it was okay to legally change her last name to Bostick. I immediately said yes. When I mentioned it to Daddy, he said he would be honored for her to have the family name. The change was accomplished when she turned 18 in 1987.

After college, she worked as Regional Manager for a clothing company, but found the required travel was just too much for her, so she got a job as Court Coordinator in the Travis County District Attorney's office. That's where she met the love of her life, David Castañeda.

– – –

Back at work, I was making some progress on getting people and projects to move to Houston. We had teamed with TRW to bid on the NASA Orbital Maneuvering Vehicle (OMV), a space tug that once deployed from the Space Shuttle, would ferry satellites from/ to the Shuttle and the Space Station. Our team won the contract. Grumman, as a sub-contractor to TRW, was to build the tele-robotic front end which would be used for the actual capture and retention of satellites. John Mockovciak, the program manager for Grumman had already agreed that he and several of his key people would move to Houston once we had the office building complete and we would use the Grumman Houston facilities for manufacturing.

Our teaming agreement with TRW was that we would have 25% of the total project and we had paid that share of the proposal costs. Mockovciak came to me several months after the contract was awarded and said we were being short-changed by TRW. According to his calculations TRW was only giving us about 8% of the work. I told him to get all the facts, put together a presentation and I would then go to Redondo Beach, California, the TRW headquarters, and talk to Daniel Goldin, their VP and General Manager. The next week I was off to talk to him.

Upon arrival at Goldin's office, his assistant asked me to wait in the conference room and Mr. Goldin would join me shortly. I waited about 35 minutes and he finally showed up. All he said was, "I'm ready to hear what you have to say." No "Hello, how are you?" and certainly no apology for making me wait. The presentation Mockovciak had made for me was expected to take about ½ hour, assuming there would be some questions and comments throughout. Goldin said nothing while I was talking, so I was finished in about 15 minutes. When I ended the presentation, he scooted his chair back, stood up, said, "So, sue me." and then walked out of the room. I went back to the Grumman Board of Directors, told them the story and they agreed to sue TRW. According to the Grumman lawyers, we had a great case, but NASA canceled the OMV program before the lawsuit could get to court.

Little did I realize that would not be my last encounter with Dan Goldin. He was appointed as Administrator of NASA a few years later. At his going-away party at TRW, he said, "Now I can get those Grumman bastards!" He was still very sore about losing the Space Station Engineering and Integration Contract to Grumman. After about a year and a half as Administrator, Goldin terminated Grumman's integration contract and gave the responsibility to Boeing, the prime manufacturing contractor.

– – –

Unfortunately, we did not win the Space Station development contract. Boeing won the overall contract, but NASA was so impressed with our crew quarters proposal, that they directed Boeing to hire us as a subcontractor.

That limited our need for facilities at Ellington, so the Grumman board approved the construction of one office building, along with a long-term lease on several adjoining acres, with the hope that we could move other programs there. In October 1986, Grumman announced plans to move part of the Space Systems Division to Ellington field. The groundbreaking ceremonies were held on August 24, 1987. This consisted of several luminaries from Grumman and the city of Houston making speeches and driving a bulldozer to start demolition of the old abandoned buildings, including what was once the Officer's Club. We held many splashdown parties there during the '60s, so I was sad to see it go, but happy that Grumman was going to replace it with "my" office building. I salvaged an "Off Limits" sign from the debris and it now hangs over the entrance to our game room.

Bussolini and Buxton, of course, took credit for the whole thing. Paul Gaines, Ed Carl, Bob Sheets, Gary Stone and I just stood on the side and said to each other, "I sure am glad 'they' could pull this off." Mayor Whitmire did give me a nice plaque commemorating the event.

**Me by sign for our new facility at Ellington**

— — —

Bob and Sue sold their trailer house on Lake Possum Kingdom and bought a big lot on the water with two houses on it. Monte and Carolyn Land shared in the purchase and moved into the smaller house, with long-range plans to tear it down and build a larger one. They moved over the Thanksgiving holiday 1986. When we would visit the new lake house, Bob always had a project underway. One of the first ones was to build a carport in front of the existing garage and convert the garage into a workshop. Another was to replace most of the boards on the walkway out into the lake. I loved working with Bob. He had a law degree but thought like an engineer. He designed the carport himself and I thought it was a masterpiece.

– – –

Mike and Andrea Sheets had been best friends since their pre-kindergarten days. The Sheets initially lived just around the corner from us in Nassau Bay. We attended the same church and shared many social events. They continued their friendship throughout college, Mike going to Trinity and Andrea to Baylor. After graduation, Mike stayed in San Antonio and worked for Harte Hanks, a marketing services company, while Andrea went to work for Interfirst Bank in Houston. They talked to each other about not being able to find an acceptable boyfriend/girlfriend. Finally, they got around to realizing that Andrea was looking for someone just like Mike, and Mike was looking for someone just like Andrea. The next question was, "Well, why don't we date each other?" At first, the thought of this was somewhat revolting. It would be like brothers and sisters dating each other! On second thought, they said, "Let's try it." When I first heard that they were going to date, I was excited, but worried that being best friends might not turn into true love. However, it did, and when they announced their engagement, I was extremely happy. Andrea was already like a daughter and now she truly would be a part of the Bostick family.

They set the wedding date for April 25, 1987. The ceremony was held at the Clear Lake United Methodist Church. Allan Restrepo was Mike's Best Man and Judy Neal was Andrea's Maid of Honor. Reverend Judd, the Trinity University Chaplin, officiated. I think all of Mike's friends had a good time in our spa the day before the wedding. I know I did.

**Mike & Andrea's wedding**

— — —

Senator Paul Simon (unfortunately not the singer) of Illinois announced in early 1987 that he would seek the Democratic nomination for President. My friend Dick Morrison was a strong backer and told me that Simon wanted to come to Houston and make a pro-manned spaceflight speech. Dick asked if I would write some ideas for the speech. At first I said, "No way, because I'm a Republican!", but after thinking about it for a few days, I said that I would give him some ideas in the hope that it might help the space cause. Shortly thereafter, I received a call from Simon's campaign manager saying he would like me to write an entire speech, so I started. In the speech, I paid tribute to the wisdom and foresight of President Kennedy, praised the accomplishments and technological spin-offs of NASA and stated the importance of continuing our expansion of the space horizon. Just as a tickler, I threw in the idea that NASA should receive authorization and appropriation for a two-year budget, allowing more effective long range planning and saving a lot of budget request time. After sending it to the campaign manager, he called me to confirm that he had received it and would give it to the Senator for his consideration. He cautioned me that the Senator would likely do a major re-write, but might include some of what I had proposed.

Several weeks later, Senator Simon scheduled an appearance at the Nassau Bay Hilton and invited dignitaries from Houston and across the state. Out-going Texas Governor Mark White attended. Several NASA officials, including JSC Director Aaron Cohen, were there also. There was to be a reception after his speech, so I didn't get a chance to meet him ahead of time. Vickie and I stood in the back and anxiously waited to see if he said anything remotely like what I had proposed. A few minutes into his speech, I realized that he was reading it verbatim! As he spoke, I at first felt proud that he obviously liked my speech, but then I became disgusted that he didn't have enough knowledge or strong feelings about space to change a single word! During the reception that followed, when Dick introduced me, he said that he started reading what I had proposed, with the intent of changing it to fit his beliefs and speaking style, but that he liked it so much he decided to say exactly what I had proposed. About a year later, out of money and after a poor showing in the primaries, he dropped out of the race. That was fine with me because I was a strong supporter of George H. W. Bush, who ultimately won.

– – –

In her junior year at A&M, Kristi met Russ Ray, an Agricultural Economics major and dairy farmer from Floresville Texas. When I first met him, I instantly liked him. He was a fine-looking young man with obvious morals and ethics and treated Kristi with respect. What more could a father want? In January 1988, when Kristi told me they were engaged and wanted to marry that summer after graduation from A&M, I was very happy. After meeting Russ' parents, brother and sisters, I was even happier. I felt as if they were my own family.

While planning for the wedding reception, I could tell that Kristi felt awkward in telling me what she would like to have, apparently afraid I would think it would cost too much. I just told her to have it where she wanted, with the band she wanted, and with the food she wanted. It was her wedding reception and I completely trusted her to make all the arrangements. My main concern was it would be an event she and Russ would happily remember.

The ceremony was on July 9, 1988, at the Clear Lake United Methodist Church with "Brother Buddy" Miller and Reverend Cliff Poe (from the Floresville First Baptist Church) officiating. Russ' brother Tom was his Best Man and Kristin Allen was the Maid of Honor.

**Kristi & Russ' wedding**

Their plan was to move to Floresville and build a home on the "Ray Compound" beside Russ' parents and his Uncle Carl. Russ would continue to work at the Ray Dairy Farm. They initially rented a house in Floresville, next to a drive-through restaurant named "The Spot." A stray dog, which had been hanging out at The Spot, started hanging out at their house. They quickly adopted her and named her Lady. Vickie and I helped them do some much needed remodeling of the rent house, mainly wallpaper and painting.

After living there for a while, they (I think primarily Kristi) decided that the dairy farm life was not for them. After much discussion between them, Russ applied for a job with Dell Computers in Austin and was accepted. Initially his parents were not too happy about him leaving the farm.

– – –

In June 1989, I was asked by Grumman to attend the Paris Air Show at Le Bourget airport. They even paid for Vickie to go with me. I was to spend most of the time at the Grumman chalet, answering questions about our role on Space Station, and promoting similar work with the Japanese and the Europeans. Also, I was to give a presentation at an AIAA conference there, and attend a 20th anniversary celebration of Apollo 11 with the prime crew in attendance. Mid-morning of the first day, June 8, I received a call from Gene Maranarie, the NASA Assistant Administrator for Public Affairs saying that Armstrong and Collins were threatening to leave because the public was driving them crazy. He asked if I could "hide" them at the Grumman chalet so that they would stay for an appearance they were scheduled to make that night at the anniversary banquet. So we hastily put together a private luncheon for them, using the menu already established for the next day. Arnie Aldrich, who was then the NASA Space Shuttle Program Director, brought them over. During the luncheon, one of the Grumman executives came in with about a dozen copies of a picture of Dave Scott on the moon during Apollo 15 and said that unfortunately, he didn't have any Apollo 11 photos left, but would they please sign the ones he had. I almost died! I was supposed to be protecting them from such infringement on their time! To my surprise, they graciously signed all of them except one. Michael Collings then said, "Since tomorrow is Jerry's birthday, I think we should sign one for him." He then signed his name and wrote "To Jerry-Happy Birthday" at the top. Armstrong and Aldrin then also signed it and the three of them and Arnie sang Happy Birthday to me. It is one of my most prized possessions.

After lunch, Armstrong, Collins, Aldrin, Aldrich and I went out on the back porch to watch an air show being conducted by the Russians. A MiG-29 Fulcrum did a couple of steep climbs straight up over the runway, cut the engines at almost stall speed, flipped over and started a free-fall toward the runway. The pilot would then restart the engines and pull up parallel to the runway at about 300 feet. Pretty spectacular! On the third such run, one of the engines failed to restart and the remaining one was not sufficient to break out of the vertical dive, so the pilot ejected at about 300 feet. We watched the ejection seat speed off to our left, but never saw the parachute deploy. The plane crashed only a couple hundred feet away from us and erupted into a fireball. All five of us swore that the ejection seat parachute never opened and that the pilot surely was dead. Later we got word that the parachute did open and the pilot survived with only minor injuries. Apparently, what happened was that when the pilot ejected, we followed it until the plane crashed and then looked back at it, therefore not seeing that the chute did open at about 20-30 feet off the ground. Just proves that eye-witnesses are often unreliable!

That afternoon I spent a lot of time talking to Neil. Most of all, he wanted to tell me all about a new tractor he had purchased for his farm in Ohio. He said he wanted to write a technical book about the Lunar Module and asked if I could get some specification documents, manufacturing drawings, test results, etc. I told him I would try my best, so he gave me his phone number, his fax number and his mailing address. Over the next few months, I was able to round up a lot of what he was looking for and mailed it to him. He later told me that he had given up on writing the book, but was using all the information I sent him in his classes at the University of Cincinnati.

The most interesting conversation I had with Neil that day was about his spending several days with Charles Lindberg at his home in Hana, Maui, Hawaii shortly after the Apollo 11 world tour. Neil said, "He taught me how to be a private person." to which I responded, "But you were <u>always</u> a private person." He said, "Yea, but he taught me such things as not giving autographs and not ever publishing the names of your children." This caught me by complete surprise because I had never heard anything about that visit.

I couldn't get in touch with Vickie in time for her to join us for lunch, but she came out later in the afternoon and literally stood in front of Neil, with his permission and appreciation, at the reception before the banquet that night, protecting him from the crowd. That was no small feat for a 5' 3", 100-pound person, but she did a magnificent job.

The Apollo 11 crew left the next morning, moderately pleased with how things had gone. Arnie and I delivered our speeches at the AIAA conference that day, along with Yuri Semenov, whom I had met in Moscow some 12 years before. Arnie and I had a lengthy discussion with him about why the Buran program was cancelled after only one flight. He said it was a mistake for them to fly it unmanned because of the additional cost of going that way. He was very frank and blunt as to why it only flew once; they ran out of money!

Seeing the Buran, which had flown its single flight some 7 months before, was very interesting. It flew in to the air show on an Antonev An-225, which was eerily similar to our Space Shuttle

Orbiter on top of its Boeing 747 carrier aircraft. Because the Buran had air-breathing engines on the back, its wings were a little further back than on our Orbiter. Other than that, it looked like a carbon copy of the Orbiter, and it should have, because the Russians used our plans! The Russians didn't have to steal our plans, they got all of them from NASA and its contractors through Freedom of Information

Act requests. This included unclassified documents on airframe design, materials, flight computer systems, propulsion systems and even the software used for design analysis.

**Buran at Paris airshow, June 1989**

— — —

When the office building at Ellington was completed, we had an open house to which we invited NASA, City of Houston and Grumman officials, including John O'Brien, who had succeeded George Skurla as President. O'Brien was not happy. He thought the building was much too elaborate and that my office area was much too nice. Jake Bussolini tried to convince him that Grumman had saved a bunch of money by adapting architectural plans from the existing Boeing building in Clear Lake, but O'Brien didn't seem to be impressed.

Alex Alexandrovich retired from Grumman in 1989, and was replaced as President, Space Systems Division by John Harrison, previously with Honeywell. This was not a smooth transition for me. John was much more interested in military than civil space. He brought with him Bob Puff, who served as an intermediary between me a John. It was clear that Puff wanted my job. This new management team at Grumman, from the Board of Directors down, was interested in home runs. They wanted big projects worth millions of dollars. I had trouble getting any bid money for small projects. My argument that several singles or doubles were as good as a home run, was not well received.

One of the disagreements that I had with Harrison was why, as a subcontractor for crew systems to Boeing on Space Station, we were not bidding on the waste management system (potty). I maintained that it was a lose/lose situation. No matter how well we might be able to build such a system, it would be very expensive and wouldn't satisfy all of the astronauts. The last thing we needed was bad press over a space potty. The issue was elevated to Robert Nafis, Harrison's boss. We ended up having to make a presentation on the subject to the Grumman Board, then headed by John O'Brien, who had succeeded George Skurla.

I reminded the Board of problems and astronaut complaints about the Space Shuttle potty, and of the bad publicity that Grumman had received about the very expensive ashtrays ($660 each) in the E-2 aircraft. The Board agreed with me and concluded that it was wise to not bid on the potty. My relationship with Harrison went downhill from there.

One thing that I did with the Space Station workforce at Ellington, was to put the designers, the manufacturing people and the quality assurance people all in the same room. At first, they all objected… "That's not the way we do it." After a couple of months, I walked into the room one day and several people were all huddled around a computer aided design/ computed aided manufacturing (CAD/CAM) system. I heard one of the manufacturing guys tell the design team, "If you could make this fillet 3/8 inch rather than 1/2, we can build it at about half the cost." The designers said, "No problem." I just grinned and walked away. Shortly thereafter, ex-astronaut Don Peterson, whom I had hired as our human factors (how easy are things to reach and operate?) expert, asked if he could move his desk into the room also. The concept, which had never been tried before at Grumman, was soon adopted company-wide.

However, Harrison, Puff and I were just not getting along. John Mockovciak, one of the long-term Long Islanders who had agreed to move to Houston, complained to me that Puff was taking up all of his time asking stupid questions and challenging the way he was doing his job. When I heard that the Space Station Engineering and Integration contract with NASA was not going well in Reston Virginia, and that new people were being brought in, it caught my interest. Tom Kelly would be the new boss, with Ed Smylie as his deputy. I let it be known that I would consider moving to Reston if there was a job for me. I visited Tom and Ed in Reston and when Tom offered me a job as Vice President and Deputy Director of Technical Operations, I didn't hesitate to accept. In addition to Tom and Ed, both of whom I highly respected, my friend ex-astronaut T. K. Mattingly would be one of my division chiefs.

In confirmation of my suspicion about Bob Puff, as soon as I announced that I would be leaving to take the job in Reston, Harrison appointed Puff as my replacement.

— — —

As Daddy approached his 80th birthday in January 1990, my sister Mary, Vickie and I tried to think of something special we could do for him. He had no hobbies or vices, so it was not easy to come up with ideas. Vickie said that since he was always watching the Nashville Network on TV because he loved country music, maybe we should take him to the Grand Ole Opry in Nashville. Wonderful idea! I called my friend Bill Bailey, then a constable in Harris County, but previously a disc jockey at radio station KIKK in Pasadena. He once won Country Music Disc Jockey of the Year.

He said he would call the General Manager and see what he could do. In a few days he called back to tell me that he had arranged for six free tickets to the Opry on the front row. He said the manager would be expecting us and to ask for him when we arrived. As soon as we were seated, the manager came and asked me and Daddy to go with him. He took us to several dressing rooms of the people appearing that night, and then to the rear of the stage where we could watch closely. Then Roy Acuff, the "king of country music", introduced Daddy to the audience and had him come to center stage. All of the performers that night were really nice to Daddy except Mel Tillis, who just walked right past him without saying a word or shaking his hand. Earl Scruggs, of the Foggy Mountain Boys, who was having his own birthday party in his dressing room, invited us to share his cake. While on the stage, I noticed Johnny Lee standing not far away. He sang the song *Looking For Love In All The Wrong Places* in the movie *Urban Cowboy* and had his own night club in Pasadena. I walked over to him and introduced myself. He said he was not performing that night, but had just come to the Opry to see what was going on. When I told him about Daddy, he insisted that he meet him and then adopted him for the rest of the night, taking him around and introducing him to each new performer. I think it was one of the best days of Daddy's life.

– – –

Before moving to Virginia, Vickie found a lump in her right breast. A biopsy proved inconclusive, but she wanted the lump to be removed. We had long discussions about the surgery and she was clear to the surgeon and me that if it was malignant, she wanted to remove the entire breast. Sue came down and was at the hospital with me when the surgeon came out and said he was 99% sure it was malignant, but the lab was performing a test to confirm. Soon he came to tell us that the lab test was conclusive. It definitely was malignant. He reiterated with us what Vickie had told him about a complete mastectomy, and asked if we still agreed. The answer was yes. She recovered very quickly and was ready to move to Reston later that year.

- - -

In the fall of 1990, I rented an apartment in Reston and began work. Some within Grumman had assumed (hoped) that because Ed Smylie and I were Mississippi State graduates, as was Bob Moorehead, the NASA Space Station Freedom program manager, we could improve the evaluations that Grumman had been receiving. Wishful thinking! Ed and I were on good terms with Moorehead, but he cut us no slack. If anything, he was harder on us than anyone else.

I started looking for a house to buy nearby. My friend Helga Meyer still lived in Lakevale, so we used her as our real estate agent. Each weekend she showed me potential houses. The first one we looked at was very nice, but with a smaller den than I would like. The others we looked at were terrible! Very depressing....old, dirty and too expensive. When Vickie came up to join the search, she was shocked to find that there were so few viable options. Without me expressing my opinion, she chose the first one at which I had looked, so we made an offer, which was accepted.

While I was still living in the apartment, Grumman held a reception at the Smithsonian Air and Space Museum to unveil an F-14 that was going on display there. As I was driving to the reception, I was listening to the radio. I stopped for a traffic light on Constitution Avenue on the south side of the White House and as I was looking to my left at the White House, the radio started broadcasting a live report from the President. He announced that Air Force F-14s had just been deployed to begin a bombing attack in Iraq. It was the official beginning of what they called Desert Shield, later called Desert Storm or the Persian Gulf War. I felt really weird listening to the President announcing the beginning of a war while I was on my way to see one of the airplane types that was involved. When I arrived at the museum, everyone was gathered around a television getting updates on the war. Much to my surprise, Secretary of Defense Dick Chaney was actually there, but he spent most of his time on the telephone. I would have given anything to know who he was talking to and what he was saying.

– – –

The move from Clear Lake to Reston was eventful, in that I wanted to take the Bricklin and leave it in Bedford Virginia with Terry Tanner for some much-needed work (see page 192). Pulling the Bricklin on a trailer behind our Cadillac was more of a chore than I had anticipated. I had driven the hills of Tennessee several times before, but never pulling that much weight. For some of the high hills, I would accelerate to 80/85 miles per hour going down a hill in order to make it up the next one. Several times, with the accelerator to the floor, we would end up barely moving at the top. It reminded me of pulling our boat up the hill leaving Norm Prince's cabin on Lake Travis. On the second day of the trip, Spook, who was riding in the back seat with Meagan, finally noticed that there was a trailer behind us, and started barking at it. What a relief it was when we made it to Bedford and could unload the trailer.

– – –

Living in Reston was something that Vickie and I both enjoyed. The previous owners of our house had made a lot of nice improvements. He was a commercial airline pilot and she was the head flight attendant for the same airline. On their travels overseas, they purchased a new mantel for the fireplace and wood to replace the handrail on the stairs plus all kinds of plants for the yard, including many varieties of tulips from Holland. The first year we were there, it was exciting to see what would come up next. It snowed a lot and we didn't even complain about shoveling snow. We built a snowman each year. Spook and Meagan were leery of the snow at first, but soon were running and jumping in it.

**Our Reston house during first snow**

In the fall, we had tons of leaves that we raked and hauled to the Fairfax County dump. The dump was one of our favorite places! They had a large field when you could dump leaves and limbs and get free mulch in exchange. For the other trash (garbage), they had a very large brick building with about a dozen big garage doors. We could just back the truck into one of the spaces and dump it all out on a very clean floor, then a small front-loader would push it into a huge pit where dump trucks were parked. When the trucks became full, they would drive the load down into Virginia to a sanitary landfill. They also had several stations outside the big brick building where you could dispose of anything…batteries, paint, etc. and recyclables such as cans, glass and paper.

Before our first Christmas in the house, Vickie decorated a normal Christmas tree for the den. For the living room, she erected a dead tree branch and decorated it with all kinds of Texas stuff: stars, cowboy hats, Dallas Cowboy footballs, boots, etc. For tinsel, she used rope. We had an open house for the neighbors, who kept staring at the tree. We told them that was the kind of Christmas trees we had in Texas, and I think they actually believed us until they saw the real tree in the den.

We had a lot of visitors while there; Mother and Daddy, Joe and Mary, Robert, Bob and Sue, Mike, Andrea and Dylan, Buzzy Griffin from Houston, and Jim Newcomb from Clear Lake among others. Vickie enjoyed showing them around D.C. After several tours, she would drop the visitors off at a particular site and tell them she would pick them up in an hour, just long enough for her to go the Hawk and Dove for a beer. Unfortunately, I was working such long hours that I rarely was able to go with them on the tours.

Bob's brother, Vickie's Uncle Doodie, joined us on a tour of Capitol Page School, the Library of Congress, the House of Representatives (where Bob and Uncle Doodie got to sit in the speaker's chair), and the Supreme Court. Mike's college friend Charles Eskridge, who was a Clerk in the Supreme Court, gave us a wonderful tour. Bob's big thrill was to sit in the Chief Justice's chair, which is not usually allowed. It meant a lot to Bob because he was authorized to try a case there. A thrill for all of us was a tour of "the highest court in the land", a basketball court on the top floor where Justices and Clerks often played. While in Page School there, I had good friends who were Supreme Court Pages, but they never mentioned the basketball court.

Working there was something else! On the good side, I was happy to be working with Tom Kelly, Ed Smylie and T. K. Mattingly. On the negative side, it appeared that the NASA Space Station Freedom management did not want a systems integrator. They wanted to be the integrator and just have the Grumman team do whatever they told us to do. Ed and I did what we could to try to convince Bob Moorehead, the NASA manager, to let us do the job we were hired to do, but we made little, if any, progress. This had been the big problem when Fred Haise was the Grumman team manager. He would sometimes yield to Moorehead but still receive poor performances grades and bonuses. Tom Kelly was sent by Grumman President John O'Brien to be more firm and not yield to the daily directions from NASA. He tried! We all tried. We all worked 10-12 hours a day, including Saturdays and usually 4-5 hours on Sundays to prove to NASA that we could successfully carry out the requirements of our integration contract. The problem was that NASA had no intention of allowing us to do our job. They just wanted to give us daily instructions and do it their way. It didn't help that the Space Station contractors, Rockwell, McDonnell Douglas and Boeing, kept telling Moorehead that they didn't need an integration contractor.

– – –

While in Reston, Aunt Beece died on June 23, 1991. I went to her funeral at the Belmont Methodist Church two days later. I was really sad over losing one of my favorite people. When I got back to Mother and Daddy's house, we got a call from Russ saying that Kristi had given birth to a healthy and beautiful little girl, who they named Lauren Joy. My first grandchild! While driving to the Memphis airport that afternoon to catch a flight back to Reston, I kept thinking about how good God was. On the same day we had buried a great lady, He had given us another one. While waiting for my flight I wrote a letter to Lauren telling her how happy I was and promising her I would be there for her whenever she needed me. That started a tradition of letters to the nine grandkids to follow, to be opened on their 16th birthday.

About a month later, on July 23rd, I heading for California to attended a Space Station meeting at the McDonnell Douglas facility in Huntington Beach. When I arrived at the LA airport car rental place, I had a message from Mike saying that Andrea was in the Santa Monica hospital ready to give birth. I checked into my hotel and then went immediately to the hospital. Colette was already there. I stayed the rest of the night there. Just after noon the next day, I waited outside the door while a fine baby boy, Dylan Travis, was delivered. Colette came and got me immediately after his birth. Per chance, I was the fourth person to hold him, after the doctor, Mike, then Andrea, then me. I took him from Andrea and took him to the sink, where Colette and I gave him his first bath. What an experience and what a handsome young boy!

In March 1992, when Lauren was nine months old, Vickie flew to Austin to stay with Lauren while Kristi and Russ took a well-deserved vacation in Hawaii. Russ won the trip for exceeding his sales quota at Dell. Kristi was very nervous about leaving Lauren, but not nearly as much as Vickie. She wouldn't take her eyes off Lauren because she thought, "If anything happens to her while under my care, the whole family will kill me!" She even slept on the floor just outside the door to Lauren's room. Lauren was obviously in great shape when Kristi and Russ returned, so they were happy and relieved. Also much relieved, Vickie told them that she was going out on the deck to have a cigarette and a glass of wine, neither of which she had indulged in since they left for Hawaii.

— — —

Also while in Reston, we were able to take some very enjoyable vacations to Possum Kingdom with Bod and Sue. One notable one was in July 1992. They had just purchased a new SeaDoo, which was a lot of fun. Bob was always building something and I enjoyed being his helper. On this trip, he was building a carport in front of their new house. Kristi, Russ and Lauren visited for a few days, so Bob, Monte Land, Russ and I spent a lot of time erecting the carport. When we got too hot, we would just go jump into the lake or take a quick SeaDoo ride. On July 4th we had our own fireworks display, orchestrated by Amanda Land. Only just over one year old at the time, Lauren seemed to really enjoy it.

– – –

Division President Tom Kelly got so frustrated that he gave up and was replaced by Connie Blyseth, who tried to improve things by bringing in some of his "tough" guys from Bethpage. It soon became obvious that we should start making plans for revamping our contract, and even consider the possibility of losing it altogether. When Dan Goldin became the NASA Administrator, that possibility seemed almost certain. He didn't like Space Station Freedom and he didn't like Grumman. Connie asked me to go back to Houston as the General Manager there and also serve as Assistant Program Director.

Goldin became the NASA Administrator on April 1, 1992, April fool's day! We were all aware of his hatred of Grumman and of his pronouncement at his TRW going-away party that "Now I can get those Grumman bastards!" We just wondered what and when he would do to try to get rid of us. Within a year and a half, he terminated our integration contract and gave the responsibility to Boeing. His prime excuse was that we had allowed the total budget to reach $20 billion and the number of Shuttle flights required for assembly to grow to 16. When the International Space Station was finally completed, the cost was $58 to $72 billion, depending on how you count operations cost, and required 34 Shuttle assembly flights. I guess our plan was not that bad after all!

We began plans to sue NASA for what was in our mind an unlawful contract termination, but when Grumman merged with Northrop in 1994, Northrop dropped the suit planning. They agreed with us that it was a winnable suit, but didn't want to offend NASA because it might jeopardize future contracts.

Dan Goldin was not only successful in terminating the Grumman space station integration contract, but also with bringing in the Russians to change from Space Station Freedom to International Space Station. No one at JSC was happy with him, but he didn't care.

In January 1993 we sold our Reston house and moved back to Clear Lake. Since we had such a short notice, we asked Terry Stone to find us a rent house for one year giving us time to look for something to purchase.

— — —

The year 1993 was also eventful away from work. Once back in Clear Lake, Vickie and I built a dollhouse for Lauren and a barn for Dylan. They both were fairly detailed and took a lot of time, which we both thoroughly enjoyed. They were hinged so that they could be opened to expose the rooms/stables. Vickie went to every craft store in Pasadena and Houston looking for just the right furniture,

**Lauren's Dollhouse**

appliances, flooring, curtains, wallpaper, animals, etc. She even found miniature doorknobs and tiny wooden shingles for the roofs.

By now Kristi, Russ and Lauren had moved into a house on Rustic Rock in Austin, which didn't have an outdoor deck. Having built several decks over the years, I gladly volunteered to help Russ build one. We rented an 8-foot trailer to put behind his Ford Bronco for hauling supplies from Home Depot. On the last trip, we got several 12-foot boards, which were really too long for the trailer, but we thought they would be okay if we drove slowly. Just a few miles down Highway 183 the trailer hitch starting lifting the rear wheels of the Bronco! We were only going about 25 miles per hour, but the Bronco/trailer combination began to go sideways. Luckily, we didn't hit any other vehicles, but the Bronco turned over. As soon as we figured out which way was up, we got out and thought both of us were unharmed. A wrecker came and pulled the Bronco and trailer to their house. We loaded all the spilled lumber onto the back of the wrecker. Later that night, my left shoulder began to hurt, so Kristi took me to the emergency room at Seton hospital, where they determined that my collarbone (clavicle) was fractured. They put me into a brace and gave me pain pills, saying they thought

**Dylan's Barn**

it would heal on its own. It didn't. Once back in Houston, I saw an orthopedic surgeon who finally had to operate and remove a small section. It has caused me no problem since.

The deck came into play for another memorable event. For Lauren's 2nd birthday party, Kristi planned a big party out on the deck. She rented a Barney costume for Vickie to wear. Barney was a purple dinosaur who had an extremely popular TV show for kids. (He was really annoying!) Most of the kids at the party loved Barney (Vickie), but a few were afraid. What we didn't realize was that it was about 20 degrees warmer inside the costume and Vickie almost passed out. I took her inside and when I took the costume head off, steam came pouring out. We told the kids that Barney got sick and had to leave.

— — —

For Thanksgiving 1994, Vickie and I visited my parents in Mississippi. Mother had recently had a stroke and spent several days in the Tupelo Hospital. By phone, Mother, Daddy, and sister Mary had told us she was much better but when we arrived, we could see that she was still somewhat paralyzed on her left side and occasionally seem confused. We went to Pickwick for Thanksgiving dinner, so at least she didn't try to cook. A couple of days later, we got a call from Mike saying that their second son, Jordan Taylor, was born and mother and child were both healthy. Of course, we were all thrilled. Daddy, upon hearing that, gave me his mother's old clock and asked that I keep it and give it to Jordan as a wedding gift. Back in Houston, I had it refurbished (all jewel bearings replaced) and it is still operating well.

Soon after we left Mississippi, Mother had to reenter the hospital. I returned to visit her there and after talking to her doctor, concluded that she needed to go into an assisted living facility. Daddy would not even talk about it, but I lined up visits to several in the area and told him I wanted him to go with me to choose one. He said an emphatic no. The morning I was scheduled to see the places, Daddy cooked breakfast for the two of us and then as I was leaving, he put on a jacket and said, "I guess I'll ride with you." We first went to the Magnolia in Iuka where he looked around and said nothing. Next, we went to the Landmark in Booneville. Again, Daddy just looked and said not a single word. We were scheduled to see another in Tupelo, but as we were leaving Booneville, he said he had seen enough and he wanted to go to the hospital and see Mother. I took that to mean that he was even more convinced that he wanted to take Mother back home and that he could take care of her himself. When we got to her hospital room, he said to her, "Well, I've found a real nice apartment for us to move into." I couldn't believe my ears and said a silent "Thank you Lord!"

Daddy and I went back to Booneville and put down a deposit on an assisted living apartment at the Landmark for the two of them. In early 1995, Vickie and I helped them move in, making at least five trips with Vickie's truck loaded to the brim. Daddy put their Golden home on the market and it sold fairly quickly. On our last trip there, Daddy stood on the back porch, looked out into the pecan orchard and said, "I sure have made a lot of tracks here." After he went inside, I stayed on the porch and cried.

– – –

We soon were to have a third grandson. Preston Thomas Ray was born on February 8, 1995 in Austin's St. David's Hospital. We were able to be there the day after he was born and were impressed with what a handsome young man he was, how sweet Lauren was to her little brother, and how nice the room was. To say that I was a proud Grandpa would be an understatement!

— — —

When the Grumman/Northrop "merger" was made final in April 1994, it quickly became obvious that it was a buy-out by Northrop and they had no intent of keeping the Grumman people around. Almost all Grumman officers were demoted, including me. I became Director of Business Development for the new Northrop Grumman Technical Services Division headed by Fred Haise (a reduction in title, but not in pay). They had a contract with JSC for operation and maintenance of all the computing systems there. Grumman had staffed the effort with mostly Long Island people and were getting low performance grades. Fred wanted me to try to figure out how to fix it, but my recommendations were too drastic in his mind; get rid of most of the Long Island folks and bring in people known and liked by JSC management. One of my recommendations was to hire Lyn Dunseith, who had retired from NASA. Fred agreed, but soon learned that Lyn agreed with all of my recommendations. The head of the effort was Bud McKinzie, who asked Lyn and me to take a look at the new thing called "internet." Was it anything that could be beneficial to the computing world and should they be using it? After a few weeks, Lyn and I presented our conclusion to McKinzie: Yes, the internet had the potential to be a very useful tool for such things as the dissemination of information within NASA and to the public, conducting information about potential hires, and for ordering supplies and equipment. We recommended that we try it out internally for a few months and then recommend it to NASA. McKinzie almost threw us out of his office, saying, "The internet will never be anything but a bunch of porn sites, and you guys are totally wrong!" The meeting ended on that outburst. As Lyn and I were walking down the hall in disbelief, he said, "Maybe it's time we really retire." Within a couple of months, we both did.

Retirement from what was then Northrop Grumman was an ordeal to say the least. Grumman had promised me that when I retired they would count my NASA time as Grumman time and guaranteed that my retirement would be at least as much as if I had stayed at NASA. I had received no retirement from NASA (they did return the contributions I had made) because I was three years short of the required 25 years, so this was very important to me. Northrop said "No way. We are not obligated to live up to such promises, if they were made." Fortunately, I had saved all the paperwork and sent it to them. They said that was all nice but what Grumman had promised me was not technically allowable, because as a US government contractor, they could only offer government approved "defined benefit" retirement plans. I ended up having to hire an attorney, Dick Morrison. Most of the folks with whom I had dealt at Grumman had retired, but we able to track them down. God Bless George Skurla, who was living in Florida at the time, because he said, "Hell yes, I promised him that and you (Northrop) had better figure out a way to make it happen." After several weeks of battling back and forth between Dick and their lawyer, they finally agreed to supplement my government approved "defined benefit" retirement with an annuity that would match what I was asking for. On March 15, 1996, I officially became retired.

\- \- \-

# Chapter 7

# UNITED SPACE ALLIANCE

I enjoyed the idea of what I thought was going to be retirement. For one thing, I was happy to be away from all the crap going on at Northrop Grumman. Mainly, I was happy to have time to spend with Lauren, Dylan, Jordan and Preston, to be followed by Ryan just a couple of months later.

In June of 1996, Dylan was in Austin with Kristi, Russ, Lauren and Preston. He had flown there with Linda who was in California for Ryan's birth on May 17. We visited with them there and then Dylan drove back to Clear Lake with us to spend a few days. At that time, we had a Buick Roadmaster (we called it the Road hog) with a system that would count down the mileage remaining on trips. This was before GPS, so you had to get the mileage from a map and insert it into the system, and then it would tell you how many miles you had to go to get to your destination. Dylan loved playing with it and soon he would look at how fast I was driving, how many miles we had to go and figure out how long it would take to get there. This from a kid a month short of being 5 years old!

While in Clear Lake, the three of us went to AstroWorld, an amusement park in Houston operated by the Six Flags organization. I think we rode every ride they had. My fondest memories are that it rained, but Dylan didn't mind. He said he was already wet from the River Adventure ride, so what did it matter. We ate hot dogs in the rain. We laughed a lot. One ride was a twisting, looping roller coaster inside a mountain where it was completely dark. To tell the truth, it was pretty frightening. When the ride was over and we got out on solid ground, he went to Vickie and said, "I will never get on that ride again!" It was one of the most fun days of my life and I think Dylan enjoyed it also.

We had purchased a toy kitchen, refrigerator and sink for Lauren to play with, but Dylan enjoyed it as much as she did.

After a few days, Dylan, Vickie and I flew to California to see our latest grandchild, Ryan over Father's Day. I felt so fortunate to now have five wonderful grandkids.

— — —

Soon after retiring I began to get phone calls from my friend Glynn Lunney. He was the Program Manager of the Space Flight Operations Contract (SFOC) with NASA, responsible for operation of the Space Shuttle. Glynn said there were a number of things he needed help with, and thought I was the right person to assist them in transitioning some non-SFOC tasks such as flight software and flight crew equipment, currently the responsibility of IBM and Boeing, respectively. I told him I appreciated the offer, but I was very happy being totally retired. After three or four more calls from him, I finally agreed to go to work for him, if he would promise me that he would retire himself within the next couple of years. He said he fully intended to retire in April 1998, about a year and a half away, and I could retire again at the same time.

So in September 1996 I was hired by United Space Alliance as Assistant Program Manager. It turned out to be one of my most enjoyable jobs. I was happy to be working with Glynn once again and I felt a freedom like I never had before. I could do almost anything I wanted to do the way I wanted to do it, as long as Glynn agreed. He was the only one I tried to please. Howard DeCastro had recently been hired as Deputy Program Manager and was very suspicious that Glynn had brought me in to assume his job when he retired, or to become the head of Flight Operations upon Harold Draughon's departure. Glynn and I laughed about that and just let him worry. Also, the IBM and Boeing managers of the projects we were transitioning to USA thought I was out to get their jobs. Paul Smith, who was CEO at the time, asked me to move to Washington and be the USA chief lobbyist. I respectfully declined, but he was furious. My feeling was, "So, fire me."

One benefit of working there was that I was eligible to purchase Chrysler Corporation automobiles at the fleet price. Soon after I started, I bought my first Jeep Grand Cherokee.

We were successful in completing the transition of the flight software and flight crew equipment work. I had hired Clay McCullough, retired from NASA, to help me with the crew equipment and Jay Baumgartner, retired from Grumman, as my budget manager. They were a tremendous help.

– – –

Away from work, we were going through some bad times with Bob. In late September 1996, just after I went to work for USA, he was diagnosed with lung cancer. He and Sue came to our house in Clear Lake and he went to MD Anderson hospital for diagnosis confirmation and formulation of a treatment plan. They stayed with us until early January 1997 while he went through radiation treatment. He never complained to us and kept a good spirit considering what he was going through. Through Thanksgiving and Christmas, we all struggled with the idea that he might not be with us for long, but kept it just under the surface. I am convinced that Bob knew he wasn't going to live long, but we didn't talk about it openly. His son Jeff came for Thanksgiving.

Just before Thanksgiving, Sue and I drove to Possum Kingdom to winterize the house, boat and SeaDoo. It was a sad trip, but good for me, and I think her, to let it all hang out and talk openly about what might be ahead for Bob. We cried a lot.

In early January 1997, Bob and Sue went back to their home in Arlington. Bob wanted to go to the lake one last time, so the four of us, plus Marnie and David, made the trip. Bob was pretty feeble by then and had to be carried up the steps.

Vickie stayed with them in Arlington and I went back to work at USA. A couple of weeks later, Bob passed away, February 6, 1997. He was only 63 years old and had been retired for a little more than 2 ½ years. That's when I committed to full retirement as soon as I fulfilled my commitment to Lunney. We had planned a lot of things to do together. His death hit me hard. He was my best friend. I learned so much from him. We discovered that engineers and lawyers have a lot in common. They both think logically and methodically and they plan for contingencies. His funeral was at the First Baptist Church in Arlington. Kristi and Russ came, which all of us really appreciated. There was an overflow crowd; the sanctuary, fellowship hall and some classrooms were full and people were standing outside. The procession from there to his final resting place, Greenwood Mausoleum in Fort Worth, was overwhelming. Because Bob had been Assistant District Attorney in Tarrant County, City Attorney in Arlington, Texas State Legislator and a State District Probate Judge in Tarrant County, he knew almost every law enforcement officer in the State, and most of them showed up. Interstate Highway 30 was closed to traffic going west. We stopped counting police cars at 25. They had every exit and entry ramp blocked. When we arrived at Greenwood, on both sides of the entrance road there were hundreds of police officers and patrolmen all standing at attention and saluting as the hearse went by. As we were walking into the mausoleum, Kate

Day, Lisa and Lloyd's youngest daughter said, "Aunt Vickie, is Elvis buried in here?" Bob would have said, "That was a <u>hell</u> of a funeral!"

— — —

Just over a year later, in April 1998, Glynn and I both retired from United Space Alliance.

— — —

## Chapter 8

# RETIREMENT

In July 1998, just over a year after Bob passed away, Vickie, Susan and I went to France. The four of us had planned such a trip for years. We arrived in Paris the day they were having a parade on the Champs Elysees for the French soccer team, which had just won the World Cup. After the parade passed, we, along with thousands of others went out into the street. Vickie started doing the wave. Others just looked at her at first but soon caught on. Within a few minutes, the wave proceeded down the Champs from the Arch de Triumph to Place de la Concorde. Way to go Vickie!

After two days in Paris, showing Susan many of our favorite places, we rented a car and headed south. We visited Versailles, and then drove on to Chartres, where we spent the night. I saw a brochure there for Leonardo da Vinci's home in Amboise, where he spent the last three years of his life. It wasn't on our itinerary, but it wasn't far from our planned route, so I definitely wanted to go there. What a fantastic place! IBM had constructed about 40 models, including helicopters, parachutes and tanks, from his drawings. What a guy he was! Not only a fantastic artist (Mona Lisa, The Last Supper, to name a few), but also an unbelievable engineer who saw a future of automation no one else could imagine. I could have spent days there, but we had to press on to our next stop, Auberge de Capucin Gourmand (Inn of the hungry rabbit!), in Tournon, Saint Martin, owned by our friends Michel and Monique Pelligran.

Linda and I first discovered their restaurant in Paris in 1981, and Vickie and I had also been there. I had recommended their restaurant to so many friends that they created "The NASA Room", with autographed pictures of astronauts, flight controllers and other NASA officials covering the walls. In the early '90s they closed the Paris restaurant and moved to Tournon Saint-Martin, about 250 miles south, where they opened an inn and restaurant. We had a great time there; wonderful food, too much wine, and conversation into the wee hours. After a fantastic breakfast the next morning, we headed east toward the wine country of Burgundy.

By now, we realized that our rental car was much too small. By the time we got all of our luggage in, there was just a tiny space for Susan in the back seat. She called it "My hole." Despite her being uncomfortable, she enjoyed the beautiful countryside; vineyards, fields of sunflowers, and beautiful old castles. We stopped often to let her stretch her legs and to have a glass of the local wine.

From the Burgundy region, we headed north toward Paris. At one stop, Susan was excited to see "Texas burger" on the menu, and ordered it. When it came, it had a fried egg on top! Most of the places where we ate did not have ice for the drinks. We spent one night in Montrachet. The hotel bar there actually could make a "CC & 7", Canadian Club and Seven-Up. And, they had ice! Susan was happy. One of my favorite stops was in the Pouilly-Fuisse region. To my surprise, there are two separate little villages, just a few miles apart, with those names. Between the villages is a quaint little restaurant, Au Pouilly Fuisse, with outdoor tables. We lingered there over wine, cheese and bread. Along the route, we toured many vineyards and castles. We could have spent weeks there, but we only had four days to get back to Paris.

Once again in Paris, we stayed at the Hotel Saint-Louis, on Saint Louis island in the Seine. From there it was an easy walk to Notre Dame, Sainte-Chapelle and our two favorite sidewalk cafés, the Brasserie de l'Isle St. Louis and Les Deux Magots, where Hemmingway and Picasso once hung out.

After two days there, it was time to head back to the U.S. We had a wonderful time, but we all missed Bob. Susan said, "Next time, get a bigger car!"

– – –

Vickie and I had already started looking for a retirement home. We wanted to be on the water somewhere with the yard sloping down into the water. No bluffs requiring long steps. If a lake appeared on the Texas state map, over the next several months we visited most of them. Our house in Clear Lake was placed on the market and it sold before we had found a lake house. Being very short on time, and thinking we wanted to be somewhere in central or south Texas, we split up to find a rental house we could live in while completing our search for a permanent place. Vickie went to Austin and I went to San Antonio. After a couple of days, we each had found a possibility. By phone, we concluded that the one Vickie had found in South Austin was the right choice, so she rented it for one year (1999) and we went back to Clear Lake to arrange for the move.

The rental house in South Austin was more than adequate while we continued our search. Previously we had looked in Meadowlakes/Marble Falls, but had ruled it out because we thought the houses were too close together. The more we looked, the more we realized that we were going to have to compromise on something. There was no perfect place. When our realtor convinced us to look at a house in Meadowlakes, we reluctantly agreed. As soon as we entered the front door and looked out on Lake Marble Falls, we knew it had real possibilities. After Vickie discovered that it had a large master bedroom with his and her closets <u>and</u> his and her bathrooms, she was sold. Then I discovered a garage downstairs with an air pump system in exactly the right spot to air up the Bricklin doors. As we were walking to the realtor's car, we agreed to make an offer.

After a few back and forths on price, a contract was accepted and we closed on the Meadowlakes house March 31, 1999. We left the closing, bought some fried chicken, a bottle of wine and had a picnic on the floor of our new home. It was good that we had nine more months in our rental house, because there were a number of things we wanted to do before moving in, such as new carpet, a bookcase/entertainment center, and a backyard fence. We were all moved in by Christmas that year.

One of the first things we did after we moved in was to look for a church. We visited several in Marble Falls and fell in love with St. Peter's Lutheran. Neither of us were Lutheran, but we felt at home there and are now convinced that God brought us to Marble Falls to be members of St. Peter's.

The house did not have a boat dock, so I was eager to get one. The bank to the lake was covered in small trees and brush. That was my first challenge. Once I had it all cleared off, I built a small retaining wall at the back of the yard and built steps down to where the boat dock would be attached. I had drawn plans for a dock which would accommodate two SeaDoos, and that would float up 25 feet in case of flood. I loved doing all of this physical labor. I found it so satisfying to be able to look at the end of the day and see what I had accomplished. Having spent most of my career at a desk, I found great enjoyment in building things with my own hands. When it was time to start the boat dock however, I realized that there was no way I could do it myself, so I found a dock builder who built it to my drawings.

In December 1999, just after the boat dock was completed, we purchased a new SeaDoo from the dealer at Possum Kingdom. It was a 1998 model that had been sitting in their showroom for almost a year, so they gave us a good deal.

We also constructed a game room on the lower level of the house. Vickie and I tore down the existing wall that divided the space into two rooms, tore the sheetrock from the walls and installed rough cedar, installed large windows, ran TV and telephone lines into the new space and retiled the floor. Then we purchased a slot machine, a shuffleboard and an Apollo 13 pinball machine. Over the years, I think all the grandkids enjoyed it. I know that we did.

– – –

In the meantime, Marnie and David eloped and were married in the Chapel at the Monte Carlo hotel in Las Vegas, on May 26, 1998. (On May 24, 2003, just two days short of their fifth anniversary, they affirmed their vows at our church in Marble Falls. Cole was the ring bearer and seemed to really enjoy the ceremony. Marnie was pregnant with Case at the time.)

– – –

Mother and Daddy were still living in the Landmark assisted living facility in Booneville. We visited them at least twice a year and they seemed to be happy there. They had three good (well, nutritious if not good) meals a day and were well taken care of. I called them almost every day. On April 5, 2000, I called and the phone was finally answered by the lady there who cut their hair. When I asked how they were doing, there was a long pause, and then she said, "Oh, Jerry, I'm so sorry to tell you that your Mother just passed away." She had just taken a shower and walked out into their room, smiled at the ladies there to help her, and dropped to the floor. The hairdresser said she tried to revive her, but there was no pulse. At least she went peacefully with no pain, for which I had always prayed.

Her funeral was the next weekend at the Golden Chapel United Methodist church. She was buried in the Ridge cemetery in Itawamba

County where her's and Daddy's parents are also buried. While there, we got a call from our animal clinic where we had boarded Spook, saying that he was in cardiac arrest and had no chance of surviving. They said they could keep him alive until we returned, but he would be unconscious, or they could remove the respirator and allow him to die. Vickie and I thought it was best to let him go ahead and die. The clinic staff buried him on a nearby ranch.

– – –

On May 23, 2000, Marnie gave birth to their first son, Cole Alexander Castañeda, at the Seton Medical Center in Austin. We were there to see him within a few minutes afer he was born, and were proud grandparents again, and happy to see mother and son in good shape. I was sad that Mother was not alive to see him.

– – –

Starting in 1964, I was selected to be a part of the NASA Longitudinal Study of Astronaut Health (LSAH), a program that would compare astronaut's health to that of mere mortals. Of course, I was in the mere mortals group. It was a good deal, because I got a free extensive physical examination every six months, which took two days. It started with a blood draw followed by a treadmill test, eye and hearing exams, a proctoscopy (not my favorite), electrocardiogram, and just about everything else you can think of. The final session was with a doctor who did a further examination and went over all the test results with me. I was able to stay in the program even after I left NASA, but only received exams once a year.

In the summer of 2000, I went for my annual exam and also to attend a party that Gene Kranz was throwing to celebrate the publication of his book, *Failure Is Not An Option*. One of the first things they did at the NASA clinic was the electrocardiogram. I noticed that the test giver was wearing a new contactor badge. When it became obvious that he was having a difficult time getting a reading, I thought, "Well, that's what you get when you go with the lowest bidder!" After a few minutes, he left to go get a nurse, who tried again. After putting new leads on and trying several times, she said she was going to get a doctor. Soon, two doctors came in and asked if I was feeling all right. After looking at the charts the nurse had taken, they asked me to follow them to their office. Once there, they told me that I had had a heart attack or was in the process of having one. They said that if I were still a NASA employee, they wouldn't let me leave the clinic. They would order an ambulance and take me to a cardiologist at the hospital. They made me promise that I would go see one as soon as possible.

That was on a Friday afternoon, so we stayed in Clear Lake for the weekend and went to the Kranz parties. He had one Friday night at his home in Dickinson and one Saturday night at the air museum in Galveston. Sunday we drove back to Marble Falls. I called Kristi to get the name of her cardiologist. Monday morning I called Dr. David Terreson and got in to see him that afternoon. After an extensive electrocardiogram and listening to my heart, he said I had not and was not having an attack, but my aortic valve had a severe leak and needed to be replaced with an artificial one.

Of course, that was pretty shocking news and my engineering instincts took over. I wanted to know every detail of the procedure and what kind of artificial valve would be used. He said he would not recommend a pig valve because they only last about 15 years. He said that the surgeon, Dr. Mark Felger, preferred a St. Jude's valve. I did a little research on my own and found that the St. Jude's valve contained metal and that after installation you could not have an MRI. The only valve I could find that had no metal was a Sulzer valve made of carbon-carbon composite, the same material on the wing leading edges and the nose cone of the Space Shuttle Orbiter, and it was manufactured in Austin. That was good enough for me. When I told Drs. Terreson and Felger of my selection and why, they just looked at each other and said, "Whatever!" Russ worked with a guy at Dell, a previous employee at Sulzer, who was able to get a sales demo of the exact valve I needed. I still have it.

That was just the beginning of my driving all the doctors crazy. I talked to Dr. Felger in detail about the surgery, the anthologist, and the operator of the heart/lung machine that would keep me alive while my heart was out of the loop. I wanted to know all about the procedure, the equipment used, and most importantly to me, the risk.

Satisfied that I completely understood the surgery, I went home and calculated the risk of the entire procedure. The most risky aspect was the anesthesiology. I calculated that, overall, I had a 13% chance of dying. To some, that may seem low, but to me it was terribly high. At NASA, where we assessed risk almost every day, our target was what we called five nines...99.999% reliability. When that could not be achieved, and it usually couldn't, we built in redundancy. If a piece of equipment had a high probability of failing, we put in three of them.

So, facing only an 87% chance of survival, I had to conclude that there was a very good chance that I was going to die. With several weeks to go before the surgery, I did what I could to make sure everything was in order before my death, even to making funeral arrangements. Once all of that was done, I started thinking about what heaven would be like. I wondered what my mother, who had passed away a few months earlier, would be like. What age would she be? Surely, she would be free of all her ailments. I wondered the same things about my father-in-law Bob.

After a couple of days trying to figure all this out, God sent me a very comforting message: "Stop worrying about this. Heaven is a wonderful place and all will be explained to you once you are here." He led me to 1ˢᵗ Corinthians 13:12; "For now we see through a glass darkly; but then face to face; now I know in part; but then I shall know even as also I am known." Did I hear an actual voice? No. Did the Holy Spirit overcome me with those words? Yes. That's the only way I can explain it, but God <u>did</u> very clearly speak to me, and I was completely at ease about the surgery, however it might turn out, from that point forward. Of course, I did survive and have had no heart problems since, probably due to my selection of the right valve!

Just a few days before my surgery, I received a phone call from my friend astronaut Dave Walker. Gerry Griffin had told him about my impending surgery, so he called to assure me that everything was going to be all right. We talked for a long time, but he never mentioned that he had been diagnosed with incurable cancer. I did not know about the cancer until he died the following April. What a guy who would call to cheer me up and never mention that he knew he was soon to die!

– – –

In April 2001, I drove to Mississippi to check on Daddy. He had agreed that he would drive back to Texas with me and spend a few days. In the meantime, I had arranged through Rob Sheets, Andrea's brother who worked at the time for Mercury Marine, to purchase a Mercury Mouse boat from a dealership in Fort Worth that had gone out of business. I figured the grandkids would enjoy it. On our return to Meadowlakes, we went by Fort Worth and picked it up. Even though I had explained to him that it was a little boat for kids, Daddy had a hard time believing I would buy something that small.

During his visit with us, I took Daddy to Fredericksburg to see the LBJ National Park. We went first to the museum, looked around at the exhibits and watched a short film. Johnson's home was not open to the public then, but you could drive in front of it. When I asked Daddy if he would like to drive by, he said he really would like to. As we drove by, he asked if we could drive around to the back. I wasn't sure that we could, but when I got to the back of the house, he said, "Stop right here." As soon as I stopped, he got out of the car and started walking. Having no idea where he was going, I followed him to a runway. Daddy said, "This is where we landed when I came here." I had forgotten that back in the 1960s when Johnson was President, he had invited all of the Agricultural Stabilization and Conservation Service state presidents to his ranch for a bar-b-que. Daddy was the President of the Mississippi ASCS. He seemed to enjoy standing there and recalling memories from years ago.

While on that visit, I even got him to ride in the mouse boat! I think all of the grandkids have enjoyed it over the years.

— — —

After Spook died, we said we would never have another dog. In September 2001, we went to the street market in Marble Falls, where all kinds of vendors set up little shops. As we were walking along, Vickie said, "Do not look to your right!" Of course, that made me want to look. The SPCA had a booth with several puppies. Closest to us was a crate with two little puppies, who turned out to be brother and sister. They were supposedly half Cocker Spaniel and half Border Collie. Despite what we had agreed about getting another dog, we adopted the little girl puppy and named her Molly. She is by far the best dog either of us has owned.

— — —

On September 11, 2001, Cole was visiting us. He was too young (not yet 16 months) to understand what happened that horrible day. Vickie woke me to tell me that a plane had crashed into one of the World Trade Center towers. I got dressed quickly and went downstairs. It was unknown then whether it was a private or commercial plane that had crashed into the north tower. Cole wanted to go outside, so I took him in my arms and went to the back porch. Just as we got there, I heard on TV that another plane had crashed into the south tower. By then, it was obvious that the crashes were intentional. Within another half-hour, a third plane crashed into the Pentagon. I was truly scared. What was going on and what would happen next? I told Cole (which he completely understood) that I would do everything I could to protect him.

– – –

Vickie's mom Susan remained in their Arlington house after Bob died. One night in late 2001, we called and asked her if she had ever thought of moving to Meadowlakes. She said that was the craziest thing she had ever heard. "Why would I want to do that?" Early the next morning she called to say that she had been thinking about it all night and that if we really wanted her to do that, she would consider it. We previewed several houses with a realtor and selected three as possibilities. When she came to look at them, she selected the one that we also liked the best. She moved in January 2002.

One of the main reasons we wanted her near us was so that we could take care of her as she grew older. As it turns out, it has been the other way around. She is healthy as a horse and takes care of Vickie and me! After visiting the Methodist church several times, she decided to join St. Peter's, which made us happy.

– – –

On November 12, 2003, Case David Castañeda was born at St. David's North hospital in Austin. Of course, we were there and very happy to welcome him to the family.

– – –

Unfortunately, in 2004 Vickie discovered a knot in her left breast, 14 years after having cancer in her right breast. This time, as before, she wanted to have the knot removed, even though a biopsy proved inconclusive. Once the knot was removed, it was found to definitely be malignant, so once again, she elected to have a mastectomy. When we were looking for a retirement home, nearness to doctors and hospitals was not on our priority list. Maybe we should have considered that, because since living in Marble Falls, both of us have spent a lot of time in Austin hospitals. After her second mastectomy, Vickie had four hip replacements, left and right within 1 ½ years, and then both had to be replaced due to a manufactures recall. In addition to my heart valve replacement, I had surgery and radiation treatments for prostate cancer, plus a double hernia operation.

– – –

After Mother died, Daddy started talking about moving to the Magnolia in Iuka. He said he wanted to go back to Tishomingo County. Mary and I finally agreed and took him there to look at an available apartment. He said he liked it and put down a deposit. I went back in Vickie's truck and helped him move in 2002. He seemed to really enjoy it there, but after being hit by a bus and suffering several bruised ribs, he moved into the main building where he could get assistance. I phoned him there every day, but often had to call several times before I could reach him. He enlisted in every activity they offered; Bible study, dominos, exercise, etc., and of course didn't miss any meals.

Mike, Andrea and all the boys were able to be there for his 95th birthday party in January 2005, which made him very happy. He and Ryan started planning his 100th birthday party. Unfortunately, that never happened. Eight months later, Daddy was killed in a car wreck.

He was headed to his bank in Golden to get his weekly spending money and free newspaper when a gravel truck pulled out in front of him in the little community of Midway. The Mississippi highway patrol officer who investigated said there were no skid marks, so Daddy apparently never saw the truck. His report assigned no fault on either party. When I told him that the Cadillac had an anti-skid brake system, which if it worked would leave no marks, he seemed surprised. I told him that the car also had a "black box" that recorded speed and accelerator and brake application. He said he had not checked that but he would. After not hearing from him in several days, I called him again. He said he went to where the wrecked car was, but was unable to get to it. When I told him of several errors in his report, such as the year of the car and Daddy's address, he became defensive and questioned why I was being so particular! I told him I just wanted the record to be correct and clear that it was not Daddy's fault. He said his report was final and he would not revisit the investigation.

– – –

Marnie and David's third son, Clay Robert Castañeda, came into this world on July 10, 2005 with a scare. He was born 12 weeks early at St. David's North hospital. Of course, we were all very concerned, but after 30 days in the neonatal intensive care unit, he was declared healthy and allowed to go home. Marnie stayed with him the entire time. Now, she had caught up with Andrea…three boys. The Robert in his name is in honor of his great-grandfather, Robert Burnett.

– – –

For Christmas 2005, we received the gift of a lifetime from Mike and Andrea: an all-expense paid trip to France! They had already made reservations for first class airline travel and for hotels and restaurants, starting in Paris and going to southern France and back, a total of eleven days. They had also arranged for Metro tickets and a rental car. All we had to do was pack our bags and enjoy, which we did the next August.

The flights to DeGaulle airport in Paris were wonderful; plenty of room and great food. The first four nights we stayed in the Hotel DeVigny, near the Arc de Triumph and just half a block from the Champs-Elysees, a nicer hotel than we were used to in France. Our room had a large entryway with a hallway between the bedroom and bath to the right and a large sitting area to the left. Everything was tastefully decorated. The bathroom was huge, with double vanities and a Jacuzzi! It was so nice that Vickie took pictures.

We did our usual things in Paris; ride the Metro and have great meals, good wine, croissants and fromage. We even found a Starbucks (That's okay in France, but McDonalds is a no-no). One night we ate at Brasserie L'Alsace on the Champs. We sat outside under a canopy with what we call "California heaters." We had onion soup, escargot and vin blanc. Does life get much better than this? For our last night in Paris before leaving for the countryside, we asked the concierge about restaurants nearby that he would recommend. He made reservations for us at Chez Catherine, just four blocks away. That turned out to be a great recommendation. The appetizers, salads and main courses were all fantastic, but then came the dessert. Vickie thought she had died and gone to chocolate heaven. She had a small round chocolate cake sealed in a chocolate glaze, topped with chocolate sorbet and chocolate flavored spun sugar! While she was pigging out on her chocolate, I had an assortment of four different strawberries; fresh with a balsamic glaze, strawberry muffin, cold strawberry parfait, and strawberry gelatin. We usually are not dessert eaters, but in this case, we cleaned our plates.

The next day we picked up our rental car, A VW Passat, and headed for Mionnay, just outside Lyons. There we stayed at Alain

Chapel, a quaint inn with a beautiful courtyard. That evening, we had the best meal of our lives in their restaurant. A true seven-course meal that lasted about three hours! I don't think either of us have ever eaten as much or enjoyed it so well. Each course was served so attractively that we didn't want to disturb it. We drank more wine than we should have, but our room was only about 50 yards away, so we made it fine.

After one night there, we drove further south into Provence to Hotel Crillon le Brave, a charming hotel well off the beaten path. Just before arriving at the hotel, we had stopped at a rest stop along the way and noticed that one of our tires had a big blister on it. I carefully drove on and called the rental car company from the hotel. That turned out to be a chore because of the language difference. The hotel clerk didn't understand "tire" or "blister", until I took her outside and showed her what I was talking about. When talking to the car company, she used "le pneu" for tire, and "le ampoule" for blister. Apparently, they didn't immediately understand but finally agreed to send someone out to fix the problem. When he arrived, there was no jack in the trunk of our car, and no spare tire! After a long conversation with his office, of which I didn't understand anything, he said he would bring us a different car, but it would be the next morning. That was fine with us.

The suite in which we stayed overlooked valleys of vineyards and had a luxurious bathroom, which warranted taking pictures again! Our meals that evening and brunch the following morning were outside on a large patio. Wonderful food again!

Sure enough, after a filling brunch, a replacement rental car was awaiting, a VW Golf with a manual transmission. The roads were narrow and winding, so the stick shift was a lot of fun to drive.

About halfway to our next destination, Chateau de Mercues, near Toulouse, we passed the Mediterranean. It was a cool day, but we couldn't resist taking off our shoes and wading. The Chateau turned out to be a beautiful 13th-century castle, with a real moat, on a mountain top overlooking lush countryside. Our room was on the top floor, so we had a fantastic view. The room was furnished with antique furniture and had an ancient wood floor with a design of the universe inlaid with different colored wood. We stayed there two nights and enjoyed every minute of it. For dinner one evening, we had a fruit and cheese plate. One of the cheeses, Cantal, was the best I had ever eaten. The waiter was very patient in explaining what it was and where it came from. His description of the cows from which the milk comes, what they are fed, and how long it is aged, reminded me of the description of how Jack Daniels whiskey is made…very precise. Ours was Cantal Vieux (old), aged for one year. I have tried to find in it the U.S., but the oldest I can find has been aged for six months. It's good, but not as good as one year.

On Sunday, after a great brunch in the courtyard, we drove into the nearby town of Cohors looking for a church. We found a Catholic church, where the service was in French, of course. We actually were able to understand a little of it. We had communion there, which we were not supposed to, but both of us have a problem with denominations that do not serve communion to others, so we did it anyway. After church we found a nice sidewalk café, where we found Mexican beer and Fritos! Quite a change from what we had been feasting on, but very enjoyable.

The next morning we headed back to Paris, where we stayed at Hotel Terrass in the Montmartre arrondissement. Another great hotel. We had an early dinner in the open-air restaurant on top of the hotel, and then left for Montmartre. I love all parts of Paris, but this is my favorite. It's hard to beat Sacre Coeur and the adjoining village where artists still hang out and you can get the best crepes in the world.

Sadly, we had to depart the next afternoon for home. Thanks Mike and Andrea for the best trip anyone could ever hope for!

— — —

In April 2008, Vickie and I went to Washington, DC for a Capitol Page School reunion. They asked me to give the keynote address. I didn't worry too much about it until I saw who was there. There were three current Congressmen and Judge Andrew Napolitano, the Senior Judicial Analyst for Fox News. Vickie said I did fine.

— — —

Kristi, Russ, Lauren and Preston went to Uganda in July 2009. Kristi was the Missions Director at their church, PromiseLand West, at the time and went to minister to several different groups and churches in Kampala and to determine the feasibility of taking a group of church members there in the future. While visiting an orphanage, all four of them fell in love with two little girls, who were sisters, ages five and seven. Upon their return, they prayed about adopting the girls and became convinced that God wanted them to do that. When they told us of their decision in October, I had no reservation because I have always completely trusted Kristi's judgement.

After going through rigorous tests and un-ending paperwork, preliminary arrangements were made with the U.S. and Ugandan governments to finalize the adoptions. Kristi and Russ planned to depart the U.S. on April 19, 2010 to make a Ugandan court date on April 23rd. Unfortunately, there was a volcanic eruption in Iceland a couple of days before and all flights to or through Europe were cancelled due to massive clouds of ash. Kristi called every airline listed in the phonebook trying to find one that would allow them to meet their court date. She had no luck until the day before they were originally scheduled to depart. I was in the parking lot of an Austin restaurant when I received a call from her saying that she had found seats for them on Emirates Airlines, flying through Dubai that would get them there on time. When we ended our conversation, I uttered a short prayer saying, "Thank you, God! You must really want this adoption to happen!" Immediately, God said back to me, "Yes, I do, and it will happen."

To say the least, the adoption process did not go as smoothly as planned. They finally got legal adoption approval from the Ugandan government, then they only needed Visas from the U.S. government for Patricia and Rose, the sisters. Kristi ended up staying in Uganda for over 20 weeks, before finally getting the Visas. This involved many meetings with the U.S. Embassy staff there. They questioned everything! Who were their parents? Why were they up for adoption? Once it was proven that the birthparents were deceased, the embassy staff questioned the status of other relatives. Were the birth certificates valid? I kept thinking, "If the Ugandan government has already approved the adoption, why are they asking all these questions?"

After about seven weeks, Russ had to return to Austin. This was without a doubt, the worst time in my life. Even though Kristi was 44 years old, she was still my "little girl." The U.S. government was telling her she would have to stay there for two years before they could give Visas to the girls. We were able to communicate sporadically via phone, e-mail and Skype. She had meeting after meeting with the embassy, Ugandan officials and relatives of Patricia and Rose. The time difference between Texas and Kampala was eight hours, so if I knew that she had a meeting at 10 a.m. Kampala time, I was up at 2 a.m. so that I could "be with her." How could I sleep through an important meeting, even though it was 5,000 miles away? I even got my passport in order and applied for a Visa to go be with her. When Mike found out I was doing that, he gave me the first son-to-father lecture I had ever had. I needed it! I still was recovering from prostate cancer and finally had to agree with Mike that making the trip was a dumb idea.

Lauren and Preston did go back to be with her from mid-July to early August. That made it even worse on me. Not only were my little girl and my future granddaughters stranded there, but now two of my grandkids were there. It was a dangerous place! Just a few days before Lauren and Preston arrived, a group of Islamist suicide bombers attacked two places where folks were watching the World Cup soccer match on TV, killing 74 people and injuring as many more. A restaurant less than one mile from where they were staying, was bombed.

I sat out on our upstairs porch every night praying and looking at the stars. I told God, "I know you told me that the adoption would happen, and I completely trust you, but it's been a long time now, and next Tuesday would be a good time." On a daily basis, I read the devotional from *Jesus Calling*, a book that Kristi had recommended and was also reading each day. Somehow, it made me feel closer, knowing that she was reading the same devotional each day.

Finally, after intervention by a Washington D.C. lawyer, in early September the Visas were approved and they headed home. On September 9, 2010, Patricia and Rose became official U.S. citizens upon landing at D/FW airport, their first time on U.S. soil. Later that day, there was a large crowd of family and friends awaiting them at the Austin airport. One of the worse times in my life quickly turned into one of the happiest times, when Patricia, recognizing me from Skype, came running down the stairs screaming "Grandpa Jerry!", came to me and gave me a big hug.

A month later, we all went with them to Travis County Court to legally change their names to Ray. What a great addition to our family!

— — —

After my heart surgery, I started thinking about a "bucket list"; things I would like to do before I departed Earth. Number one on my list was to deliver a sermon at church. It was something which I had thought about for several years. I did that at St. Peter's in October 2011, for both the early and late services. Kristi, Russ, Lauren, Preston, Patricia and Rose came for the late service. My subject was "Talking to and listening to God", about the power of prayer and the importance of listening to God. Second on my list was to skydive. I did that in San Marcos Texas with Preston when he turned eighteen in February 2013 and again with Mike, Dylan, Jordan and Ryan in Santa Barbara California in May 2014 when Ryan became eighteen.

**Preston and I after landing**

**Bostick boys after landing: Jordan, Mike, Jerry, Dylan, Ryan**

Another thing on my list was to drive a NASCAR Sprint series racecar. I did that in April 2014. Ten guys from our St. Peter's Bring Your Own Bible (BYOB) bible study group went to Texas Motor Speedway and each drove. Allan Restrepo was able to join us, which made it even more special. Kristi and family were there to watch. In retrospect, I was too cautious and only averaged 113 mph on the 1.5-mile track, with a top speed of 160 mph. I want to do it again at Talladega Superspeedway in Alabama where the track is 2.66 miles long, and can hopefully go faster.

**Allan & I suited up**

**Ready to race**

# EPILOG

God has blessed me with an incredible life, and the ten of you are my greatest blessing. I have wonderful memories throughout your lives so far. I remember when you (with the exception of Patricia and Rose, who didn't come into my life until you were ages five and seven), as babies, slept at our house without your parents. We had monitors, over which we could hear all the sounds you made. Each morning I would get up early and take the monitor with me downstairs so that I could be closer to you when you awakened. Usually, the first thing I would hear was "Granny Vick! Grandpa Jerry!", letting me know you were awake. When I opened your door, I was always welcomed with a smile. An exception to this was Clay. He would always wake up and start looking at a book or playing with a toy and talking to himself. Sometimes this would go on for a half-hour before he would call for one of us. I loved it!

Patricia and Rose, since you were too old for monitors, we did things like pizza parties on the floor or sleeping in a tent in the back yard. You always seemed to be very comfortable with us, which made us happy.

I have fond memories of being at your house on Christmas morning to watch you run to the tree to see what Santa brought and of playing board games and putting together puzzles with each of you. Outside, we had fun playing bocce ball and croquet. One of my favorite outdoor activities was lying on the ground at night, looking at the moon and talking about how to get there. I also enjoyed playing with you in the game room and on the SeaDoo and Mouse.

Unfortunately, for the past several years, we have not been able to spend as much time together as I would like. There are many reasons for that: Lauren and Dylan working in New York; Jordan, Preston and Ryan in college; the Castañeda boys moving to Rockwall; and mine and Granny Vick's health.

I hope I haven't bored you to tears with this book. As I said in the preface, I just wanted to put on paper some things that happened during my lifetime, and to let you know how important all ten of you are to me.

I love every one of you so much!

Grandpa Jerry…the kid from Golden

**Grandkids in 2008 before Patricia & Rose**

**Grandkids in 20012 without Castañeda boys**

# Appendix 1

(From the Capitol Courier, March 22, 1956)
**Vice President's Room in Capitol
Has Historic Chandelier, Desk, Mirror**
*by Jerry Bostick*

*Situated at the east end of the Senators' Lobby on the Senate side of the Capitol is the Vice President's Room, filled with a wealth of precious memorabilia. Finished in 1859, the room has been used as a private office for the Vice President by every holder of this high post since that date. The first to occupy it was John C. Breckinridge of Kentucky.*

*The chandelier over the Vice President's desk was purchased in Paris by Thomas Jefferson when he was ambassador to France. It is made of Bohemian crystals, and has all sterling silver clips and chains. It had gas and candle type of lighting prior to being wired for electric current. The story concerning the chandelier relates that Jefferson placed it the White House shortly after becoming President, and it remained there until Theodore Roosevelt became President. With all the windows open in the hot weather, the wind would blow in and make the prisms on the chandelier tinkle. This made President Roosevelt nervous and he had the chandelier removed and placed over the Vice President's desk in the Capitol with the comment that the Vice President never had anything to do and the tinkling of the prisms would keep him awake.*

*The desk in the center of the room was first used by President McKinley. After his assination it was stored in the basement of the White House until 1917. One day President Woodrow Wilson, when exploring rooms which he had never before seen, found the desk. He had it removed to his office for his personal use and used it for his work for the balance of his term in office.*

*Over the clock is a small gold mirror which is known as the Dolly Madison mirror. As the story goes, Mrs. Madison bought the mirror for $50 in American money while visiting k. There also was a $30 customs fee when it arrived at the port of New York. Mrs. Madison charged it to the official account and the government paid the fee. An investigation was later started as to whether or not the government should pay the $80 but was finally cancelled after a cost of $2800.*

*The large picture of George Washington hanging on the wall is considered one of the most valuable paintings in the Capitol. If the painting could be valued in dollars and cents, the art critics in Washington believe it would be worth nearly half a million dollars.*

*Among other historic articles reposing about the room are a bookcase from the time of Buchanan, a French gilt clock from the Polk administration, and an antique gilt mirror purchased by John Adams.*

# Appendix 2

(From the Congressional Record, June 19, 1957, page A4845)
*Valedictory and Salutatory Addresses at*
*Commencement Exercises at the Capitol Page School*

## EXTENSION OF REMARKS
## OF
## HON. FRANK CHURCH
## OF IDAHO
## IN THE SENATE OF THE UNITED STATES

Wednesday, June 19, 1957

*Mr. CHURCH. Mr. President, one of the very minor irritations I have felt since coming to these Halls, was the absolute lack of any occasion upon which I might give fatherly advice. But on June 10, in the House Ways and Means Committee room, that lack was remedied. I was privileged at that time to address the graduating class of the Capitol Page School, on the occasion of their commencement exercises. I was deeply pleased at being asked to make this address, but I even more enjoyed listening to the valedictory and salutatory addresses of Mr. Jerry Bostick and Mr. George Weaver. It seemed to me, as I listened, that these young men symbolized the earnestness, the courtesy, and the devotion to duty which unfailingly characterizes the service rendered by our young associates here at the Capitol.*

*I should like again, today, as I did on June 10, to wish these graduates productive and rewarding lives, filled with much success and happiness.*

*I ask unanimous consent that the addresses by Mr. Bostick and Mr. Weaver and the list of the members of the graduating class of the Capitol*

*Page School for 1957 be printed in the Appendix of the Record, following these remarks.*

*There being no objection, the addresses and list were ordered to be printed in the Record, as follows:*

## *VALEDICTORY ADDRESS BY JERRY BOSTICK, CAPITOL PAGE SCHOOL, COMMENCEMENT EXERCISES, HOUSE WAYS AND MEANS COMMITTEE ROOM, JUNE 10, 1957*

*Distinguished guests, Mr. DeKeyser, members of the faculty, and friends. I realize that graduation ceremonies similar to ours are taking place in every community at this time of year, but I feel confident that no graduates have been given better advice or have heard sounder words of wisdom than those expressed by our distinguished speaker, Senator CHURCH. Thank you for taking time from your busy schedule to speak to us this evening.*

*Tonight we are bringing to a close our training in the essentials that will help us as we undertake more advance training, which in turn will further mold our lives. The years immediately ahead present a greater challenge than ever before to all of us and we are determined to do our part in providing progressive leadership. We, therefore, pledge that we will do everything possible to spur our country on to a full realization of its magnificent potentialities. This can be done if we will forever keep in mind the words of the English writer and critic, John Ruskin, who said, "It is not how long we live, but how well we spent the life we lived that counts."*

*The opportunity to be graduates of the Capitol Page School and of working from day to day with the lawmakers of this Republic will forever be among our most cherished memories. The many unique experiences and wonderful associations we have been privileged to have here will bear fruit in our lives and in our work. We hope that we can show our appreciation to our sponsors by using these experiences to further the welfare of our Nation in the years to come.*

*We fully realize that perhaps we would be saying nothing of a brighter tomorrow if we had not had the patience and understanding shown us by parents, teachers, and associates. To those who have assisted us so greatly we pay our humble respects.*

*Only the future will tell whether we achieve the high standards which have been set before us. With Divine guidance we hope to contribute toward America's ultimate goal—peace, preparedness, and prosperity.*

## LIST OF GRADUATES, 1957 CLASS OF THE CAPITOL PAGE SCHOOL:

*Jerry Creel Bostick*

*Charles Vernon Bush*

*Allen Warren Davis*

*Lawrence Colin Fernsworth*

*Richard L. Fruin, Jr.*

*George Ward Gaines*

*Robert M. Jacoby*

*Drew M. Johnson*

*Jed Joseph Johnson, Jr.*

*Frederick Phillip Kessler*

*Warren Lee McElvain*

*Frederick Jerome Saunders*

*Terrance M. Scanlon*

*William Eugene Smith*

*Julien Gillien Sourwine*

*E. John Watson*

*George Arthur Weaver*

*Roger Stephen Williams*

# Appendix 3

# MOVIES AND TELEVISION

**Apollo 13**...When Mike called me in early 1994 asking if I knew that Jim Lovell was writing a book about the Apollo 13 mission, I replied, "Yes, and his co-writer is Jeffery Kluger." There was a brief silence on the phone and then he asked me how I knew that. I told him that I had just gotten off the phone with Jeffery, and that he and Lovell had called me several times with questions. Mike seemed surprised, but said he had a 12-page synopsis of the book and thought it would make a great movie. I assumed that he meant a documentary, but he said no, he thought it should be an historical docudrama, and that he was going to recommend to Ron Howard, his boss at the time, that they option the rights to the book. I told him I thought that was a terrible idea and it would turn out like *Houston, We Have a Problem* or *Marooned*, two docudramas about the mission that I hated. He assured me that Ron, as the director, would make it as historically accurate as possible, but still entertaining.

By the end of that day, Imagine Films closed the deal on the film rights to the upcoming book. When Mike told me about the deal, he said that Ron also hated the previous docudramas and that he wanted to hire Gerry Griffin, Dave Scott and me as technical advisors. How could I refuse even though I still had remaining doubts?

Bill Broyles and Al Reinert were hired to write the script, based on Lovell's book. As part of their preparation, they asked if I would meet with them and tell them "what flight controllers do." We met for lunch at Pe-Te's Cajun BBQ, just across the street from Ellington

Field. When they asked me if any flight controller had ever panicked, my reply was, "No, when bad things happened, we just calmly laid out the options, and failure was not one of them." I immediately sensed that Bill Broyles wanted to leave and assumed that he was bored with the interview. He said he thought it was time to wrap it up, and they left. Much later, I learned that when they got into their car to return to Houston, Broyles screamed, "That's it! That's the tag line for the whole movie...Failure Is Not An Option!"

Before the filming started, Ron Howard asked Gerry and me to conduct a four-hour "Flight Controller class" for the actors. He wanted us to tell the Mission Control Center actors what flight controllers do, what astronauts do, and what happened on the mission. In typical fashion for us, we didn't over plan the presentation. We agreed that I would start out with the trajectory aspects, beginning with launch, Translunar Injection (TLI), transposition and docking and mid-course corrections up to the time of the onboard explosion. Then Gerry would take over and tell them what happened, why it happened and what problems the controllers and the astronauts then faced. Beyond that, we would just wing it based on questions the actors might have. That's as much thought as I had given it until the plane ride to Los Angeles.

When I started seriously thinking about what I would say, I had some dire reservations. I figured that the actors would just sit there and say to themselves, "I know my lines, I know how to act, so who is this NASA nerd up there telling me all this?"

**The limo that met us at the airport
(Note the license plate)**

When we actually gave the presentation, I learned that I could not have been more wrong about the actors' attitude. They were like sponges, absorbing every detail and wanting to know more. The planned four hours ran into a day and a half. Finally, Ron said, "I know you guys are enjoying this, but we have to stop and make a movie!"

Gerry and I were in our normal NASA mode and were always early for whatever was planned. If we had a call to be on the movie set at 7:30 a.m., we were there at no later than 7:15. Each day, we noticed that Ron was already there; looking at camera angles, going over the script and in apparent deep thought. Previously, we had asked Mike what we were supposed to do as Technical Advisors. He said, "Just stand in the background and don't say anything unless asked.", so that's what we did. On the first day, after a few minutes, Ron asked us a few questions. That went on for several days until Ron finally said, "I kind of like you guys being here to help me plan what we're doing for the day, so could you be here 30 minutes early from now on so that I can go over everything with you?" So, from that day forward, we were always already on the set when Ron arrived.

The control center set, located on Stage 27 on the back lot of Universal Studios, was unbelievably accurate. It was dimensionally correct to within one inch, the consoles were exact copies, the carpet was exact down to the coffee stains, the displays on the consoles and the front screens were copies of the real ones. Often Gerry and I felt like we were in a time warp. At least twice during the filming, I left the set at the end of the day and looked for the elevator, because the real control room for Apollo 13 was on the third floor in Houston. Once when asked about where he slept, Gerry pointed south and said, "Well, I lived just across the street there, so I went home as much as I could.", before realizing he was not in the actual control center.

We both were impressed with the control center actors and with the astronaut actors, Tom Hanks, Bill Paxton, Kevin Bacon and Gary Sinise. Even though we were filming control center scenes, in which they would not appear, they were there almost every day. Usually in making movies, the script supervisor would read the astronaut lines if the script called for them to be talking to the control center. Tom Hanks actually got up on a ten-foot ladder in the front of the room and read his lines himself! He, being an absolute space nut, would engage us in space trivia questions. He could name the date, the crewmembers, and where he was on launch day, for every manned space mission from Al Shepard through the Challenger Space Shuttle flight. Gary Sinise was the perfect actor to play T. K. Mattingly. They both are very detailed and want to understand precisely everything they are doing. After Gary's first day of filming, he asked me to stay late and go over the remaining parts of his script with him. We spent at least three hours, with him asking hundreds of questions.

Ron had an absolute compulsion for accuracy. When Gerry and I would point out some things that were not 100% accurate in the script, like Gene Kranz not being the only Flight Director, he would listen attentively, and say, "You are right, but we're making a movie and I can't have 19 main characters, so we have to consolidate some things." He invited us to go with him each day and review the "dailies", the shots that were made the previous day. He seemed to value our opinion.

For some reason, Gerry had to leave a few days before we ended the control center filming. On the day we shot the end of the mission where the spacecraft stayed in communications blackout much longer than normal, I was the only advisor there. When Ron got everything all set up; actors in place, cameras at the correct angles and lighting just right, he came to me and said, "I want you to direct this scene." When I replied that I didn't know anything about directing, he told me that since I was the only one who was actually there when it happened, to just tell the actors how you and the other controllers felt. So, I told them how tired, but happy we were that we apparently had saved the astronauts, but when we stayed in communications blackout for so long, we started thinking that maybe the heat shield had cracked or the parachutes didn't open and we had lost them. I told them that we went from great satisfaction, to great depression, and then to elation when we finally got a call from the spacecraft saying the chutes were open and they were fine. After shooting the scene once, Ron asked if the actors were okay with it. Ed Harris, who played Gene Kranz, said, "I'd like to do it one more time. Please have Jerry come up here and give us his pep talk again." Of course, because of my superior direction, I think it is one of the best scenes in the movie.

Dave Scott and I joined the cast and crew at Ellington Field when they were filming the micro-gravity scenes in the NASA KC-130, fondly called the "vomit comet." Dave and I volunteered to fly with them, but NASA would not allow anyone to fly who was not certified, which required several days of training. Dave, of course, had been certified and had flown on the plane several times before his Apollo 15 mission, but NASA said the certification was outdated.

Vickie and I were invited to the wrap party at the Ragin Cajun restaurant and bar in Clear Lake once the filming was complete there. At the party, a stranger came in with several movie posters and t-shirts to get Tom Hanks to sign them. Tom said he would if he could keep one of the t-shirts. He then asked Vickie if she wanted him to autograph it for her. She asked that he sign it "To Marnie", so he did.

After all the filming was complete, in March 1995, I was asked back for "looping", which I called dubbing. It's a process where they re-record the actors voices over the film footage, if the original recording was not up to specifications. It's a pretty involved process because the lip movement and the re-recording have to be synchronized. The main actors that day were Tom Hanks and Ed Harris. Ron conducted the exercise via a video link from his home studio in Connecticut. The rest of us were at Glen Glenn studios in Hollywood. Tom had to leave early because the Academy Awards were scheduled for that night. (He won the Best Actor award for *Forest Gump*). Ed Harris and I took frequent breaks to go outside and smoke, as we had done during the filming. I had noticed that his shoes and pants were covered with paint blotches, so I finally asked about them. He said he had been practicing for an upcoming movie that he would direct and play the lead role of Jackson Pollock. Pollock was an American abstract painter, known for slinging a big brush toward the canvas. *Pollock* turned out to be a pretty good movie.

In mid-afternoon, I was standing outside our studio sound stage reviewing an upcoming scene, when I heard someone coming down the hallway screaming, "I know the whole world is a stage, but where is stage 6?" It was Steve Martin, dressed in a tuxedo, there to pick up his date for the Academy Awards that night, Diane Keaton. I directed him to stage 6, just down from us, where she was looping *Father of the Bride II*, in which she would star along with Steve Martin and Martin Short.

We were invited to the World Premier in June 1995 at the Samuel Goldwyn Theater in Beverly Hills. It was an outstanding event and we were proud of Mike. After the premier, there was a reception where we got to mingle with all of the cast and crew, plus several invited guests such as John Travolta and Henry Winkler, Fonzie from *Happy Days*. He accidently ran into Vickie, spilling his drink on her. He profusely apologized and said he would be happy to pay to have her dress cleaned, to which she responded, "That's all right, Fonz. No harm done."

Soon thereafter, we also attended a premier in Pasadena Texas, at a theater just a few miles from Clear Lake. Everyone gathered at Space Center Houston and road buses to and from the theater. At that premier, I sat between Fred Haise and Gene Kranz. I was worried about how they would react to the movie. Fred had declined to co-author the book by Jim Lovell and really didn't want to have anything to do with the movie, so I was especially worried about his reaction. Besides, he was my boss at the time! He didn't say anything during the premier, just sitting stoically. When we boarded the bus to go back to Space Center Houston, he and his wife Patt took the seat directly behind Vickie and me. By that time, I was sweating b-bs. Did he like the movie or was he offended? After a short time, he tapped me on the shoulder and said, "I didn't chew gum." Bill Paxton, who played him in the movie, was always chewing gum. That's the most critical thing Fred ever said to me about it.

Later that night, I introduced T. K. Mattingly to Gary Sinise, who portrayed him in the movie. I also was nervous about how T. K.

would react. I soon saw that they were cut from the same cloth and were very interested in each other's careers. They got along great and I left them, still talking, in the bar at 2:00 a.m.

I still keep up with most of the control center actors. They meet each Thursday in the Los Angeles area for lunch, if they are not working. The group usually consists of Googy Gress, Chris Ellis, Andy Milder and Joe Spano. Occasionally, Ron and Clint Howard and Dave Scott drop by. I meet with them every time I go visit Mike, Andrea and the boys.

Overall, I think the NASA community was well pleased with the movie. I was! Just like on the actual mission, we had an extremely dedicated group of people working on a very difficult task, who would settle for nothing but the best.

As far as impact on me personally, the movie stimulated great interest among the public, worldwide. Maybe the rapid development of the internet at about the same time had something to do with it, but I saw a tremendous increase in autograph requests. In previous years, I would get maybe three or four requests through the mail for autographs; mainly on stamp covers and a few pictures. Since the movie and/or the internet, I now average about two such requests a week. I am always happy to oblige and have only charged for autographs three times; Autographia in London, the Astronaut Scholarship Foundation and Spacefest. On each of those occasions, I gave the money to our church. I feel very fortunate to have participated in America's space program and have no desire to profit from it.

The greatest part of doing the movie for me was to get to work with Mike. I learned a lot about what he did as a producer and he learned some about what I was doing during all of those days away from home during space missions.

**Griffin, Hanks, Howard, me and Mike on Control Center set**

**From the Earth to the Moon HBO miniseries**...Soon after the Apollo 13 movie came out, I learned that Tom Hanks had reached agreement with HBO to do a miniseries on which he had been working for some time. He told me what he was thinking about while we were filming *Apollo 13*. He ignored at least two of my inputs; do one complete episode about Gemini 8 and don't do one on astronauts wives.

Mike was one of the producers for the series, so I was thrilled to once again be a technical advisor. I reviewed and commented on the script for all 12 episodes and was on the set for filming of three of the shows. Each episode was directed by a different person (David Frankel did three). The first one that was filmed and the first to air, was *Can we do this?*, directed by Hanks and mostly filmed in the original Mercury Control Center in Florida. It was thrilling and depressing at the same time. The building had a leaky roof and had been used mostly for storage of surplus equipment for the last few years. We were able to spruce it up a little and it looked fine on film.

I learned very quickly that there is a big difference in making movies and TV shows. TV shows are usually low budget and filmed very quickly. No re-shoots unless the first shot is totally unusable.

The series won an Emmy, a Producers Guild Award, and many others. Mike received an Emmy statue and I got a certificate of appreciation from the Academy of Television Arts & Sciences.

**Armageddon**...A couple of years later, I was asked to be a Technical Advisor on the film *Armageddon*, directed by Michael Bay. I quickly saw how different directors operate. Michael Bay rarely did more than one shot of any scene. The first day that I was there, they shot a scene where the Flight Director, played by my friend Chris Ellis who portrayed Deke Slayton in *Apollo 13*, was doing a roll call of the flight controllers. He said Eva, as in a girl's name, rather than the individual letters E-V-A (Extra Vehicular Activity), as it should be. I pointed that out to Bay, but he said, "That's fine. I'm not going to reshoot it." On many occasions he would ask me a question, I would answer it, and then he would say, "That's boring! I'm not going to use that!" In my opinion, he was much more interested in excitement than accuracy.

One very good thing about this experience was that I became friends with Billy Bob Thornton. I am fully aware of his reputation in those days as a drug using, rabble-rousing guy, but he seemed to go out of his way to be nice to me. He asked me a lot more questions than Michael Bay did, and usually took my advice, even if it meant a change in the script. When he did say something not in the script, Bay usually noted the change, but said it was okay. An example of this is a scene in which he was in a conference room explaining to the flight crew how they would approach the landing on the asteroid. The set included rather crude models of the earth, moon, asteroid and the Shuttle that they would use for the landing. Michael Bay asked me to run through the scene, showing how the approach and landing would occur. The first thing I said was, "Now let's keep the laughter to a minimum. I know this is not to scale". Then I described how they would swing around the moon and land on the asteroid. When the scene was shot, Billy Bob used my exact words and Bay didn't seem to mind. In fact, he thought it was funny and that I had finally done something to help.

One day Billy Bob told me that his girlfriend was coming to the set the next day, but he had a full day, so he would appreciate it if I would stick with her and show her around. Of course, I agreed. The next morning he introduced me to her as Laura. I did as he had requested and spent the entire day with her, trying to explain how movies were made. That night I told Mike about it and he informed me that it was Laura Dern, the star of *Jurassic Park*. I felt like an idiot for not recognizing her and for assuming that she didn't know how movies were made. I had not recognized her because she looked a lot different with no make-up.

The next morning Billy Bob said that he had a "bone to pick" with me. He said that Laura had a wonderful time with me and now liked me better than him.

Other actors who were very nice to me included Ben Affleck (his friend Matt Damon came by the set frequently), Steve Buscemi, Jessica Steen and Michael Clarke Duncan. Michael Duncan was a huge guy who played "Bear" in the movie. In person, he was the opposite of this rough character. He came to me almost every day, put his arm around me and asked what he was supposed to do next. Of course, I was happy to work once again with some of the *Apollo 13* actors; Chris Ellis, Googy Gress and Andy Milder.

On the opposite end of the scale was Bruce Willis. Even though he knew my name, every time he wanted to ask me a question, he would yell, "Hey NASA man!" After many days of that, I answered "Yeah, boy actor, what do you want?" He did tell me that he probably deserved my response, but asked that I not do it again. From then on, he did call me by my name. He got upset because the producer published a memo addressed to all the people who were to be interviewed and filmed for *The Making of Armageddon*. Since the list of addressees was in alphabetical order, my name was first, and his was last. He made them reissue the memo with his name first.

What I learned from working on this movie was that *Apollo 13* was unusual, in that all of the cast and crew got along well and worked as a team, just as we did years before in mission control. There were no prima-donnas. The same cannot be said about *Armageddon*. I should have stopped consulting on movies after *Apollo 13*!

The best part of doing this movie was getting to spend some time with Mike, Andrea and the boys. The hotel where I stayed in Century City had a swimming pool on the roof, so Dylan and Jordan enjoyed coming over and swimming with me. Ryan was too little at the time.

— — —

TV Documentaries...Over the years I have appeared in a number of television documentaries including:

> *The Century, with Peter Jennings*, on ABC
> *Failure Is Not An Option* and *Failure Is Not An Option II, Beyond The Moon*, both on the History Channel.
> *Race To The Moon; The Daring Adventure of Apollo 8* and *Earthrise: The First Lunar Voyage*, both on PBS.

I never enjoyed doing those. I found it terribly distracting to be surrounded by lights so bright that I couldn't usually even see the person conducting the interview, and by the camera, reflector screens and microphones sticking in my face.

I recently did one, *Go Flight: The Untold Story of the Heroes of Mission Control*, which will not air until sometime in 2016. Apparently, the technology has improved over the years, and that filming was not nearly as intrusive as previous ones. They even let me wear my glasses!

# Appendix 4

# "BAD" HABITS I DEVELOPED ALONG THE WAY

Most of the "bad" habits which I developed over the years can be attributed to my time at NASA, but not all.

Number one has to do with being on time. My Daddy always said, "If you aren't 10 minutes early, you're late.", so I already had this habit before joining NASA. It certainly was reinforced there, first by Cliff Charlesworth ("If you have a slow horse, get an early start.") and later by George Low, who was known to lock the door to a meeting room at the scheduled time. People soon learned to be on time. I still am somewhat obsessed with this habit. If someone tells me they will be somewhere at an appointed hour, I fully expect them to show up before or on time.

Closely associated with number one is my number two, not doing things when promised. If someone tells me they will do something by next Tuesday, I expect them to either do it by then or let me know when it will be done. At NASA this was cause for not ever trusting that person.

Number three on my list is telling the truth. My parents preached this to me as a child. "Always tell the truth, even if it hurts." and, "Oh what a tangled web we weave, when first we practice to deceive." This too, was reinforced at NASA. I quickly learned that Chris Kraft was intolerant of people who tried to cover up mistakes, and totally intolerant of anyone who lied to him. I developed the same philosophy and sorted out who I could or could not trust. You can deceive someone without lying, but both are unacceptable.

Number four is to say as much as you can in the shortest amount of time. Although we had no specific training on this subject at NASA, when we were flying space missions, especially the early ones, we had a very limited time of voice contact and had to get our messages across as succinctly as possible. Even though I did not ever directly talk to an astronaut in orbit, I many times gave the CAPCOM a note to read up to the crew. It had to be clear and short. "Turn on your C Band over Hawaii." Associated with this habit is to never just say "What?" when you don't understand exactly what someone has tried to tell you. At NASA if someone said, "We will have telemetry contact over Carnarvon at GET 25:18:54.", and I didn't understand the time, I would say, "Repeat all after GET." That way, they didn't have to say the whole sentence over again. All I didn't understand was the time. Away from NASA, I have modified this somewhat. If someone says to me, "I saw Joe Blow at the hardware store and he said to ask you about Bible study and call him at his office." If I understood everything except where I was supposed to call him, I would just say, "Call him where?" Most people, unfortunately, still will repeat the entire sentence. It's a small thing, but it drives me up the wall!

Number five has to do with meetings. My NASA experience taught me that meetings should have a specific agenda and all discussion should only be about what's on that agenda. In addition, when the agenda is completed, the meeting is over, regardless of the time remaining. Most of my non-NASA meetings seriously violate these rules, and I have to continually remind myself that I'm dealing with volunteers and I can't enforce these rules. I'm getting more tolerant, but not yet completely.

Appendix 4

My sixth "bad" habit is how one should say numbers. At NASA, we never said "fifteen" or "fifty", because they sound so much alike. The proper usage is "15" (one five) and "50" (five zero). I still have that habit today, and wish that other people did, especially when relaying phone numbers. An obvious exception is when talking about ages; it's okay to say "fifteen" or "fifty." At NASA, we also did not say letters, such as A, B, C. We always said "Alpha, Beta, Charlie." This is rarely a problem away from work, except when talking about such things as confirmation numbers and e-mail addresses.

- 387 -

# Appendix 5

# VOLUNTEER ACTIVITIES

Over the years, I have been involved in many volunteer activities with churches, service organizations, universities, non-profit professional associations, cities and communities. I have always had a sense of obligation for such activities, and felt that there has to be something in life besides work. I really got started in 1964 when we moved to Clear Lake/Nassau Bay. At times, I have had to realize that I was becoming too involved in these activities and to back off. I still have a hard time saying no when someone asks me. Here is a list of the major ones.

Lions International: Secretary and President, Bay Area Club; Zone Chairman, Houston District

Clear Lake United Methodist Church: Church School Superintendent; Vice Chairman, Administrative Board; Adult Sunday School Coordinator

Clear Lake National Bank: Consulting Board

Space Center Houston: Founding Committee

American Institute of Aeronautics and Astronautics: Senior Member

Armed Forces Communications and Electronics Association: Member

National Contract Management Association: Member

American Astronautical Society: Director-At-Large, Southwest Section

Bay Area United Way: Advisory Board

Bay Area Auxiliary, Assistance League of Houston: Advisory Board

University of Texas: Aerospace Engineering Visiting Committee Member

University of Houston-Clear Lake: Development and Advisory Council Member

Mississippi State University: Research Advisory Committee Member

Houston Chamber of Commerce: Aerospace and Technology Task Force Member

Clear Lake Area Economic Development Foundation: Executive Board; Chairman of Membership Development; President

Texas Space Grant Consortium: Charter Member, Board of Directors

Houston Proud: Board of Directors

Honorary Constable, Harris County, Texas

NASA Alumni League, JSC Chapter: Board of Directors, Vice President

Texas Space Commission: Charter Commissioner

St. Peter's Lutheran Church, Marble Falls: Member, Building Committee; Vice President, Congregation Council (twice); Church School President; Youth Sunday School teacher

City of Meadowlakes: Floodplain Administrator; Deputy Emergency Management Coordinator

Older Adults Rural Services: Volunteer Driver

Lower Colorado River Authority: Lake Marble Falls Advisory Panel

Central Texas Groundwater Conservation District: Charter Director

I enjoyed most of these activities, while some were somewhat disappointing. My church activities were mostly enjoyable and rewarding, especially at St. Peter's. The University experiences were mixed. The University of Houston-Clear Lake was a very good experience. The Chancellor at the time was Tom Stauffer and he welcomed suggestions for improvement. The University of Texas Engineering Department was almost the opposite. They really didn't want any advice, but just liked the idea of having "influential" people on the committee and didn't want any criticism, constructive or otherwise. They did not appreciate my criticism of their desire to cut back on elective courses. The Mississippi State Research Advisory Committee was very successful. The professors there were doing some great research, but they never applied for any patents on their work. After a couple of years, we were able to turn that around and the patents proved to be a good source of revenue. The two state boards, Texas Space Grant Consortium and the Texas Space Commission, were impressive at the start, with hearings before my confirmation and then swearing-in ceremonies on the House of Representatives floor. However, neither was ever funded. In each case, we had to borrow office space from other state agencies and they were eventually dissolved due to lack of funding.

One problem that I had with each of these activities, and still do, was that the meetings tended to go long and often got off the agenda subject. See Appendix 4.

Made in the USA
San Bernardino, CA
31 August 2016